Bound 1962

FRENCH MUSIC

FRENCH MUSIC

*From the death of Berlioz
to the death of Fauré*

By
MARTIN COOPER

LONDON
OXFORD UNIVERSITY PRESS
NEW YORK   TORONTO

Oxford University Press, Amen House, London E.C.4

GLASGOW NEW YORK TORONTO MELBOURNE WELLINGTON
BOMBAY CALCUTTA MADRAS KARACHI KUALA LUMPUR
CAPE TOWN IBADAN NAIROBI ACCRA

First edition 1951
First issued in *OXFORD PAPERBACKS* 1961

Printed in Great Britain by Richard Clay and Company, Ltd.,
Bungay, Suffolk

TO

MY WIFE

CONTENTS

LIST OF ILLUSTRATIONS

ACKNOWLEDGEMENTS

My first debt of gratitude is to the late M. D. Calvocoressi, who helped me with advice and information when I first planned this book. Richard Capell read the manuscript and gave me much valuable advice on many matters, from presentation to typography. Edward Sackville-West helped me substantially in compiling the 'Other Arts' column of the end-tables. Felix Aprahamian was generous in putting scores at my disposal. M. and Mme. Tony Mayer helped me to obtain the illustrations I wanted from France. Finally the library staff of the Paris Conservatoire and the British Museum were always helpful, often under considerable provocation.

Thanks are due to the following publishers for permission to quote extracts from copyright musical works: Chappell & Co. Ltd. (André Messager); J. & W. Chester Ltd. (Germaine Tailleferre); Choudens (Alfred Bruneau, André Messager); Durand et Cie (Claude Debussy, Vincent d'Indy, Gabriel Fauré, Darius Milhaud, Maurice Ravel, Camille Saint-Saëns, Florent Schmitt); Éditions Maurice Senart (Darius Milhaud); Éditions Salabert (Florent Schmitt); Hamelle et Cie (Vincent d'Indy, Gabriel Fauré); Heugel et Cie (Gabriel Fauré, Jules Massenet); Rouart, Lerolle et Cie (Georges Auric, Pierre de Bréville, Ernest Chausson, Guillaume Lekeu, Albert Roussel); La Sirène Musicale (Arthur Honegger, Francis Poulenc, Georges Auric); Universal Edition (Darius Milhaud).

M. C.

St. John's Wood,
February, 1951.

INTRODUCTION

FRENCH music is not generally popular in England, for it lacks the quality which most endears any work to the public. It lacks, that is to say, a strongly flavoured emotional content, either moral and uplifting as in Beethoven or introvert and lowering as in Tchaikovsky. In general the musical public probably agrees with W. J. Turner, who thought Debussy a purveyor of 'first-class bonbons and you can't live on bonbons all the time . . . and as for Ravel, Florent Schmitt, Dukas, Roussel and all the other French composers whose music I have heard, they seem to me to be merely clever'. In the same essay Turner stated his major premiss, one which the majority of French artists of all descriptions would reject. The function of art, he writes, is to reveal the soul of man; and he goes on to say, quite truly, that if this be admitted Debussy's is a 'singularly one-sided, incomplete and inadequate revelation. . . . It is the sublimity of the soul that makes the music of Beethoven and Bach so immeasurably greater than that of Wagner and Debussy.'

This is not a book on aesthetics, a treatise on the sublime or a study of racial characteristics; and it is not my wish to contradict Turner's contention. But it is important to grasp the fact that, for good or for evil his view of art is not generally held in France, by composer or by public; and that to seek in French music primarily for a revelation of the composer's soul or for marks of the sublime is to look for something which the French consider a by-product. This instinctive shying away from the obviously great, high-sounding aims no more betokens artistic cynicism or impotence than the refusal to make a display of personal temperament and characteristics argues a lack of personality or character. The French composer is consciously concerned with the two data which no one can question—his intelligence and his senses. Music has remained in France longer than elsewhere the art of arranging sounds in agreeable and intellectually satisfying patterns. Every composer worthy of his name will inevitably reveal himself, his character, in his music; but this revelation is a by-product to the French, whereas to Turner and the majority of English music-lovers it is of primary importance. The French composer is unhappy with such a word as sublimity, which suggests to him a

single, and by now a largely conventional, form of excellence.
He would prefer the humbler search for perfection in all forms,
however small, and would be more prepared to find the sublime
in a perfectly finished and balanced piano prelude than in a work
planned on a larger scale, with more obvious pretensions to great-
ness but less aesthetically satisfying. In fact, the primacy accorded
in England to what are in reality moral values in a work of art is
generally refused in France; and the attempt by d'Indy and other
followers of César Franck to bring French musical feeling more
into line with that of England and Germany in this matter only
resulted in a violent reaction, which has been more significant in
the history of music than the movement which prompted it.

The regarding of a piece of music as an artefact—a thing of
planned shape, dimensions, colour and consistency—rather than
as the expression of an emotion whose end is in itself, brings the
French composer nearer than any other to the plastic artist. The
pictorial element, varying from the most naïve to the most sophisticated, has been a permanent feature in French music, closely connected with that traditional association with the dance which has
distinguished French music from that of Italy, where the basic
element has been the human voice. Again the ordinary English
music-lover's sympathies are alienated. England's musical tradition is largely vocal and the human voice is the ideal conductor of
that warm, specifically human, emotional quality which English
listeners ask of music. Pictorial music is valued, as by Beethoven,
inasmuch as the emotional reaction takes precedence over the
pictorial, the feelings of the seer over his suggestion of the things
seen, the pictorial. A composer who, like Ravel, boasts that his
music is *mehr Malerei als Empfindung*—more scene-painting than
sensibility—is felt not only to have blasphemed but to have put
himself beyond consideration as a great composer. And yet nothing
could be more illogical. No one really supposes that the composer
can, even if he would, keep his personal reactions out of his music,
for the most crassly representative art is but nature or 'reality' seen
through a temperament; and in taking the temperament for granted the French are doing no more than accepting the facts.

The qualities for which French art is famous—logic, clarity,
moderation and balance—are the corollaries or the direct results
of this deliberate restriction of field, this concentration on the data
of the intelligence and the senses and this instinctive mistrust of the
vague and large-sounding. Those French artists who have proved

exceptions to this general rule show a bad head for heights. How uncertainly, for all their boldness and ardour, do Berlioz, Hugo, and Balzac range among the peaks of the spirit! In the early years of the period with which this study deals, a great foreign influence, that of Wagner, swept into French music and for a short time set a fashion which was at odds with the national character. At the same time a reaction against the routine and superficiality of Parisian musical life centred around César Franck, a Belgian by origin, whose traditions were ecclesiastical rather than national, those of the Catholic church organist rather than the French secular artist. Both Wagner and Franck, parallel and complementary influences in French music, deflected the interest of a whole generation away from plastic, pictorial, or architectural, interests towards that of emotional expression. Duparc's 'Je veux être ému' was this generation's motto and their emphasis on emotion marks off Franck's pupils both from their contemporaries (except those few who were wholly under the spell of Wagner) and from the French tradition in general. Just how far César Franck was a creation of his pupils it is difficult to say, but his influence on French music was wholly their work. D'Indy assumed the role of a musical Savonarola, castigating superficiality and complacency in the name of Franck, the Pater Seraphicus. His foundation, the Schola Cantorum, was a home of musical Puritanism, a Port-Royal or house of the prophets; and d'Indy's Catholicism and regionalism coloured his whole conception of music in an exactly opposite sense to the fashionable metropolitan paganism of Paris in the eighteen-nineties. The whole movement connected with the Schola was partly a reassertion of the provinces against Paris and partly a recrudescence of the Jansenist spirit, familiar in religious thought and in letters but hitherto unknown in music. If Port-Royal in the seventeenth century proved the home of saints and scholars rather than of creative artists, the same was true of the Schola Cantorum. D'Indy won converts, but though he formed many artists none of them came to artistic maturity until they outgrew the influence of the Schola. Roussel's relation to the Schola was very much that of Racine to Port-Royal; and before his death d'Indy himself had abandoned his aggressive Germanic earnestness and was writing chamber music whose qualities are the traditional qualities of French art.

César Franck is probably still the most highly rated French composer among the ordinary concert-going public in England.

(It is significant that he was at one time W. J. Turner's favourite composer.) But the music of his pupils and disciples has never won much favour. It is as though French music were fated to displease the British public; for instead of appearing 'merely clever' the music of Franck's disciples sins by an excess in the opposite direction and embarrasses the listener by the tremulous plangency of its emotionalism. Even in the song, which Debussy considered the only unambiguous home of melody and straightforward emotional expression, the English public meets many difficulties. There is the highly stylized diction or declamation in Debussy, the rarefied and sophisticated musical atmosphere in Fauré and the exotic note in Ravel. In fact the best French songs generally appeal to the more highly-trained chamber music audience than to the lovers of *Lieder*. Throughout the whole range of French music, too, though especially in the sphere of the song, there is a strong sensual element which embarrasses and even repels the unsophisticated Englishman. Modesty is demanded in different contexts by the two nations; and the French find the emotional immodesty of much of the German and Slav music admired in England as embarrassing as the English find a frank preoccupation with physical passion. Fauré sets Verlaine's

> C'est l'extase langoureuse,
> C'est la fatigue amoureuse.

Debussy chooses Baudelaire's

> Tes beaux yeux sont las,
>   Pauvre amante!
> Reste longtemps sans les rouvrir,
> Dans cette pose nonchalante
> Où t'a surprise le plaisir.

Roussel, in a less voluptuous age, happily sets such a line as

> Que la ceinture d'or sous les seins nus se noue!

and these examples could be multiplied endlessly. Try to translate such lines into English; they are untranslateable. The words they require have quite different associations in English—medical or 'naughty' (which our grandfathers significantly called 'French'). Not only the right words, but the right mood is lacking. On the other hand the music to which Fauré, Debussy and Roussel set these immodest words is chastened and modest compared with the love music of *Tristan* (where in the text the physical realities of love are replaced by neuter abstracts), with the suppressed sensuality of Brahms or the acrid salaciousness of Strauss. English prudery is mistaken by the French for hypocrisy, because it is shocked by the statement in plain words of sentiments and sense-impressions which are welcomed provided they are disguised in vague generalities or idealistic trappings. The English find French frankness in such matters crude, unromantic and embarrassing; and this difference in taste and approach has played a considerable part in preventing French vocal music from becoming popular with the general public.

But only with the general public. The refined palate, both sensual and intellectual, of the more sophisticated classes, in England as elsewhere, is delighted by the French music of the last seventy years. The modern musical arbiters of elegance—Stravinsky, Constant Lambert, Virgil Thomson, Casella, Falla—have been French enthusiasts without exception. The typical sophisticated eclectic taste of the present day, embodied by Stravinsky, even proclaims as admirable models the early Gounod, Delibes, Bizet, Chabrier and Messager—all music dismissed by the more naïve music-lover as cheap or superficial compared with Brahms and Strauss. An admiration for Satie is an article of faith among the sophisticated, whether they know his music or not; and this is simply because Satie is the quintessence, the *reductio ad absurdum*, of the French protest against the opulence and luxury—both emotional and purely sonorous—which characterized Wagner's music and in one form or another threatened to deprave the whole of music. Satie was the perfect protestant, the purge after the banquet, a historical necessity; but a negative rather than a positive force. It is abundantly clear what his music is not, less easy to state its positive qualities; but in any case it is necessary to have a Gallicized palate to appreciate his particular flavour.

French music since 1870 has been of great importance historically. Of the three giants who overshadowed the middle years of the nineteenth century, from 1830 to 1880, Wagner has eventually proved most conservative in his influence; it was Berlioz and Liszt who were pregnant with the 'music of the future'. Wagner's achievement was complete and self-contained, while Berlioz and Liszt always suggested more than they achieved, opening avenues which they themselves never penetrated. The Russian composers of the eighteen-sixties and eighteen-seventies took up many of these suggestions; they made a new use of colour and turned for inspiration to musical and literary elements quite outside the German romantic field of vision—to the East, the Slavonic folk-song or the music of the Orthodox Church. By 1890 this Russian music was beginning to be known in France and it played a large part in determining the development of Debussy, Ravel, Dukas and Schmitt. In the eighteen-nineties, while Strauss was squeezing the last drops out of the Wagner-Liszt tradition in his tone-poems, Debussy was inventing a new musical language and a new aesthetic, in which an important element was the Russian music which had developed from the crossing of the Berlioz-Liszt strain with the native Slavonic elements. Liszt was the common term, the man with three nationalities, who was Hungarian, French and German in turn and ended his life recognizing the claims of a supra-national religion as stronger than those of any nationality. But it was through France that Russian music influenced Western Europe and for thirty years after 1890 France was, for good and for evil, the country where musical history was being written, the scene of that evolution whose pattern every other country has eventually followed.

This historical significance lends an interest even to the years immediately following 1918. The reaction against tradition was inevitable and anyone who is impatient with the music of Satie, Poulenc or Milhaud should read through Strauss's *Symphonia Domestica*, Schönberg's *Gurrelieder* and Mahler's *Eighth Symphony*. There could be no fruitful development along those lines—'not that way, that way madness lies'. In Vienna the reaction was more apparent than real; the old emotions were volatilized under heavy intellectual pressure but they remained the same, only in a gassy instead of a liquid form. In Paris the revolution was more drastic and there was a short-lived attempt to break away from the whole tradition of emotional expression. But the next twenty years were spent in the search for a substitute, a search which all now admit to have been vain.

This book does not attempt to deal with the new movements and personalities which have entered French music since the death of Fauré in 1924. The last chapter merely pursues the careers of the composers already mentioned in earlier chapters. By 1924 the movement which originated in Paris had spread to every European country and France lost her unique position. It is plainly more difficult for a foreigner to judge among composers of the second and third rank than among those who have been acclaimed outside their own country. Foreign studies of contemporary music often devote considerable space to British composers of whom many of their compatriots have scarcely heard and do no more than mention in passing figures of great local significance. This difficulty is increased in dealing with living composers, who are rated not only differently by their compatriots and foreigners, but even by different groups of their compatriots. I have not tried to achieve a spurious French outlook in writing this book; it has not been submitted to French criticism nor have I taken trouble to discover the latest quotations in the Parisian aesthetic stock-market for the various composers concerned. The book will therefore in all probability seem naïve and provincial to any French reader, as callow as many foreign studies of English art or literature seem to us. Since the book is meant for English readers, this does not greatly concern me. I have tried to write with as much objectivity as possible of a period which is not only important to the general understanding of contemporary music but also rich in music which I find personally sympathetic. I make no extravagant claims for any individual composer; but I believe that few countries at any period have been richer in the best music of the second rank. Taste, intelligence and skill cannot replace the individual genius or, divorced from largeness of character, create works of the first magnitude; but widely diffused they can ensure a very high average standard, a musical culture only inferior to that which is formed round the greatest constellations.

I

BERLIOZ was fortunate to die without witnessing the miseries of the Prussian War and the Commune. In 1869 it was only the politically conscious in France who realized that after Austria, France's turn must come, sooner or later; and Berlioz, never at any time a serious politician, was by then in any case too ill and broken to take an interest in public events. The complete failure of *Les Troyens* had finished him; he could struggle no longer against indifference and misunderstanding, and in March he died. The great generation of French romantics was breaking up. Delacroix had gone in 1863, Baudelaire in 1867, and Théophile Gautier only just survived the war, to die in 1872. The deliberate frivolity of the Second Empire, the shameless place-seeking and corruption of Napoleon the Third's régime, had had a double effect on the artistic world. The serious artist, Berlioz or Baudelaire, turned his back on public life in a gesture natural to those who inhabit and cultivate exclusive, 'private' universes. The less serious, but more extravert, artist such as Offenbach, frankly enjoyed, even if he did not make direct use of the comic indignities of the Second Empire. Offenbach's operettas were so rooted in this well-dunged soil that they virtually disappeared with the régime, and Offenbach never lived to witness his only subsequent success, the *Contes d'Hoffmann*. Auber, director of the Conservatoire since 1842 and Imperial Maître de Chapelle since 1857, died during the Commune—a witness of the revolutions of 1789, 1830, 1848 and finally 1871, who maintained through them all his reputation for charm, wit, kind-heartedness and his brilliant if superficial artistic gifts.

On the surface it was the end of an era; but in reality the seeds of the new, post-war world had begun to germinate long before 1870. The great figures who were disappearing had been prophetic. Romanticism had mingled with the Parnassian ideal of dispassionate objectivity in Baudelaire, with the beginnings of a new conception of technique in Delacroix. Flaubert, who lived on until 1880, was the typical bridge between the old and the new dispensations, a Janus who faced backward to the romanticism of his young days and forward to the realism which was to become the new slogan of the eighteen-seventies. Berlioz stood alone, too individual to fall into any classification; and when a new French music was born, like a phoenix from the ashes of the war and the Commune, the names that first became famous were mostly those of young men who lacked both academic distinctions and influential positions in the musical world. The Société Nationale de Musique was founded on 25 February 1871, only a few days before the Prussians marched down the Champs-Élysées; and it must have seemed almost ironical to adopt, at the moment of France's greatest humiliation, the proud motto of ARS GALLICA. Many years later the chief founder of the new society, Camille Saint-Saëns, described for another generation the state of French music in the late eighteen-fifties and early eighteen-sixties, only ten years before.

'The young musicians of to-day', he wrote in 1900, 'would find it difficult to imagine the state of music in France when Gounod came on the scene. The *beau monde* thought of nothing but Italian music; the last ripples of the tide on which Rossini, Donizetti, Bellini, and the wonderful generations of singers who had interpreted their works, had sailed to take Europe by storm, were still sensible; and the star of Verdi, veiled as yet with the morning mist, was just appearing above the horizon. The real public, that is the *bon bourgeois*, recognized no music outside the opera and French comic opera, which included works written for France by distinguished foreigners. There was a universal cult, a positive idolatry, of "melody" or, more exactly, of the tune which could be picked up at once and easily remembered. A magnificent period such as the theme of the slow movement in Beethoven's Eighth Symphony was seriously described as "algebra in music". . . . Fifty years ago *Robert le Diable* and *Les Huguenots* were spoken of in a voice of hushed awe, *Guillaume Tell* with a kind of pious unction. Hérold and Boïeldieu were already accounted classics and the laurels of the French school were disputed by Auber and Adolphe Adam. Enthusiasm for Auber went to fantastic lengths and it was forbidden to point to the evidences of careless workmanship which must inevitably appear in any music which is turned out at such speed and in such profusion as his. Outside these two large groups there existed a small circle of professional and amateur musicians who really cared for and cultivated music for its own sake, secret worshippers of Haydn, Mozart, Beethoven and occasionally Bach and Handel. It was quite useless to try and get a symphony, a trio, or a quartet performed except by the Société des Concerts du Conservatoire or by one or two private chamber music societies.'

Saint-Saëns was thirty-six in 1871; he could remember the years of which he was writing and he spoke from bitter experience. But it should be said in justice that, bad as things undoubtedly were, they were perhaps not quite as bad as Saint-Saëns remembered them. The facts points to a little, very natural, exaggeration in his picture of French musical life. There were quite a number of chamber music societies who performed the classics, even if they did not ask for modern works to include in their programmes. There was the Société Alard Franchomme, founded in 1848: the Société des Derniers Quatuors de Beethoven, founded in 1851: the Société de Musique de Chambre Armingaud (in which Lalo played the viola), founded in 1856: Lamoureux's Séances Populaires de Musique de Chambre, founded in 1859: and the Société de Musique de Chambre Jacoby-Vuillaume, founded in 1864. Saint-Saëns's description seems really to apply with more justice, therefore, to the eighteen-forties, when he was a child.

The badness of the state of affairs at the Opéra, on the other hand, could hardly be exaggerated. Between 1852–70 precisely five new French works were included in the repertory: Félicien David's *Herculanum*, Ambroise Thomas's *Hamlet*, Gounod's *Sapho*, *La Nonne Sanglante* and *La Reine de Saba*. The repertory consisted of Rossini's *Guillaume Tell*, Meyerbeer's *L'Africaine* and *L'Étoile du Nord;* Donizetti's *Lucia di Lammermoor* and *La Favorita;* Auber's *Muette de Portici;* and Halévy's *La Juive*. Most of these works dated from the eighteen-thirties or forties and it was this extraordinary time-lag in producing even foreign works which earned the Opéra its name of 'la musée de la musique'. At the Opéra-Comique conditions were not much better, except that the works performed were mainly French. Boïeldieu, Adolphe Adam and Auber provided most of the repertory; and the same privileged composers represented modern French music, David's *Lalla Roukh* being given in 1862 and Thomas's *Mignon* in 1866. The younger composers had no outlet for their work except the Théâtre Lyrique where the success of Gounod's *Faust* in 1859 encouraged Carvalho to take a comparatively bold line and gradually to introduce more modern French works into his repertory. Gounod was the favourite and his *Philémon et Baucis* was given at the Théâtre Lyrique in 1860, *Mireille* in 1864 and *Roméo et Juliette* in 1867. After Gounod came Reyer, whose *La Statue* was given in 1861: Berlioz with *Les Troyens à Carthage* (1863): and Bizet with *Les Pêcheurs de Perles* (1863) and *La Jolie Fille de Perth* (1867). The foundation by Pasdeloup in 1860 of the Concerts Populaires, cheap Sunday concerts, introduced

Parisian audiences by degrees to the symphonies of Beethoven, to Mendelssohn and Schumann, and later to occasional modern French works, such as Bizet's *Souvenirs de Rome*, which was performed (and hissed) in 1869. This was the extent of the serious musical life of Paris outside the Société des Concerts du Conservatoire, which remained semi-private and strictly conservative. There was very little good orchestral music, no *lieder*, not much chamber music; and the little there was met for the most part with indifference or hostility. It was the age of the catacombs and very few observers could have foretold the sudden blaze of musical activity and life which was to spring up in the eighteen-seventies.

Faust made Gounod easily the foremost French composer of the day in 1860. Born in 1818, he won the Prix de Rome in 1839 and the friendships he formed there influenced not only his own personal style of composition but also the subsequent history of French music. Mendelssohn's married sister, Fanny Hensel, introduced him as a student in Rome to the works of Bach, Beethoven and her own brother, to the classics of German literature and particularly to Goethe; so that it was natural, when the time came to decide the allotting of the last years covered by the Prix de Rome, that Gounod should be anxious to know Germany and German music at first hand. He spent the year 1842-3 in Vienna, where he heard a great deal of German music, including Beethoven, and had two masses of his own performed, which was a great honour for a French composer in those days. From Vienna he went to Berlin, where he met the Hensels again, and then to Leipzig, where he made friends with Mendelssohn himself and attended his rehearsals of the Gewandhaus orchestra, which at that time was probably the best in Europe. It was not until May 1845 that Gounod returned to Paris, bringing with him a conception of music which was to become overlaid, but never quite obscured or forgotten. Ardently pious, he had come under the influence of Lacordaire while he was in Rome, and in Paris he became organist to the Missions Etrangères in the Rue du Bac. His piety had its counterpart in his music. He was already in love with the bland, serene simplicity which he was so often to carry to the verge of banality, and over; but his experience of Germany and his friendship with the Mendelssohns had given him an ideal of solid musical workmanship as well as an attitude towards the artist's 'calling' which breathes the full German romantic earnestness. 'Pour lui, l'art est un sacerdoce,' young Bizet wrote of Gounod, adding a touch of malice, 'c'est lui qui l'a dit.' This simple, well-founded piety, religious and artistic, was something new in the world of Parisian music; and the fathers of the Missions Etrangères soon complained that their congregations found the works of Bach and Palestrina, offered to them by the young organist, rather severe after the showy and theatrical church music to which they were accustomed. It was something unheard of that a Prix de Rome should be interesting himself in Bach and Palestrina rather than in Auber and Meyerbeer.

In 1847 Gounod began studying for the priesthood; but he changed his mind before long and set to work instead on his first opera, encouraged by his friendship with Pauline Viardot the singer, whom he had met first in Rome and then again in 1851. *Sapho* was cleanly and firmly written and genuinely dramatic; the characters were alive, even if they were rather sentimentally conceived. Above all, there was no hint of Rossini nor of Meyerbeer; Gluck seemed rather to have been Gounod's ideal, as Adolphe Adam pointed out. Berlioz found *Sapho* too 'fierce' (a curious distinction for any work of Gounod) and remarked, rather enigmatically, that 'a musician must before all else write music', while Théophile Gautier complained that there was no ballet. The music for *Ulysse*, written the following year, was a failure, although it contains well-written things, charming without being frivolous, and again, like *Sapho*, wholly French. Gounod was discouraged and in his next opera *La Nonne Sanglante*, he made an attempt to captivate the public by choosing a melodramatic libretto after the manner of *Robert le Diable*. That was in 1854. Three years later Gounod had a nervous breakdown which looked for a time as though it might develop into a permanent mental derangement, but he recovered so completely that in the three following years he wrote three of his best works. *Le Médecin malgré lui* (1858) is witty, light-handed and perfectly adapted to Molière. Here and in *Philémon et Baucis* (1860) Gounod is at his best, as he really was rather than as he wished to be—an elegant musician, with a charming lyrical gift, a genuine instinct for what may be called 'chamber' drama, and a discreet and well-balanced sense of the orchestra. *Faust*, his masterpiece, was also his undoing. Vast popularity combined with his religious feelings—something of a desire to play the prophet—to make him concentrate on the grand manner, the large scale. Scudo, critic of the *Revue des Deux Mondes*, had touched Gounod's ambition when he wrote of *Philémon et Baucis*: 'Formal details, niceties of orchestration and stylistic charm will not make any composition dramatic if passion, forthright ideas and variety of colour are only conspicuous by their absence.' This was an only slightly veiled appeal to Meyerbeerian standards and in due course Gounod retraced his steps to the musical orthodoxy of the day and produced *La Reine de Saba* and *Roméo et Juliette*. After starting as a Wagnerian suspect—that is to say, as an original musician— Gounod became steadily more fashionable and Italianate during the eighteen-sixties until his flight to England at the time of the war and his ten-months' stay here (September 1870–July 1871) introduced him to the English taste for oratorio and turned his thoughts back to religious music. *Mireille* (1864) was an oasis, a fresh, natural, charming work with no hint of the vast, showy machinery of the Opéra; but it had little success and no successor.

After 1870 Gounod wrote only three operas: *Cinq Mars*, *Polyeucte* and *Le Tribut de Zamora*. Otherwise he devoted himself to oratorio, spending the last twenty years of his life producing those grandiose and blandly banal *objets de piété* by which alone, with the exception of *Faust*, he is remembered outside France. The gay, finely wrought smaller works of his middle life were forgotten, as Tennyson's earlier lyrics were for a time forgotten. *Faust* played in Gounod's development the same role as *In Memoriam* in Tennyson's. The phenomenal success of a single work put both of these great artists on a false trail, so that they spent the rest of their lives pouring their naturally lyrical gifts into epic moulds. Both were excellent craftsmen, but at the end of his life Gounod could have echoed Tennyson's pathetic complaint that 'he was the greatest master of English living and had nothing to say'.

'Il s'écoute phraser,' said Blaze de Bury of Gounod and it was not a deliberate pose. The pretentious, pontifical side of his character had always been there. While he was working on the composition of *Roméo et Juliette* he wrote to a friend: 'Au milieu de ce silence il me semble que j'entends me parler en dedans quelque chose de très grand, de très clair, de très simple et de très enfant à la fois.' As he grew older this side of his character grew out of all proportion and he became famous in Paris for his deliberately mystifying remarks, although one may suspect that *obiter dicta* such as 'les enfants, ce sont les roses du jardin de la vie' represented a more genuine, less deliberately cultivated side of his character.

It would be wrong to allow these weaknesses to obscure Gounod's real merits and the part which he played in the re-establishment of a genuinely French musical ideal among French musicians. In his *Portraits et Souvenirs* (Paris, 1900) Saint-Saëns summed up Gounod's qualities as they appeared to his fine critical judgement:

'Expressiveness was always his ideal: that is why there are so few notes in his music . . . each note sings. For the same reason instrumental music, "pure" music, was never his forte. His aim in orchestration was to discover beautiful colour and, far from adopting ready-made the methods of the great masters, he applied himself to the study of timbres and tried to invent new combinations suited to his own ends.'

Later in the same essay Saint-Saëns makes an instructive comparison between Berlioz and Gounod.

' "What an elegant man Berlioz is!" said Gounod to me one day. Berlioz's elegance was not visible at first sight . . . it is hidden in the web, the very flesh of his music . . . and this is the exact antithesis of Gounod, whose style is irreproachably elegant on the surface, but sometimes conceals a basic vulgarity, rather like a streak of plebeian blood which imparts a muscularity and acts as a safeguard against the nervous instability inherent in good breeding. It is the antidote to insipidity. . . .'

Finally Saint-Saëns describes the characteristics of Gounod's later works (i.e. roughly those after 1870).

'He tried to minimize the number of modulations in his music, on the ground that it was a mistake to use such a powerful aid to expressiveness too freely. . . . His aim was to obtain the maximum possible effect with the minimum of apparent effort, to reduce the representation of external events and objects to a minimum and to concentrate all the interest on the expression of feelings.'

This was indeed the tradition of Gluck, as Adolphe Adam had remarked of *Sapho* as early as 1851. It was not the attitude of the composers who founded the Société Nationale, and even if Gounod had been on the spot rather than in England it is doubtful whether he would have been as sympathetic with the new school as he would have been twenty to twenty-five years earlier. Berlioz summed up his opinion of French music in 1855 in the following words: 'Apart from Saint-Saëns, a fine musician nineteen years old, and Gounod, who has just written a very fine Mass, I can see nothing but ephemeral insects hovering over this stinking morass which we call Paris.'

Camille Saint-Saëns was born in 1835 and was thus Gounod's junior by seventeen years. He was a pupil of Halévy at the Conservatoire but failed to win the Prix de Rome. An early passion for Mozart soon ripened into an enthusiastic admiration for the 'classical' music in which Paris was so poor, and at the age of eighteen Saint-Saëns had written his first symphony, followed in 1855 by a pianoforte quintet and a year later by a second symphony. These early works show a musicianship, a purely technical facility and a sense of instrumental style which was without parallel in the music of the eighteen-sixties, not excepting that of Gounod himself. In 1858 Saint-Saëns was appointed organist of the Madeleine and three years later he began to teach the pianoforte at the École Niedermeyer, where he had Gabriel Fauré and André Messager as pupils. He was a brilliant pianist, with the same facility and sense of style in performance as in composition, and his first three pianoforte concertos (1865, 1868 and 1869) contain more original, more personal music than the symphonies. With Berlioz dead, Auber dying, and Gounod fled to England, Saint-Saëns found himself in 1871 virtually doyen of French music at the age of thirty-six. He had been ignored or abused by the official musical world, at least as a composer; and it was inevitable that when he came to found the Société Nationale the men whom he collected round him should be those who had themselves felt the weight of official conservatism, who looked to the new gods—to Liszt among foreigners and to Gounod and Saint-Saëns himself in France—for encouragement and leadership. These were the young; and the average age of the first members of the Société Nationale was something in the early thirties.

In 1871 Saint-Saëns himself was deeply impressed by Liszt's musical personality, although the style of the first two symphonies and the first pianoforte concerto recalls much earlier models— Mozart, Weber, Mendelssohn, and occasionally Beethoven. Even when the texture of the orchestration was more modern—as in the slow movement of the second symphony, where the strings are muted and the cor anglais has a predominant part; or the second movement of the concerto—the musical thought remains fundamentally derivative. In the following passage from the first symphony, for instance,

Ex. 1

Mendelssohn and Weber have about equal honours. There are more daring moments in the second symphony; and such phrases as:

Ex. 2

sempre più appassionato

seem to anticipate by nearly thirty years the 'serene anxiety' of César Franck. In the concerto, again, originality appears in details. The ornamentation of the slow movement is often quite out out of the ordinary run of virtuosic filigree work, and such a passage as the following:

Ex. 3

contains the seeds of devices which are genuinely harmonic, not merely decorative, and were not found fully developed until nearly forty years later, when Ravel used them in his *Jeux d'eau* (1901).

These are admittedly exceptions. It was not until the second and third pianoforte concertos that Saint-Saëns began to write thoroughly original works rather than brilliantly prophetic passages in fundamentally derivative settings. In the second concerto the writing is far more sure, more loosely knit and at the same time warmer than in the first. The ornamentation and the passages in double octaves show the influence of Liszt, but this has been properly assimilated, and the whole work is one of the earliest examples (the Introduction and Rondo Capriccioso for violin and orchestra, is another) of those well-written, well-designed and always pleasing compositions of which Saint-Saëns was to produce so many during his long lifetime. The thought is very seldom profound, occasionally it is even trivial; but the manner is unfailingly charming, full of musical breeding, spirited and un-portentous, and it had a great influence on the formation of the new ideals of the eighteen-seventies. There was very little other orchestral music to serve as a model and Saint-Saëns's idiom answered—and still answers—to qualities fundamental in the French musical character, to the desire for balance, the hatred of pretentiousness, the love of fine workmanship and the respect for tradition.

In the third pianoforte concerto Liszt's influence is even more marked than in the second, and that of Beethoven has grown at the expense of the more elegant Mozart and Mendelssohn. In the *cantabile e legato* of the slow movement there is more than a hint of the emotional warmth and richness of texture (even the chromatically falling bass) which have become associated with the name of Franck:

Ex. 4

and the whole work is the mature expression of a magnificently musicianly, if not strikingly original, character.

Gounod and Saint-Saëns, then, were the pillars supporting the new edifice of French music, unlike each other and yet both essentially French. Gounod's passion for expressiveness and his preoccupation with orchestral colour were well balanced by the classical purity of Saint-Saëns's style and his feeling for linear design. Both were fully aware of their debt to the German schools, predominantly romantic in the one case, classical in the other; but neither was anything but French in outlook and feeling. Gounod's appreciation will show how Saint-Saëns appeared to the most gifted of the older generation.

'Saint-Saëns possesses one of the most astonishing musical organizations that I know,' he wrote. 'He is a musician armed with every weapon. He is master of his art as no other composer is; he knows the classics by heart, he plays with and makes light of the orchestra as of the pianoforte, which says a great deal. He is neither finicking, violent, nor emphatic. He has no system, belongs to no party or clique; he does not pose as a reformer of anything; he writes as he feels and makes use of what he knows.'

In fact, it is almost possible to divide French music of the next fifty years into the two traditions, that of Gounod and that of Saint-Saëns; and although the greatest individual works spring from a crossing of the traditions or stocks, it is probably true to say that most French composers until 1914 showed—at any rate in their general outlook—a natural leaning towards one of the two traditions rather than the other. Thus, in their different ways, Massenet, Franck and Fauré may be said to derive from the Gounod tradition, while Chabrier, Dukas and Ravel (in ways even more different) can be related to that of Saint-Saëns.

In 1871 the war with Prussia and the Commune had left France shattered. Whatever might develop out of defeat and grim hatred, it could never be a repetition of the brilliant, frothy extravagance of the Second Empire. For a short while, at least, the overpowering predominance of the opera was broken, for opera needs money and a stable social system. Here was an opportunity for the more austere musical forms of orchestral and chamber music to gain a footing in Paris, and it was in these forms that the members of the Société Nationale first distinguished themselves. By 1872, it is true, Offenbach was back and producing five operas in that one year alone; but it was no longer the same thing, and the operetta furore of the year was created by none of these but by Lecocq's *La Fille de Mme Angot*.

More typical of the time were Saint-Saëns's symphonic poems and chamber music and the sudden, tragic flowering of the young Alexis de Castillon, which was cut short by his death in 1873. In those last three years of his life Castillon wrote as much chamber music as many composers produce in a lifetime; for Franck had found the means of releasing a whole flood of musical energy which Castillon's first teacher, Victor Massé, had only succeeded in damming. It was only in 1868, when he was thirty years old and despairing of finding himself musically, that Castillon was introduced to César Franck by his friend Duparc, who was already one of Franck's pupils. The war interrupted his studies and ruined his health, so that he died at thirty-five, but not before he had produced a piano quintet, a string quintet and pianoforte trio, a

pianoforte quartet and concerto, and a violin sonata. Castillon
was still an amateur when he died, but an amateur of the most
fertile and promising kind, with ideals which might have
won him a place beside the greatest of Franck's disciples if he had
lived. A passage such as the following, from the first movement of
his string quartet, shows the intensity of his music, his obvious
admiration of Beethoven and the ideal of vigour and expressiveness which he shares with d'Indy.

Ex. 5

Saint-Saëns's first violoncello sonata does not show the same feeling for chamber music style as, for instance, Castillon's violin sonata. The pianoforte is too preponderant, with frequent tremolando
passages which sound badly; and the influence of Beethoven
appears unassimilated, more in the exterior features of the writing
than in the musical thought. The violoncello concerto in A minor
is a brilliant and wholly successful piece of its kind. It is original in
design, a trifle monotonous rhythmically but full of decorative
charm. Saint-Saëns opened up more fertile ground with his symphonic poems, in which he followed, without imitating, the example of Liszt, whose influence we have already seen in the third

pianoforte concerto. The *Rouet d'Omphale* is the most simple of all
Saint-Saëns's symphonic poems, consisting of no more than the
most elementary ternary form (ABA). *Phaéton* is in every way more
ambitious. The opening chords on the harp give the half-exotic,
half-mysterious atmosphere, and the trumpet and trombone
theme of the ride, beneath the brilliant gallop of the strings, and
the very Lisztian emotional passage are worked together in a
double ternary form of a simple kind (ABC, ABC) into what is
really the most successful of all Saint-Saëns's symphonic poems.
The *Danse Macabre* is the best-known of the four and contains,
besides some very effective programme music of the purely pictorial, un-psychological kind, a brilliant orchestral device. The
midnight clock, with which the work opens, is represented by a
single D, held for twelve bars by the horn, struck twelve times by
the harp; and this gives both the realistic and the poetic or atmospheric side of the picture in the simplest and neatest way possible.
The last of the four, the *Jeunesse d'Hercule*, is the longest and formally
most complicated, to correspond with the more elaborate programme. Musically it is on a level with the *Phaéton*; and it is interesting that it is in these two that the influence of Liszt is most in
evidence. The opening of the *Jeunesse d'Hercule*, the long, wandering thread of thirds in the muted violins

Ex. 6

and even the rather broken structure of the whole work show
Saint-Saëns in an unfamiliar light, more emotional and less dapper
than usual. The fourth pianoforte concerto is the climax of his
orchestral production in the eighteen-seventies. The pianoforte
dominates the whole work, in the grandiose romantic style, rang-
ing through the most diverse moods, capricious and emotional, as
different as possible from the delicately drawn and discreetly
coloured music of the early orchestral works. The quartet is different again, and here Saint-Saëns showed his unfailing sense of style.

The colouring is far less brilliant than in the concerto, the emotion more disciplined; and the romantic atmosphere of the first movement is succeeded by a deliberately archaic slow movement, as in the second symphony and the first pianoforte concerto.

As order returned to Paris, the theatres opened and with them the Opéra, the Opéra-Comique and the Théâtre Lyrique. The members of the Société Nationale were soon in evidence in this sphere too. As an operatic composer Saint-Saëns is remembered only by his *Samson et Dalila*, which was given by Liszt at Weimar in 1877 but not heard in France until 1890, when it was played at Rouen. It is in fact his only successful attempt at opera. His first, *Le Timbre d'Argent*, was written in 1864–5 but not given in Paris until 1877. *La Princesse Jaune* (1872) was a failure in Paris; and the directors of the Opéra, who made the unforgivable mistake of refusing to mount *Samson*, were justified in their refusal of *Étienne Marcel*, which was given at Lyons in 1879. Both *Le Timbre d'Argent* and *La Princesse Jaune* are small works, but they have neither the character nor the point of a work like Bizet's one-act *Djamileh*. The music, like everything Saint-Saëns wrote, is workmanlike and not without charm, but it is insipid and lacking in dramatic feeling. *Étienne Marcel* is a full-size opera on a French historical subject, with better moments than either of the other two but still uneven and without genuine dramatic feeling. *Samson* stands alone, though here again the inspiration comes and goes. All the Dalila music is good, for Saint-Saëns had the gift of expressing voluptuousness without losing his French sense of proportion. The heroic side of Samson, the music of the religious and military leader, is fine throughout, but especially in the last scene. Samson as Dalila's lover, her prey, is less convincing and more conventional. The choruses are fine in themselves, though they are not always strictly dramatic. What must have caught Liszt's imagination when he decided to give this unknown French work in Weimar was the unmistakable coherence of the whole work, its quality of genuine emotional unity, which can only be felt when a composer has really himself felt his subject. *Samson*, unlike Saint-Saëns's other operas, is a complete, coherent whole. It is possible to admire it or not, but the music creates its own emotional world which there is no gainsaying, and this is one of the greatest qualities which any work of art, and especially opera, can possess.

It is the lack of this quality in the early works of Jules Massenet which distinguishes him so completely from Georges Bizet. Both were most enthusiastic members of the new society. Bizet was only four years older than Massenet, but his career was almost ending as Massenet's began. Born in 1838, he won the Prix de Rome in 1857, returned to Paris in 1860 and had already produced two operas before the Prussian War, *Les Pêcheurs de Perles* and *La Jolie Fille de Perth*. It was not until 1872 that Bizet reached artistic maturity with his one-act opera *Djamileh* and the incidental music to Alphonse Daudet's *L'Arlésienne*; and three years later came *Carmen*, followed almost immediately by Bizet's death. But in these last three years of his life he had developed from a gifted student, in love with Italian opera and Gounod alternately, into a distinct personality. There is no escaping the Provence of the *Arlésienne* music; the landscape is not merely a background to the work, it is the main character, always present and perpetually active, and Bizet's music catches exactly the vigour and simplicity, the emotional torridity and the tragic fatality which underlie the uncompromising contours of the countryside. *Carmen* was Bizet's only operatic masterpiece. Only here did he get almost free of the weaknesses and concessions to convention which marred his earlier operas. Unwittingly he created a new ideal of directness and simplicity, by his 'direct action' assault on the sensibilities of his audience. Meilhac and Halévy, his librettists, had toned down Mérimée's story, but Carmen remained a revolutionary among operatic heroines of her day. Bizet's music combines in an extraordinary, instinctive way the most obviously attractive melodies with original orchestration, miraculously economic characterization and a sense of style which could make equal use of a *salon habañera*, the brass-band style of the bull-fight music and touches of contrapuntal writing scattered throughout the score. There is never a note too many or too few and each note tells. Nietzsche's enthusiasm for *Carmen* may have been partly a malicious anti-Wagnerian joke, but he was looking in the right direction to find an antidote to the cloudy giants, gods and dwarfs of the *Ring*. 'Music must be Mediterraneanized,' he said and it was in the bright light, the grace and the humanity of *Carmen* that he found his ideal.

The deaths of Bizet and Castillon were two major losses to French music, losses which could only be afforded at a time when a large and gifted younger generation was growing up, as in the eighteen-seventies. The amazing flowering of the next twenty years tended to obscure the potentialities of these two men, who died in their thirties. Bizet has been bitterly criticized and Castillon forgotten, while Massenet won the leading position as operatic composer, and the disciples of Franck claimed the honour of reconstituting French chamber music.

Jules Massenet studied with Ambroise Thomas and won the Prix de Rome at twenty-one in 1863. When he returned to Paris from Rome, the influence of his old master procured the performance of his first opera, *La Grand' Tante*, at the Opéra-Comique, and Pasdeloup played an orchestral suite at one of his concerts. But it was not until 1872 that *Don César de Bazan* brought Massenet really into the public notice. As a comic opera *Don César* satisfied the taste of the day, which was for a stereotyped farce with tender interludes. Musically it is of little interest. The first evidence of Massenet's real gifts was provided by the incidental music which he wrote for Leconte de Lisle's *Les Erinnyes* and by an oratorio, *Marie Magdeleine*, both produced in 1872. Massenet was hardly the composer to understand the mentality of Aeschylus, or even that of his French adapter; and the extent of his failure may be gauged by the fact that Electra's libation to her dead father is accompanied by the famous *Elégie*, which has since achieved international notoriety as a violoncello solo. But in itself the music is often sensitive and charming, a kind of gifted water-colour technique which it is not fair to condemn simply on the score of its being out of place as a background to the inexorable necessities and dark bloodiness of Aeschylus. *Marie Magdeleine*, with the title role taken by Pauline Viardot, had a great reception from the public. The reformed prostitute was still enjoying the vogue created by the Romantics (Victor Hugo's *Marion Delorme* and, above all, the younger Dumas's *Dame aux Camélias*) and there was almost no extreme of sentimentality to which the Parisian public would not go on this particular theme. The whole oratorio is a typical example of what d'Indy was later to call, in fury, Massenet's 'érotisme discret et quasi-religieux'. Apart from a few pseudo-classical, contrapuntal numbers and the melodramatic villainy of Judas, who urges Mary not to give up her prostitute's life, the whole work centres round the thinly veiled erotic relationship between Christ and the Magdalen, for which Massenet found an astonishingly apt idiom based on the blander passages of Gounod's *Faust*, but with a distinctly personal flavour added. It was this style, which he later modified and to a certain extent sophisticated but never really abandoned, that won Massenet the nickname of 'la fille de Gounod'. As often happens in such cases, *Marie Magdeleine* contains examples of more concentratedly 'Gounod-esque' music than any work of Gounod himself. A typical Gounod cadence occurs in the Magdalen's air 'Avez-vous entendu sa parole', which is in the key of A flat:

Ex. 7

Oui, sa clé-mence est di - vi - ne

Here everything is typical—the vocal line, the harmonization, the excursion from A flat into C major, even the words of the text. Encouraged by the success of *Marie Magdeleine*, Massenet produced a second 'discreetly erotic and quasi-religious' oratorio, *Eve*, in 1875. Here the style is more individual and the Prelude to Scene 2 consists of a melody which was to become typical not only for Massenet himself but for a whole generation of French composers who came under his influence.

Ex. 8

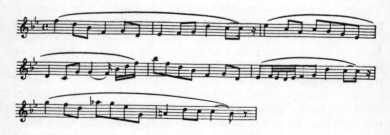

The structure is consistently two-bar; each phrase ends with the slurred feminine cadence. The whole melody is short-winded—it has no breadth, no emotional drive to force it over the meagre two bars or to modulate from the tonic. It was unquestionably inherited from Gounod, and the perpetuation of the type in French music was unhappily assured when Massenet was made professor of composition at the Conservatoire in 1878. But there are pro-

Léo Delibes
Drawing by Louise Abbéma

Camille Saint-Saëns
Caricature by Pauline Viardot

TWO PRIX DE ROME SCHOLARS

Jules Massenet
par S.Chaplin, 1864

phetic passages in *Eve*, passages which form a kind of middle term between Gounod and Debussy. Here are the comments of the Narrator after the Fall, where the whole-tone scale is hinted at.

Ex. 9

The triplet thirds are parents of innumerable passages in *Pelléas* and in the pianoforte and orchestral works of Debussy, though the four-square rhythm of the vocal part and its tendency to monotone are typical of the later works of Gounod. In his opera *Le Roi de Lahore* Massenet did little more than carry this 'new Gounodism' to the stage. The Oriental setting, with the Hindu priestess in the temple at evening and the two lovers competing for her hand, is little more than a re-telling of Bizet's *Pêcheurs de Perles*, while the Hindu paradise is almost identical with Gounod's Christian heaven, and Indra intones on a single note just as do the divine personages in Gounod's later works.

Gounod himself did not finally return from England until 1874, but his two cantatas of the eighteen-seventies, *Gallia* and *Jeanne d'Arc*, and even his opera *Cinq-Mars*, showed how deeply he had felt the events of 1870–1 as a Frenchman. Musically these works are below the best of Gounod's work in either field, opera or oratorio. Although *Gallia* has a fine opening and Gounod's heartfelt distress makes itself felt, the work as a whole is overweighted with the new style of Mendelssohnian oratorio which Gounod had encountered in England and not yet assimilated. *Cinq-Mars* is a work of transition, Gounod halting between the florid operatic style of *Roméo et Juliette* and the more individual style of the *Rédemption* and *Mors et Vita*, the 'music treated in the style of fresco' (*musique plane et peinte à fresque*) as the composer called it. *Polyeucte* was the only opera written wholly in this style, and it was a complete failure. In the words of Saint-Saëns, 'Au théâtre où la science, l'étude paraissent comiques, où les crimes les plus affreux ne sont pas sans attrait, l'amour divin est peu intéressant.' And *Polyeucte* is concerned very much with 'l'amour divin'. Simplicity is the rule.

'The long recitatives on a single note, or rising and descending by semitones, the solo parts proceeding invariably by the intervals of a third, a sixth or an octave, while the orchestral parts adhere to incessant reiteration of the same chord: these impart a monotony and a heaviness to the work which must weary the best-disposed audience.'

The *Judex* from *Mors et Vita* is a typical melody of the kind described above and its effect is nothing more than soporific. But *Polyeucte* contains some better music also, and Gounod seems in places to be returning to the ideals of Gluck, which had influenced the composition of his first opera, *Sapho*, nearly thirty years before. Unfortunately, he had none of Gluck's vigour or dramatic forthrightness, and simplicity alone degenerated more often than not into bland banality.

What French music in the eighteen-seventies lacked was a guiding personality who should collect round him the most promising of the younger generation. Saint-Saëns was too much of an eclectic and an individualist, and his personality attracted friends rather than disciples. Gounod's powers were, if not failing, at least passing through a transitional crisis; and he was a great deal in England. The necessary figure did exist, however, though he was hidden away in the organ loft of an unfashionable Parisian church; and he was not a Frenchman either by birth or, fundamentally, in feeling. César Franck was born at Liége, of Walloon parents, in 1822. The family moved to Paris in 1834 and at the age of fifteen Franck entered the Conservatoire, where he gained prizes for both organ and pianoforte. His father was ambitious and determined to make a virtuoso pianist of his brilliant son. César Franck started on this career, both as performer and composer, and there remain from what his later pupil, d'Indy, calls his 'first period' (1841–58) a number of florid and worthless pianoforte pieces and three trios, in which his real gifts begin dimly to show. In his oratorio *Ruth* (1846) Franck plainly found a genre which was sympathetic to him, one in which he could express the rather naïve and emotional mysticism which was the foundation of his character. After his marriage in 1848 he broke away from his family and their more showy ambitions for him, and settled down to an obscure life of private teaching, organist's work (first at Notre Dame de Lorette and then at St. Jean au Marais) and, in his little spare time, composition. But it was not until his appointment in 1858 as organist to Ste. Clotilde, where he was already choirmaster, that Franck's 'second period' began. During the next sixteen years Franck composed chiefly ecclesiastical music. Much of this does not really represent anything more than the *pièces d'occasion* demanded of any organist of the day. French ecclesiastical music was in any case at a low ebb in the eighteen-fifties and sixties, and although Gounod had done something to banish the purely secular, operatic style from the liturgy, the music which he put into its place does not seem to modern ears anything better than a compromise with the world. The Messe Solennelle and the Messe à Sainte Cécile contain, especially in the solo numbers, music of which the question might well be asked whether it were 'voluptuous piety or mystical eroticism' and, as we have seen, this was a genre which Massenet exploited with enormous success in the eighteen-seventies. A great deal of Franck's church music, though not fundamentally different from this, is certainly more daring harmonically and bears the mark of an original and inquisitive mind—or perhaps of a new and rather troubled sensibility. Liszt declared that the Six Pieces for organ (1862) had 'their place beside the masterpieces of Bach' and, as it were in return, Franck absorbed a great deal of the atmosphere and the theory of Liszt's own composition. The German romantics had their effect on Franck too; but it often seems that Beethoven and Schumann reached him indirectly, through the medium of Gounod and Liszt.

Franck's 'second period' as a composer reached its climax in two religious works on a large scale, *Les Béatitudes* (not performed until 1879, and then only privately) and the *Rédemption*, the first version of which was performed in 1873. Gounod's *Rédemption*, although it was not performed until 1882, was first conceived in 1868, so that he and Franck were working on the same idea at much the same time. It was in 1872, his fiftieth year, that Franck succeeded

Benoist as organ professor at the Conservatoire, and it was then that he for the first time reached artistic maturity. But he was almost completely unknown.

In his pianoforte lessons at the Jesuit College of Vaugirard Franck had as a pupil a boy named Henri Duparc, whom his family wished to study the law. Duparc was a keen musician and while he was nominally working for his law examinations he began to take lessons in harmony and composition from Franck. He was soon joined by two other young enthusiasts, Arthur Coquard and Albert Cahen, and when Duparc introduced Alexis de Castillon to Franck in 1868 the nucleus of the Franck school was formed. The little circle of pupils and friends who heard his fine playing and improvisation at Ste. Clotilde, and with whom he discussed his works during the processes of composition and revision, was well aware of his genius—though we may quite fairly assume that their critical judgement was affected by the simple goodness and personal charm that led to their naming Franck "Pater Seraphicus". But the public could know little or nothing of these gifts and graces, since Franck's music was for the most part cast in forms that made little appeal to them. To all but his small circle he was a mere teacher and organist.

Neither the *Rédemption* nor the *Béatitudes* spread his fame. The fact that they were in oratorio form told heavily against them and the music itself, which even Franck's greatest admirers would admit to be unequal, was at its best beyond the comprehension of the average audience of the day. The *Rédemption* is called a 'poème symphonie' and is divided into three parts—the first showing the pagan world and culminating in a flight of angels who announce the birth of Christ; the second, an orchestral interlude expressing the 'joy of the world in the Christian faith, triumphant in spite of persecution', and the return of paganism in the modern age, deplored in the third part by angels who weep for man's wickedness, until an archangel announces the forgiveness of God which can be won by prayer. The resemblance to Gounod is strong in the vocal part which often moves—presumably unconsciously—according to Gounod's principles enunciated some years later. There are the stereotyped intervals, the four-square rhythm and, in general, the same atmosphere of banal and unctuous piety. Only the occasional chromatic alterations are peculiar to Franck, and they seem to emphasize rather than diminish the banality. The extraordinary *salon* quality of even the best French religious music

at this time is revealed in the all too elegant phrase which Franck
assigns to the Archangel:

Ex. 10

Nous som-mes au ciel   bien   loin, bien loin de vos fan - ges

The *Béatitudes* contain better music than anything in the *Rédemption* with the exception of the orchestral interlude. They are
nevertheless a failure in the same sense. It has become a commonplace saying that Franck was too beautiful a nature to conceive of
positive evil; and it is true, in the sense that dramatic feeling, a
power of characterization, does depend on the ability to conceive
and express contrasts. The part of Satan in the *Béatitudes*, for example, is feeble and conventional in the extreme and there is no
strong contrast between evil and good, merely a beautiful, if
rather insipid, atmosphere of religious tenderness broken here and
there by descents, not into Hell, but into the duller purlieus of the
Opéra. Franck's religious feeling was profounder than that of
Gounod no doubt, but his weakness lay in his failure to subject his
works to a sufficiently high critical standard. Technically, the
chromatic effects were already becoming a marked feature of his
style, often giving his music a romantic richness of colour, its surface a beautiful iridescence. But he used them uncritically, at last
almost unconsciously, so that they degenerated from a conscious
effect into an unthinking mannerism. An example of the extremes
to which enharmonic modulation, for example, can be carried, is
provided by the Sixth Beatitude—

Ex. 11

where the richness of the harmony is emphasized by the extreme poverty of the melody and the rhythm. From his prosody alone it would be easy to see that Franck was really an instrumental composer. The text of the *Béatitudes*, it must be granted, probably occupies much the same position in literature as the religious pictures of Bouguereau in painting; but, even so, Franck's prosody is inexcusable.

With his symphonic poem *Les Éolides* and the pianoforte quintet Franck entered on his 'third period', which contains all his greatest works and lasted until his death in 1890. *Les Éolides* is the musical illustration of a poem by Leconte de Lisle, beginning:

> 'O brises flottantes des cieux,
> Du beau printemps douces haleines . . .'

and its mood is quite unlike that of the majority of Franck's works. Here (and later in the Scherzo of the String Quartet) the composer is less earnest than usual, no longer in conscious search of the sublime but more freely sensuous, more lightly armed and graceful. The chromatic effects are used less as a means of heightening the emotion and more as a kind of cosmetic, which beautifies the surface of the music and gives it an ambiguity and elusiveness as charming as the fairies of Leconte de Lisle's verses. Melodically, too, *Les Éolides* is akin to such works as Rimsky-Korsakov's *Schéhérazade*, with its technique of short, broken phrases which suggest, rather than express, emotion. In certain passages the strings are divided into eight parts, which was almost unknown in the French music of the eighteen-seventies.

The pianoforte quintet is Franck's first completely mature production. It was completed in 1879 and performed for the first time on 17 January 1880 with Saint-Saëns at the pianoforte. It is seldom a purely musical quality which endears the quintet to its admirers. The majority of Franck's works, even those of his maturity, are full of technical imperfections which offend the musically trained ear. The texture is too unrelievedly thick, so rich that it cloys the ear after a comparatively short time. The chromatic mannerisms soon become tedious, like any other ingenious effect which is overworked; and the shameless bridge passages in which, as it were, the organist improvises with one hand while he changes his registration with the other (see, for example, pages 29–30 of the miniature score of the quintet) artificially break the continuity of the musical thought or betray its exhaustion.

The strength of Franck's music, the quintet included, lies in its emotional quality, which is difficult to define but perhaps best described by Jean-Aubry's phrase of 'serene anxiety'. Anxiety and conflict—such conflict as the composer described as that between 'Light and Darkness' in the *Rédemption*—are the basic traits of Franck's mature style. The darkness is not exactly evil. It is something more negative, a doubt, some lack of tranquillity which perpetually threatens the positive serenity, the childlike confidence on which Franck based his view of the world. The moments of purely sensuous beauty which occur in all his works are again and again interrupted, often brusquely, as though they were connected in the composer's mind with the obscuring of the ideal, the disappearance of the cloud from the temple. It is this element of repression, of interior conflict, which probably accounts for the frequent breaks in musical continuity, as if the energy which should carry the music forward in a broad, unimpeded sweep were deflected elsewhere, to the rather lachrymose emotion and the too-facile piety. The slow movement of the quintet provides an example of an emotional lack of restraint common in Franck's music, removing it altogether from the French tradition and betraying the Germanic affinities of his genius. The appearance of this quality in French music had a violent effect, at first winning admiration and imitation and later provoking satiety and profound revulsion. It is perfectly exemplified in the quintet which is, to this day, cordially detested or admired, but there is no denying the power and originality of the work and the advance in the sphere of chamber music which it represented in 1880.

By a strange coincidence another northerner was writing and forwarding the cause of chamber music in Paris at the same time as Franck. Edouard Lalo was born at Lille in 1823, the year after Franck, of a family originally Spanish but French by adoption and the course of time. He studied both violin and violoncello at the Lille Conservatoire, but in 1839 he ran away to Paris and managed to find his way into Habeneck's violin class at the Conservatoire, while he studied composition and the pianoforte privately. Lalo's real musical education began in 1855, when he joined the Armingaud-Jacquard Quartet as violist and so became intimately acquainted with the music of Schubert, Schumann and Mendelssohn as well as with the classics. He did not actually compose chamber music (with the exception of a single string quartet in E flat, written in 1855) until many years later, and his opera, *Fiesque*, was only placed third in a competition organized by the Théâtre Lyrique, but performances of the ballet music (1872) and other excerpts from *Fiesque* were successful. There followed during the eighteen-seventies a violin concerto in F, the *Symphonie Espagnole*, a violoncello concerto, and the *Rapsodie Norvégienne*. These orchestral works are not Lalo's best, nor are they in themselves great music; but their piquant combination of a good, German-based technique with fresh and elegant melodies formed an excellent introduction to the more difficult and serious orchestral music which young French musicians were to produce in the near future, chiefly under the influence of Franck. The *Symphonie Espagnole* still holds a place in the violinist's repertory, but played without the orchestra it loses more than half its charm and becomes little more than a show-piece for the soloist; and this accounts for the disrepute into which the whole work— and with it, at least outside France, the name of Lalo—has fallen. The two concertos are written in what seems now an old-fashioned style; and the insipid melodiousness of the *Rapsodie Norvégienne* would be unbearable to a modern audience after sixty years of genuinely national music with which to contrast it. But more will be said of Lalo later.

Nothing has been said hitherto of the ballet, and for a good reason. At the Opéra it was considered essential that any work submitted should contain a ballet in the third act, for by that time the admirers of the ballerinas would have finished their dinners and be in the right mood to appreciate the dancing and other charms of their favourites. When *Tannhäuser* was given at the Opéra in 1861 one of the chief complaints was that the ballet occurred in the first act so that the ballet public never saw it at all. This hedonistic approach could never encourage either serious dancing or the careful composition of ballet music; and in fact the ballets in *Faust*, *Roméo et Juliette*, *La Reine de Saba* and other operas of the eighteen-sixties and even the eighteen-seventies contain the most carelessly written and unoriginal music in the scores. It was largely by chance that a genuine composer of ballet music was eventually discovered when the accompanist at the Opéra, Léo Delibes, was commissioned to collaborate with a Pole, named Minkus, in the composition of a ballet entitled *La Source*. This was in 1866, when Delibes was thirty and had already written a number of operettas and opéras-bouffes. His contributions to *La Source* completely eclipsed those of Minkus and in 1870 he was commissioned to compose a whole ballet, *Coppélia*. In 1873 Delibes produced a three-act opera, *Le Roi l'a dit*; and three years later another ballet, *Sylvia*, which confirmed his position as a composer of ballet music. He seems to have understood dancing in much the same way as the Italian composers of an earlier generation understood singing, and his music is as essentially *ballabile* as theirs is *cantabile*. The dancing was certainly that of the old school of ballet, virtuosic in grace and elegance rather than in emotional power or expressiveness. The music of *Coppélia*, for instance, is designed as the accompaniment to what is first and foremost a spectacle, a display aimed at the senses in which the emotions play a subordinate part. Colour and movement, grace and vivacity are the qualities naturally demanded by music for this type of dancing, and these Delibes had in plenty. In actual melody—the essential *cantabile*—he was not so strong and certainly not so original; and it was this that prejudiced his position as a composer of opera. His one great success in that genre, *Lakmé* (1883), owes its effectiveness to the same qualities as distinguish the music of the ballets—colour, grace and vivacity.

It is significant that between 1874–7 the Société Anonyme des Artistes, Peintres, Sculpteurs et Graveurs was formed, which included among its members Manet, Cézanne, Renoir, Degas, Pissarro, Boudin, Sisley and Berthe Morisot; and the first three 'Impressionist' Exhibitions were held (the use of the name 'peintres impressionistes' dates from 1877). Delibes probably knew little or nothing—except from the newspaper scandal—of these new developments in painting; but his were none the less some of the earliest attempts to do in music what these innovators were attempting for painting—to make colour a primary consideration instead of the chance adjunct of a work of art. Towards the end of the eighteen-seventies new movements began to appear unequivocally in literature as well as in painting. Realism, adumbrated by Flaubert, received its first thorough-going expression in Zola's *L'Assommoir*, and the vaguely Symbolist aspirations of some of the members of the Parnasse Contemporain were summed up for the first time with complete unambiguity in Mallarmé's *L'après-midi d'un faune*. Music, as often happens, lagged a little behind; but the times were ripe for changes which, if not revolutionary in form, were at any rate so fundamental that they represented little short of revolution in actual fact.

II

'MUSICAL art owes practically the whole of its progress during the last two decades of the nineteenth century and the first of the twentieth to two fertilizing influences: that of folk-music and that of poetic programmes.' In these words M. D. Calvocoressi sums up the formative influences which operated most strongly in French musical life between 1880–1900. As often happens, the surface of music gave little idea of the forces which were stirring in the depths. Massenet and Delibes owed little to either folk-music or poetic programmes, nor did the oratorios of Gounod; and these were the popular successes of the eighteen-eighties. It was rather in the minority movements that new ideas were gaining ground, in the historical classes of Bourgault-Ducoudray at the Conservatoire, in the private composition classes of César Franck and the irresponsible harmonic experiments of a 'mauvais élève du Conservatoire' who still signed himself Achille de Bussy. In these widely differing spheres there was a common discontent with the prevailing musical régime. In 1879 Franck's pupil, Henri Duparc, had taken a musically inclined civil servant, Emmanuel Chabrier, to hear a performance of *Tristan* at Munich; with the result that the civil servant threw up his post in the civil service and gave himself up to composition entirely, with strange and interesting results. In a speech made in 1878 at the Paris Universal Exhibition, Louis Bourgault-Ducoudray, who had just returned from collecting folk-songs in Greece, had gone so far as to say that 'no element of expression to be found in any tune, however ancient or remote in origin, should be banished from our musical idiom. All that may help to rejuvenate this idiom should be welcome. The question is not one of giving up any previous conquests but, on the contrary, of adding to them.' In the same year the speaker began to lecture on musical history at the Conservatoire.

In the Franck circle an enthusiastic but precise young aristocrat from the Vivarais, Vincent d'Indy, was already to the fore. A visit to Liszt in 1873, combined with the fundamentally Teutonic influence of Franck, had given rise to a large orchestral triptych inspired by Schiller and dealing with the life and death of Wallen-stein—rather overladen music, carefully written, not without emo-tional warmth and absolutely in the style of the new 'symphonic poems' which Liszt has produced in such abundance. In 1876 d'Indy made the inevitable pilgrimage to Bayreuth, accompanied by Saint-Saëns; and another symphonic poem, *La Forêt Enchantée*, bore witness to the state of fermentation which this visit produced, while a pianoforte quartet of the same year was prophetic of a new departure in French chamber music, parallel and similar to that initiated by the pianoforte quintet of d'Indy's master, Franck. Saint-Saëns, too, was returning to chamber music. With the com-position of the four symphonic poems between 1871–7 he seems to have rid his system of the predominant influence of Liszt, although his admiration was still strong and in 1878 he arranged for a con-cert at which the *Dante* and *Faust* symphonies and *Festklänge* were played. The trumpet septet and the first violin sonata indicate a turning away from the romantic and the rhetorically emotional which had engrossed Saint-Saëns during the eighteen-seventies and borne fruit in *Samson* and the symphonic poems, and a return to the fundamentally sober and classical, the witty, the well-groomed and the technically teasing which represent the com-poser's basic mentality.

One of the most striking and unexpected developments of the eighteen-eighties was the sudden blossoming of Édouard Lalo. Lalo's music is fundamentally decorative and un-romantic; and although the influence of Schumann (and even occasionally of Liszt) is visible in the Trio, the musical interest is essentially formal and colouristic rather than literary or emotional. The workman-ship is delicate and effortless, thoroughly natural and with no forced highlights. Lalo's rhythm is particularly distinctive. In the second movement of the Trio he uses the devices of broken (com-bined triple and common) rhythm which he had plainly learnt from Schumann, and in the fourth movement this reaches an almost Brahmsian complexity. In the first movement of the Sym-phony in G minor the frequent dotted rhythm enhances the im-pression of a broad and solemn declamation, a serious and coldly impassioned oratory. In the ballet *Namouna* this natural tendency to the exotic is exploited to the full, with a brilliance and charm which were lost on the majority of the audience but aroused such vociferous enthusiasm in the seventeen-year-old Debussy that he was turned out of the theatre. Oddly enough, *Namouna* is rather monotonous rhythmically, and its main charm lies in the orchestration, which recalls Bizet in its lightness, its aptness and colouring.

Lalo's one opera, *Le Roi d'Ys*, appeared in 1888. Massenet had already taken the operatic world by storm with his *Hérodiade* and *Manon*, by no means worthless works in themselves but well within the framework of the conventional musical scene and containing none of the disturbing, brilliant and forward-looking elements which distinguished the *Roi d'Ys* and Chabrier's two operas, *Gwendoline* and *Le Roi malgré lui*. These three works, together with Reyer's musically inferior *Sigurd*, were the first unmistakable evidences of Wagnerian penetration into French opera, and as such they deserve historical as well as purely aesthetic appreciation. It was impossible for alert and intelligent musicians of the eighteen-eighties to be unaware of Wagner's music, which was convulsing the whole of musical Europe; and the malcontents in every country looked to him rather as political malcontents of the nineteen-twenties looked at the Soviet régime in Russia—with a mixture of admiration, fear, envy and hope. The leading figures of French music, or those who were on their way to becoming leaders, all made the pilgrimage to Bayreuth. D'Indy and Saint-Saëns went in 1876, Duparc and Chabrier in 1879, Fauré in 1883 (the year in which the painter Fantin-Latour conceived his group of French artists and musicians which he entitled 'Petit Bayreuth'), and Debussy was to follow in 1888 and 1889. Between the reactions of these different artists there was a wide gulf, a distinction which separated them roughly into two classes. There were those who, like Lalo and Debussy, felt the enormous attraction and the liberating influence of Wagner's music, i.e. of his harmony and the richness of his instrumentation; and those who, like Reyer and Chabrier, allowed themselves to be at least temporarily won over by his dramatic ideas, including the mystical value of Norse mythology and the (essentially German) presentation of his characters' psychological development. The *Roi d'Ys* is a Breton legend which might well have commended itself to Wagner; but Lalo's treatment of the story is thoroughly French, even to the point of accepting Gounod's religious idiom as the normal manner in which supernatural personages should speak (Saint Corentin). Rhythmically Lalo's score is strong and original, and the claims of prosody and even of natural diction are sacrificed to musical considerations. In harmony the *Roi d'Ys* often appears, on paper,

more revolutionary than it actually sounds, as the following
passage shows:

Ex. 12

But it is in the orchestration that Wagner's influence is most
clearly heard. Here Lalo, like Chabrier, allowed his enthusiasm to
blind his judgement, with the result that his score was voted outrageously Wagnerian in 1888 and has been voted outrageously
noisy ever since. The Breton Wedding in the third act is probably
the best thing Lalo ever did, for it combines freshness with a
natural elegance, clear linear design with colour and feeling. In
the natural line of development from Bizet to, let us say, Ravel,
Lalo strengthened the texture and enriched the palette of the
French musical idiom by his intimate knowledge of the German
classics and his tempered acceptance of that part of Wagner's
'message' which he felt by instinct to be most assimilable by the
French genius. That, as a colourist, he was sometimes seduced by
the over-magnificence of Wagner's palette, is regrettable but not
really relevant; and he remains in many ways one of the most important links between the pre-Wagnerian music of the eighteen-
sixties and eighteen-seventies and the whole-hearted Wagnerians
of the late eighteen-eighties and the eighteen-nineties.

Emmanuel Chabrier was an entirely different temperament. An
Auvergnat, born in 1841, Chabrier spent the years from 1862 to
1880 in the Ministry of the Interior, interesting himself not only in

music but also in the other arts. He was an intimate friend of Verlaine, Manet, Banville, Leconte de Lisle and Anatole France; and
thus he acted as unofficial liaison officer in that universal *rap-
prochement* which was the natural outcome of Wagnerian enthusiasm
in the *avant-garde* of each art, finding expression in the 'musical'
conception of poetry held by the Symbolists and in that approach
to both poetry and music which could be felt in the pictures of the
'Impressionists'. Paul Dukas admirably summed up the strange
atmosphere of excitement and fermentation in the French artistic
world at the end of the eighteen-eighties and the beginning of the
eighteen-nineties:

'Impressionism, symbolism and poetic realism merged together in
an atmosphere in which enthusiasm, curiosity and intellectual passion
competed. Painters, poets and sculptors all took their material to pieces,
as it were, examined it, questioned it, changed and remade it according
to their own will. Words, sounds, colours and lines must all express new
shades of meaning, new feelings.'

At his death Chabrier possessed 8 Monets, 6 Renoirs, 2 Sisleys,
2 Fantin-Latours and 11 Manets (one of which was the famous
Bar aux Folies-Bergère).

Chabrier's actual musical instruction was haphazard and of no
great importance in his development. Two operettas produced
while he was still a civil servant, *L'Étoile* and *Une Education Man-
quée*, show an original sense of humour, sophisticated rather above
the average of the genre; a pleasant melodic gift, though nothing
extraordinary; and a barely sufficient technical knowledge. In
1881 there appeared the *Dix Pièces Pittoresques* for the pianoforte,
which mark the opening of Chabrier's career (a short ten years) as
a professional musician. After the concert at which a selection of
these pieces was played César Franck is reported to have remarked,
'We have just heard something quite out of the ordinary run. This
music is a bridge between our own times and those of Couperin
and Rameau.' And there is truth—allowances having been made
for Franck's notorious kindheartedness—in the association of
Chabrier's gay and greedy vitality, his wit and affectation, with the
eighteenth rather than the nineteenth century. The ten pieces are
unequal and full of reminiscences of Schumann and Offenbach;
but the piquant and often clumsy harmony and the rhythmic
verve, the confusion of sentimental nostalgia and almost brutal
café-concert atmosphere were something quite new and peculiar to

Chabrier. The *Valses Romantiques* for two pianofortes are more distinctly original, both in their actual writing and in the Bovaryesque parody of romanticism by an artist who, like Flaubert, was at least three-fifths a romantic himself. Harmonically they are one of the first and best examples of that 'écriture alambiquée'—the perversely complicated and over-seasoned style—which Chabrier developed to its logical and disastrous conclusion in the cantata *La Sulamite* (1885). The waltzes are felicitously humorous, and whereas in *La Sulamite* Chabrier uses his harmonic spices to heighten the emotional tension, in the valses he merely exploits them ornamentally, as piquant and unexpected turns of phrase. From 1881 onwards he was trainer of the chorus which took part in the Concerts Lamoureux; and during 1884–5 he rehearsed the choruses for the production of the first two acts of *Tristan*. But the event which, after the journey to Munich in 1879, had more effect than any other on Chabrier's musical development was his journey to Spain in 1882. 'Eh bien, mes enfants,' he wrote from Seville that year, 'nous en voyons, des derrières andalous, se tortiller comme serpents en liesse.' The vitality, the grossness and absolute naturalness of the popular music and dancing of Spain, the absence of any trace of the *salon*, delighted this coarse-mouthed, delicate-feeling Auvergnat; and it was with his *España*, produced two years later in 1884, that Chabrier won his first great success. Even now, in the full light of the more sophisticated Spanish works of Rimsky-Korsakov, Debussy and Ravel, Chabrier's *España* (from which in a sense all these other works proceed) has qualities of vigour and abandon which make it more truly Spanish, more evocative of popular Spain, than these more finely worked, more sensitive and therefore less popular works. Glinka, another composer who remained at bottom an amateur like Chabrier, had already caught something of the same quality in his *Jota Aragonesa* which, like *España*, echoes the genuine, objective reality of popular Spanish popular music, where the *Capriccio espagnol*, *Ibéria* and the *Rapsodie espagnole* belong in reality to the class of romantic travel impressions or 'années de pèlerinage'—the fine lucubrations of sensitive artists which remain foreign and subjective.

This quality of objective immediacy found another expression in the series of songs which Chabrier produced during the eighteen-eighties—humorous, half-childish works with deliberately comic titles such as *Villanelle des petits canards*, *Ballade des gros dindons*, *Pastorale des cochons roses*. His more serious songs are far less original. *Credo d'amour*, *Tes Yeux bleus* and *Toutes les fleurs* are no more than drawing-room romances with a touch of Wagnerian harmony and the angularity or gaucherie which was peculiar to Chabrier. But these humorous songs opened up a new world of music, a kind of antidote to the rapidly spreading Wagnerian pomposity which was threatening to engulf the French composers of the *avant-garde*. Saint-Saëns contributed to these same beginnings of a movement away from Wagnerian solemnity when he wrote in 1886, for the amusement of himself and a small circle of friends, his *Carnaval des Animaux*. The musical content is negligible; but this conception of music as the possible vehicle of quite frivolous humour was novel and, in its small way, epoch-making among the tone-poems and music-dramas of the Wagnerians and the symphonies and quartets of the Franckists.

Chabrier was unconsciously producing the antidote while he consciously devoted his energies to the propagation of the poison. Of Chabrier's two operas, *Le Roi malgré lui* is strongly coloured with Wagnerian harmonic progressions and Wagnerian orchestral timbres, while *Gwendoline* is a monumental essay in 'Nordic' poetry, carried out in a style so highly seasoned, so deliberately complicated harmonically, that its own composer admitted that it was more like some musical 'extract' which needed diluting in water before it could become palatable. ('. . . C'est du Liebig musical,' he wrote, 'c'est trop compact: il faudrait en prendre une boulette pour mettre dans un honnête délayage et agiter avant de servir le morceau.') The harmonic train of thought started in a French mind by the close study of Wagner resulted, in two such fundamentally different cases as those of Chabrier and Debussy, in very much the same effects; so that one is tempted to the conclusion that these were in fact the passages of the Wagnerian gospel really relevant in France. In the Prelude to the *Roi malgré lui*, for example, there is the same obsession with chords of the ninth as affected Debussy—

Ex. 13

while in *Gwendoline* there are passages of a quite uncertain tonality

Ex. 14

which lie well forward on the road leading from light harmonic experiments with the whole-tone scale to Debussy's deliberate rejection of traditional tonality. There is a great difference between the fairly frequent use of whole-tone chords, and even whole passages, such as can be found in Liszt, Saint-Saëns and Rimsky-Korsakov, and the conscious adoption of the whole-tone scale as an alternative to the hitherto accepted diatonic order. Chabrier represents the penultimate stage of this process, which provided the peculiarly French form of escape from that general state of flux into which the music of Wagner brought the world of harmony. Not that he was consistently *avant-garde*, as we have seen. His melodic gift was small and he tended either to fall into completely conventional melodic formulae, as in the final love duet of *Gwendoline*, or else to rescue himself from this predicament only by sudden, violent contortions which are merciless to the singer and do not alter anything more than the superficial form of the melody.

In the matter of operatic construction Chabrier was a Wagnerian idealist in theory, a sworn enemy of those bridges which in the old opera permitted of a general relaxation of emotional tension in the audience and a momentary recourse to conventional formulae on the part of the composer.

'I want my work to be beautiful throughout, and there are thirty-six forms of beauty. Never the same colour, and everywhere variety, shape and, above all, vitality. Naïveté, too, if possible, but that is hardest of all.'

Gwendoline is more closely knit, more 'advanced' formally than *Le Roi malgré lui*; and for that very reason it is more difficult to listen to, more turgid and intense, more of a copy of German originals. In *Le Roi malgré lui* Chabrier is far more himself, humorous and vivacious with moments of direct sentimentality, piquant and instinctively interesting. Here he solicits the audience's attention, whereas in *Gwendoline* he demands, and in the last resort fails to obtain, it.

This soliciting of the audience during the eighteen-eighties was the speciality of a single composer, Jules Massenet, who had brought it to such a degree of perfection that in his best works it assumes the quality of an artistic gift. Of the four operas produced by Massenet between 1880–90 the first two, *Hérodiade* and *Manon*, were by far the most successful. *Hérodiade* continues the tradition of 'l'érotisme discret et quasi-religieux' of the oratorios of the eighteen-seventies, *Marie Magdeleine* and *Eve*. John the Baptist's love for Salomé is at first mystical and half paternal; his love-making is conducted through a religious medium and only becomes frankly human when in the last act he is faced with death. As usually happens with Massenet, he fails in the less emotional and intimate scenes, in the political action of the story; and the feeling between the Idumaean people and their Roman conquerors, Herod's vacillation, even Herodias's enmity and jealousy, are either coldly and conventionally treated or seen through the same haze of mystical eroticism. Massenet seemed then to be incapable of any musical expression except that which is concerned with erotic, or sub-erotic, personal relationships. It was the fact that he could capitalize this weakness which makes *Manon* not only his finest work, but something very near a masterpiece. The whole of Prévost's story is set in an atmosphere of coquetry and amorous intrigue which cries aloud for the accompaniment of music, such as Massenet's, ' . . . melodies which are delicate and caressing rather than deeply felt, an orchestration rich in pretty and clever filigree work but without any depth'. From the opening scene, in which Manon flirts with her cousin Lescaut, the story is a succession of ambiguous erotic situations, none of which demands any real depth of emotion. The gentle, swaying phrase which depicts Manon's shyness and hesitation:

Ex. 15

is brilliantly suggestive: and the burst of facile emotion in the
phrase expressing des Grieux's passion for Manon:

Ex. 16

is, of its kind, quite irresistible. The reminiscence of Bizet in Example 15 returns in the famous dream of des Grieux which is a
more theatrically effective version of the tenor-baritone duet from
Act I of *Les Pêcheurs de Perles* ('Au fond du temple saint'). In the
scenes at the Foire St. Germain and the gaming-house, even in
the seminary of St. Sulpice, Massenet can legitimately preserve the
emotional atmosphere which was in reality the one string of his
lyre, because Prévost's story is a perfect emotional unity and,
whatever the scene may be, it is no more than the *décor* for
Manon's amorous escapades. One may find this ceaseless harping
on the erotic interest tedious and cloying, but it is admirably
suited to Massenet's talent and called out the very best of which
he was capable. After *Manon* Massenet produced *Le Cid* and
Esclarmonde, both inferior works. The heroic grandeur, the dark
passions and the violent Spanish chiaroscuro of the Cid's story
were about as suited to Massenet's gifts as the Nibelungenlied;
and his inability to use other colours than rose-madder and eau-
de-Nil, other scents than chypre and incense, other stuffs than
crêpe de Chine and swansdown, make *Le Cid* a pitiable affair. *Esclarmonde* shows the first influence of Wagner on Massenet's idiom, an
influence which inevitably led in the direction of spectacular effect.
Any deep understanding or assimilation of Wagner's idiom was
plainly unthinkable for Massenet; but, like Puccini later, he was
anxious and able to adopt any devices which could give his music
more modern colour and a more piquant flavour, without affecting

its fundamentally conventional and popular character. His use of rising sequences in the orchestral part and the semi-recitative of the voice is harmlessly Wagnerian; and in the decorative effects of the magic and spectacular scenes there is some Wagnerian seasoning which may well have titillated early audiences.

Apart from his actual compositions Massenet exercised large influence on the coming generation of French composers through his position as professor of composition at the Conservatoire from 1878–96. His particular melodic idiom, which as we have seen was derived from Gounod, influenced composers as far removed from him in other respects as Debussy and Ravel, and threatened for a time to become something like a national idiom. After *Hérodiade* and *Manon* the most notable operatic production of the eighteen-eighties (leaving Chabrier's two works on one side) was Delibes's *Lakmé* (1883), which Adolphe Jullien described as 'a miniature *L'Africaine* with a touch of *Armide* thrown in'. As in the ballets, Delibes's chief preoccupation is colour. The Oriental vein in French art goes back at least as far as the *Lettres Persanes* of Montesquieu and the 'chinoiseries' of the eighteenth century. It reappears in the *Orientales* of Victor Hugo and in Félicien David's *poème-symphonie*, *Le Désert* (1844) and his *Lalla Roukh* (1862). Bizet's *Pêcheurs de Perles* and Meyerbeer's *L'Africaine* continue the tradition, which combined with the wave of Wagnerian enthusiasm in Reyer's *Salammbô* and finally took a new lease of life in Debussy's *Pagodes*, the 'chinoiseries' of Ravel, in Florent Schmitt's *Tragédie de Salomé* and Albert Roussel's *Padmâvati* as late as 1918.

It is difficult to make a fair assessment of the three operas which Saint-Saëns produced during this period—*Henri VIII*, *Proserpine* and *Ascanio*. In spite of their generally high musical level they have disappeared from the repertory and the simple reason that their dramatic style is outmoded is not sufficient to account for this, for *Hérodiade* is still popular in France and *Manon* all over the world. Saint-Saëns's failure to hold the stage with any opera except *Samson et Dalila* is partly due to the very correctness and efficiency of his musicianship, which seems to militate against such strong emotional appeal as Massenet exercised, or the charm and brilliance of *Lakmé* and *Le Roi malgré lui*. *Henri VIII* is a full-dress historical opera, of the same order as *Les Huguenots*. *Proserpine* and *Ascanio* are stories of amorous intrigue with amply detailed historical background, in fifteenth-century Florence and the France of François I respectively. It is hard to find fault with them musically; but they are correct and lifeless, whereas Saint-Saëns's chamber and orchestral music, with all its faults, is thoroughly alive and individual. The Algerian Suite (1880) is one of those travel impressions which Saint-Saëns, like so many of his contemporaries, was content to leave purely subjective and only vaguely reminiscent or evocative of the country which inspired it. Of the *Carnaval des Animaux* we have already spoken, showing that what originated in the composer's mind as a private amusement was, in fact, destined to become of greater historical importance than some of his most serious and cherished works, even the third symphony which appeared in the same year (1886). A full-scale work in the grand late-romantic manner, this symphony really represents a return to the Lisztian influences which were so strong in Saint-Saëns's orchestral music of the eighteen-seventies. The opening phrase alone gives the emotional note of the work, which continues almost uninterrupted, unvaried except for successive heightenings of the emotional atmosphere, the semi-religiosity of a chorale and the addition of the organ to the orchestra. The whole score breathes the high seriousness, the vibrating emotion and the faintly self-conscious showmanship of Saint-Saëns's genuine feeling for the grander and more objective aspect of romanticism. The third symphony does credit to Saint-Saëns as a man; but it demonstrates his limitations as an artist rather than his gifts. The cosmic questionings, the tempests of doubt and the final winning through to serene conviction were not really Saint-Saëns's forte. One side of him was moved by their purely aesthetic potentialities, their grandiosity as a programme and the enviable beauty and satisfactoriness of the conclusion, but the emotion was not profound. His genius was literally superficial, in the sense that it was for the surface of things—for the fine cut of a melody, the thin but firm texture of good orchestration, for piquant harmony and a witty and urbane turn of phrase. In the depths he flounders, keeps his head respectably above water, but that is all.

On the other hand, these cosmic questionings and religious syntheses were the chosen field of César Franck and his school; and a comparison between Saint-Saëns's third symphony, in which he attempts the Franckian genre, and Franck's own symphony makes the contrast clear. The last ten years of Franck's life, 1880–90, saw the production of his chief works. The pianoforte quintet of 1880 was followed by a symphonic poem, *Le Chasseur Maudit*, *Les Djinns*, *Prelude, chorale and fugue*, and the *Variations symphoniques* for pianoforte and orchestra, the violin sonata, *Prelude, aria and finale*, the symphony in D minor and the string quartet. Franck also left two operas, *Hulda* and *Ghisèle* (unfinished), though neither of these was performed in his lifetime. The productions of these last years of Franck's life are not only of musical value in themselves; their influence on the course of French music, direct and indirect, was immense. Franck's musical mentality was not really in tune with the French genius, and his influence is comparable with that of Wagner, momentarily violent but more important historically for the reaction which it provoked than for the number of master-pieces written under its influence. The *Chasseur Maudit* is a conventional tone-poem, with a German romantic programme treated in the Lisztian manner and far less original than the best of Saint-Saëns's tone poems. The orchestration is thick, with a preponderance of brass; and the knight who was dragged down to hell for preferring hunting to church-going on Sunday is not, in Franck's hands, a very convincingly villainous figure. With *Les Djinns*, on the other hand, Franck was breaking new ground. The pianoforte concerto had become increasingly a show-piece, and Franck's conception of a work in which the pianoforte should collaborate with the orchestra, without dominating it, was new and represented a wholly healthy instinct. The emotional content of the work is typically Franckian, for it depicts the struggle between 'light' and 'darkness' in which the Djinns represent the evil instincts of man, finally overcome by the power of prayer and that mystical, luminous, instinctive faith which was Franck's greatest quality. Whereas Liszt, to whom Franck was greatly indebted, tended to attribute demonic and passionate qualities primarily to the pianoforte in opposition to the strings and the orchestra in general (*Malédiction*), Franck reverses the roles and gives the pianoforte the broad, sweeping, luminous arpeggios which symbolize the serenity of faith. The demonic, individualistic pride of the virtuoso is replaced by the single soul struggling with the vast forces of wickedness represented by the orchestra.

The four years from 1883 to 1887 represent the period of Franck's most intense pianistic activity. *Les Djinns* appeared in a two-pianoforte version in 1884, but was not performed with the orchestra until March 1885. In 1884 there appeared the *Prelude, chorale and fugue*, which was not performed until 1885 (January), while the *Variations symphoniques*, composed in 1885, appeared in a two-pianoforte version in 1886 and were first performed with orchestra in the May of that year. The *Prelude, aria and finale* was composed in 1886–7 and first performed in May 1888. If we take into account the pianoforte part of the violin sonata composed for Ysaÿe in 1886 this represents an enormous pianistic activity in a short space of time, when the composer was between the ages of sixty and sixty-five. The quality of all these works is amazingly high; each of them has lived and has added something unique to the late romantic repertory. Musically they represent a unique fusion of several strands. Franck shared with Liszt a passionate admiration for the great German classics, especially the later works of Beethoven, and this solid basis assured a generally high level of craftsmanship, a mastery—at least technical, if not always psychological—of fugal and symphonic structure which was rare in France outside his circle. Like Liszt, Franck had a fund of genuine religious emotion which determined, in his case, the nature of the whole of his output, although he suffered from the low standard of religious music and the rather facile and senti-mental piety which was the immediate reaction of too many of the faithful to the hostility of science and the vast developments of secular civilization. Unlike Liszt, Franck felt the glamour and attraction of the world distinctly less than the average artist; and, lacking this corrective, his genuine religious faith tended to find expression in a tender *vox humana* which answered the challenge of evil in a way which was 'supplicatory, but with anxiety and some agitation' (a mark of expression in *Les Djinns*). Technically, the *Prelude, chorale and fugue* and the *Variations symphoniques* are a strange, but completely individual, fusion of styles. What M. Cor-tot calls the 'côté artisan d'église' (which might maliciously, but not quite unfairly, be translated the 'church-worker side') of Franck's genius relates his music to two diametrically opposed in-fluences—the great organ works of J. S. Bach on the one hand and the pretty sentimentalities of contemporary church music on the other. While his early training as a virtuoso pianist inclined him to the floridly ornamental, his mature passion for Beethoven led him to conceive of all music as primarily an expression of soul, a philo-sophy of life, in his case half-Christian and half-romantic but wholly emotional. It is in the light of these extreme opposites that we must view the last great works of his life and also the subse-quent reaction against his music, which had such a large place in determining the direction of French musical development.

The very title of the *Prelude, chorale and fugue* reveals Franck's desire to rehabilitate the strict, seemingly austere musical forms which the romantic movement, in the first flush of its victory, had declared outworn; and to show that these forms could be used without sacrificing any of the achievements of romantic or 'modern' music. The grouping of these three movements round a single generating motif was, in fact, a purely modern device, an application of the cyclic principle which Schubert had adumbrated in the *Wanderer Fantasia* and Berlioz had used in his *Symphonie fantastique*. The introduction of a second thematic element in the chorale completed the modernity of the conception by giving scope for the element of interior conflict which replaced, in Franck's aesthetic, the more exterior dramatic considerations which weighed so heavily with the early romantics. Franck's theory, however, was not so strong as his nature, and Saint-Saëns was not without justification when he complained that the chorale was not a chorale nor the fugue a fugue. The dramatic, or perhaps more properly the psychological, element is too strong for the purely musical. Even so, it is possible that, failing to write a satisfactory chorale and fugue, Franck may yet have written a great work of art.

The element of conflict is implicit, once again, from the very start of the *Variations symphoniques*; for Franck chose a double subject, each element of which has its own development, thereby creating a double stream of expressive forces whose crossing and re-crossing give life and impact to the work. This is a parallel principle to that of the pianoforte concertos of Beethoven, in which the solo instrument is pitted against the orchestra; but in the *Variations symphoniques* the conflict is not between groups of sonorities but rather between two opposing musical ideas. The freer form of the variation is well suited to Franck's essentially emotional character which, as we have seen, found the austerities of stricter forms irksome; and the freedom with which he could establish a succession of emotional atmospheres, independent of the exigencies of exact form, gives the whole work a more natural and less constrained feeling than the *Prelude, chorale and fugue*. The high seriousness of the opening gives way, in the last variation, to something very like frivolity. Both here and in the last movement of *Prelude, aria and finale* there is a certain deterioration in the musical quality (Cortot speaks felicitously of the 'embourgeoisement' of the theme), and Franck seems to fall into the mannerisms of the pianoforte music on which he was brought up. The prelude and aria are so unpianistic as to sound like transcriptions of organ music. There are obvious pedal parts, a kind of two- or three-manual technique and patent changes of registration which makes the whole work inferior to the *Prelude, chorale and fugue*, in spite of the intrinsic beauty of the first two movements.

The violin sonata has probably done more than any one work to immortalize Franck's name. The dedication to Ysaÿe ensured that its first launching into the musical world should have every advantage, and its subsequent history has been a quick triumphal progress to the status of an undisputed classic. Perhaps the chief reason for its unbroken popularity lies in the fact that it is less involved than any other of Franck's works in an emotional or psychological programme. Here for once we are, on the whole, free from the eternal conflict of darkness and light; the atmosphere is more lyrical and the lyricism is more secular. We can forget the organ loft and the thurible on the one hand, the dimly apprehended forces of evil on the other; we are in a purely musical world. The balancing of the two instruments is beautifully managed, although the pianoforte part (especially in the first movement) is sometimes heavy. There is a soaring quality, something akin to the great bursts of moral *élan* which inspired Beethoven, in the chiming canon of the last movement which, no doubt, appeared to the composer as a divine solution to the more questioning mood of the first movement and the dark turbulence of the second.

With the symphony in D minor and the string quartet we come to the end of Franck's works. The symphony marks the peak of the first phase of Germanic influence in France and, as in the case of most climaxes, the reaction had begun some time before in the lower strata of musical life. There is no questioning its emotional power, although its musical vitality oscillates between two great extremes (cf. the first and second subjects in the first movement) and the cut of phrase is often too rigidly four-square to be satisfactory. Debussy's summing up is, on the whole, fair: 'Franck's symphony is amazing,' he said to Guiraud. 'I should prefer less four-square structure. But what smart ideas!' The reactionaries (apparently forgetting the second symphony of Saint-Saëns) declared that no work in which a *cor anglais* was employed could be called a symphony. Reactionaries are seldom wholly in the right, nor were they in this instance; but they are almost equally seldom wholly in the wrong. Franck's symphony is not really a symphony,

not because a *cor anglais* is included in the score, but for the same
reason as the chorale and fugue of the *Prelude, chorale and fugue* are
not really a chorale or a fugue. A symphony is before all else a
musical structure; it is an architectural form. In the symphony,
therefore, any emotional element that cannot be expressed in
lines and masses, any predominantly colouristic or literary element,
is not only alien and out of place, it actually saps the symphonic
character of the work. Beethoven stood at the parting of the ways,
bred in the linear, architectural school of music and looking forward to the world in which colour, tone-quality and texture were
gradually to usurp the expressive function which had hitherto
belonged to line and mass. For largely personal reasons he remained within the limits of the old world until the ninth symphony, although he often strained the natural bounds of the form.
Weber, on the other hand, who was almost his contemporary,
rejected the symphony; and in fact after 1820 the conscious
symphonists were neo-classical composers—Mendelssohn and
Brahms avowedly, Schumann and Saint-Saëns inasmuch as they
were symphonists. Franck was well trained and founded in the
forms of the classical school, but hopelessly removed from their
spirit, and his symphony—like the symphonies of Borodin or Mahler—is one only in name and, loosely, in form. To deny its musical
worth and many moments of great musical beauty because it is
misleadingly named is pedantry; but the very beauty and subtlety
of the middle movement, for example, its weird and melancholy
atmosphere, remove it from the symphonic class. It most nearly
approaches genuine symphonic status in its least original passages
—the ill-fated development section of the first movement, and the
last movement which seems to protest too much that it is the finale
of a symphony.

The string quartet is probably the work of Franck which has
won him greatest esteem among musicians. His contrapuntal
training and all his love for classical forms could here be used
legitimately, without his running the danger of being false to his
own personality. A string quartet must be predominantly contrapuntal, and Franck satisfies this demand; but the nature of the
content is not determined by strict formal exigencies, and Franck's
quartet is full-bloodedly late-romantic in character, like all his
other works. Beethoven's influence is stronger here than in any
other work, from the soaring tranquillity of the introduction to the
solemn simplicity of the slow movement and the brusque, broken

recitatives of the last movement. The scherzo recalls the Franck of *Les Éolides*, free from all doubts, conflicts and divine consolations, as capricious and atmospheric as Mendelssohn's scherzo movements. Technically, the part-writing is masterly, and if the tonal ensemble sometimes approaches the orchestral rather than the strictly chamber music ideal in volume and texture, this represents a legitimate extension of the genre, a licence which Franck is careful never to abuse.

The cantata *Psyché*, written during the years 1887-8, and Franck's two attempts at opera (*Hulda* and the unfinished *Ghisèle*) reveal a weaker side of his genius but one that was none the less typical. As in *Les Djinns*, he takes a pagan legend in *Psyché* and baptizes it. Psyché herself is the Christian soul and her lover is the divine lover of the Song of Songs. The Zephyrs and the Voices which warn or encourage her are conceived in that same semi-sensual, semi-mystical fashion which we have seen Massenet exploiting on a lower level of creation. *Hulda* was played for the first time at Monte Carlo in 1894, *Ghisèle* in 1896; and although both works contain some respectable and carefully written music, they both show beyond any doubt that Franck's gift for the theatre was negligible. The Aslaks of eleventh-century Norway and the court of the Merovingian kings of Neustria are not promising backgrounds in any case. Expressing themselves in an idiom which tends to oscillate between that of *Béatitudes* and *Tristan* they are insufferable.

Gounod in the eighteen-eighties was far from a spent force, and two cantatas, *Rédemption* and *Mors et Vita*, went at least some way towards rehabilitating a reputation which had been eclipsed since his stay in England at the time of the Franco-Prussian war. Opera had ceased to interest Gounod, and his whole attention was now devoted to the oratorio, which he had first learned to know and come to admire in that England which was proud to be a second home to Handel and to Mendelssohn and finally to Gounod himself. The *Rédemption* came as a new inspiration to the generation of English church composers who were well grounded in *Messiah*, *Elijah*, *St. Paul* and *Hymn of Praise* and asked for nothing better than a restatement of oratorio ideals and principles in a rather more modern idiom. For Gounod was not impervious to modern influences. There were some strange harkings back to the aesthetic of an earlier generation bred in the love and holy fear of Meyerbeer; but the *Marche au Calvaire*, with its little triplet fanfares and

cocky, precise rhythms, would not shock a generation for whom
opera and oratorio were most beautiful when they most closely
resembled each other. The grandiose platitudes with which the
text swarms, so soon as it abandons the actual words of the gospels,
reached their sorry height in the choral comments, where the part-
writing matches and, if anything, exceeds it in weakness and
banality. Yet it was this choral writing which formed a whole
generation of lesser ecclesiastical composers and left a mark on the
music of the Anglican rite which half a century barely succeeded
in removing.

The text of *Mors et Vita*, which is a free adaptation of the
Requiem Mass, preserved Gounod from the worst excesses of plati-
tude and banality. Musically, *Mors et Vita* is more dramatic and
more concentrated than *Rédemption*. The influence of Verdi is unmistakable in several places, as, for example, the tenor solo of the
Ingemisco and the introduction to the *Inter oves locum praesta*.

Ex. 17

By what was more probably mental affinity than conscious or unconscious borrowing, César Franck repeated almost exactly the
'happiness of the blessed' motif in the second subject of the first
movement of his symphony. This mental affinity between the two
composers is sometimes so marked that one is tempted to think
that at least a portion of Franck's music is little more than Wagner-
ized Gounod, though Franck had little use for Gounod's music.

Quite alien to these bland banalities and outside the normal
course of Parisian musical life was a strange figure, still something
of a mystery. Charles Valentin Morhange, known to the musical
world as Alkan, died in 1888 at the age of seventy-five. Very little

is known about his life or personality, except as revealed in his music. His whole existence was given up to the pianoforte, as teacher, virtuoso and composer. Liszt seldom visited Paris, it is said, without seeing Alkan, and Franck made several transcriptions of his works. By the highest contemporary standards, therefore, Alkan was a musical personality. He has been compared with Berlioz, Haydn, Cervantes, Defoe, Verlaine, Chopin, Hogarth, Rowlandson and Watteau by a single admirer (Bernard van Dieren: *Down Among the Dead Men*, 1935); a catholicity of praise which ends by conveying almost nothing beyond the writer's personal admiration. The extent of his works is considerable. They include thirty *chants*, divided into five suites, which are short and broadly melodic in a manner which varies between that of Schubert and Mendelssohn; *Douze études dans tous les tons mineurs*, a series of magnificent technical studies of varying musical worth; forty-eight *Esquisses*, divided into four suites, some mostly technical (Le Staccatissimo, Le Legatissimo), others with more fantastic names as *Les Diablotins*, *Fais dodo* and *Les Enharmoniques*; and twelve *morceaux caracteristiques*, *Les Mois*. There is a pyrotechnical study entitled *Le Vent*, a charming genre picture, *Le Tambour bat aux champs*; and an enormous *Sonatine*, which recalls both Beethoven and Weber. Throughout most of these works there is a large number of unusual marks of expression, which suggest a naïve and eccentric personality with a possible tinge of the charlatan. 'Diabolicamente', 'quasi cavalcate', even 'quasi conquistatore', have at least some meaning; but with 'quasi santo' and 'quasi santa' we are approaching the deliberate mystifications of Satie. Alkan's works seem to contain a definite, though small, vein of musical originality, which is especially noticeable in the technical sphere and is combined with a strong tendency to experiment; and a mind steeped —perhaps one should add, a hand schooled—in the classics of romantic pianoforte literature, that mind and hand constantly producing echoes of other works. We have, in fact, a nineteenth-century Busoni, devoting himself exclusively to the pianoforte and never generally famous for the simple reason that he never left Paris and very seldom played in public. The majority of his technical novelties were little more than developments of immediately pre-Lisztian pianoforte technique along almost exactly the same lines as Liszt himself carried them. The priority may be questionable, but there can be no question of the attribution of honour; for whereas Alkan wrote a handful of 'interesting' and original works,

Liszt built the results of his experiments and discoveries into a whole series of works for orchestra as well as pianoforte, which altered the course of musical history as well as that of keyboard technique.

III

FRANCK's influence was not spent when he died in 1890. The circle that had formed round him was to alter, if not to dominate, the course of French musical development for at least ten more years. Vincent d'Indy was well on the way to making a major position for himself in the musical world, and he was the most loyal and whole-hearted of all Franck's disciples. An important addition to the circle had been made in 1880, when Ernest Chausson began studying with Franck; and during the next ten years a stream of new recruits appeared—Gabriel Pierné, Joseph Ropartz, Pierre de Bréville, Charles Bordes and a young Belgian, Guillaume Lekeu. The works of these men star the history of French music for the next forty years, and in all of them there lived on, under varying forms, something of Franck's idealism, something of his careful, loving and slightly gauche craftsmanship. His death marked the end of the first period of that Germanic influence which had dominated French music increasingly since 1870 and was still to dominate it, in a different way, for another ten years. Franck's own attitude to Wagner was one of distrust. He divined a subtle poison beneath the magnificence and intoxication of the new music and, for his own part, avoided it. But for younger men, his pupils, it was less easy. They were, in any case, in opposition to the suave, Alexandrine academicism of the Conservatoire; and, though perhaps not in sympathy with complete rebels like the young Debussy, they were enough touched by the spirit of the times to feel that to be in opposition and to be Wagnerian were almost interchangeable terms. Duparc was a fervent Wagnerian and so, in a different and more personal way, was d'Indy. Chausson and Lekeu were attracted and influenced, though in their music it seems that the attraction was neither profound nor lasting, and that, had Lekeu not died at twenty-four and Chausson at forty-four, both would have shaken off what was probably no more than a passing fever. Meanwhile, no milder word than fever can be used to describe the violent enthusiasms of the late eighteen-eighties and early eighteen-nineties, which Paul Landormy contrasts with the new modes of feeling which were to replace them:

'Those were the days when admiration for the last quartets of Beethoven, the works of Wagner and the quintet and quartet of Franck knew no bounds. Feelings were violent in a way that was altogether romantic. Lekeu fainted after the prelude to *Tristan* at Bayreuth and had to be carried out of the theatre. Such were the enthusiasms of the times and the state of delirium in which people listened to music.'

Wagner had become the idol of the symbolist or 'decadent' school of poetry, the *avant-garde* of the literary world led by Stéphane Mallarmé and proclaimed by Catulle Mendès in the epilogue to his *Richard Wagner* (1886). As early as 1879 Wagner, in an interview with a journalist named Louis de Fourcaud, had aired his views on the correct development of music in France, in which he professed himself greatly interested. His theories (expanded on two occasions by Louis de Fourcaud in *Le Gaulois*, first in January 1880 and then again exactly six years later) were simply a form of musical nationalism—the cultivation of French epic and folk-songs, for which Wagner expressed a great admiration. He explained in a conversation with d'Indy in 1882 that his own early failure in Paris had been due entirely to the machinations of a German-Jewish clique (by which he presumably meant Meyerbeer and his supporters, paid or otherwise); and there was something ironical in the fact that a Portuguese Jew should have been his chief spokesman to the French musical world. Mendès was, however, not an uncritical admirer. After warning young composers against the imitation of Wagner and 'the steadily increasing infiltration of Germanic influence', he goes on to point out that it is Wagner's aesthetic theories that are valuable to the young French composer rather than his music.

'A great name . . . awaits the French musical genius who first soaks himself in the musical and poetic legends and songs of our race and at the same time assimilates all those points of Wagnerian theory which are compatible with the French genius, for he, alone or with the help of a poet, will rid our opera of the mass of outmoded and ridiculous shackles which now hold it in thrall. He will achieve an intimate unity between poetry and music, for the sake of the drama and not for mere brilliance. The poet in him will boldly reject literary ornament, the musician all those vocal and symphonic beauties which can hinder the flow of dramatic emotion. He will reject recitatives, airs, strettos, even ensembles, unless these are demanded by the dramatic action, to which everything must be sacrificed. He will break the back of the old four-square melody and his melody—without becoming Germanized—will stretch out unbroken, following the poetic rhythm. In a word, his music will become language, but a language which is music. Above all, he will use all the resources of musical science, all the promptings of musical inspiration to transform his orchestra into a great cauldron, in which the themes which represent his characters or their emotions will be mingled and developed and all the elements of the drama will be molten and welded together. While the stage action—steeped in the tragic atmosphere created by the orchestra, heroic and noble, manifold yet springing logically from a single idea—the action will move amidst violent passions, unexpected happenings, smiles and tears, relentlessly towards some great final emotion.'

In this turgid and rather hysterical vision is reflected the whole ferment caused by the music and theories of Wagner. Mendès grasped the fact that Wagner was really preaching musical nationalism and that to his French admirers this should mean a new enthusiasm for their own French legends and music, not for the Germanic tales which were the natural inspiration of the German Wagner. In fact it was Lalo's *Roi d'Ys* that fulfilled at any rate this part of Wagner's precepts rather than Chabrier's *Gwendoline* or Reyer's *Sigurd*.

The *Revue Wagnérienne*, which ran from 1885 to 1887, existed to make the other, non-musical side of Wagner's work and personality known to the French public. It was planned at Munich in the summer of 1884 by a group of French intellectuals who were attending a performance of the *Ring*. The moving spirits were Édouard Dujardin, who had been at the Paris Conservatoire with Debussy, and Théodore de Wyzewa, later famous as a Mozartian scholar. The only German scholar associated with the revue was Houston Stewart Chamberlain, but the literary rather than musical character of the whole undertaking was emphasized by the collaboration of Villiers de l'Isle Adam, Mallarmé and Mendès. The avowed object of the editors was the study of Wagner as 'poet, thinker and creator of a new art-form', and in April 1885 the third number contained a contemptuous attack on the composers who were content to learn from the music of Wagner without bothering to understand his philosophical and aesthetic theories.

'They simply continue the tradition of Meyerbeer's melodrama or Adam's operetta, which they learned at the Conservatoire, and adjust them to modern taste. These gentlemen have now discovered the scores of Wagner and, being musicians, they are struck by the ingenious nature of the orchestral development, the powerful orchestration, the harmonic richness, the brilliant use of the whole *technical* apparatus, which is all that they can see. So they borrow Wagner's principle of thematic development, his instrumentation and his harmonic idiom, which they imitate as best they can. The milder spirits among them attenuate, the bolder exaggerate these "Wagnerian" traits; all equally fail to understand them. They have discovered that Wagner uses leit-motives, so they use leitmotives and we have the "letter theme" or the "bishop theme". They have discovered that Wagner gave the orchestra an important role, so they load their scores with noisy instrumental combinations and accompany a sentimental romance with the most erudite dissonances. . . .'

And so it goes on. Massenet is presumably the composer aimed at in the passage about leitmotives, for *Manon* (1884) has a letter theme; and possibly Reyer's orchestration, as his *Sigurd* (Brussels 1884) was a direct challenge to the Wagnerians, and he was a Jew. More important is the philosophical point of view stated and elaborated, generally by Théodore de Wyzewa, in the *Revue Wag-nérienne*. Schopenhauer is mentioned and discussed, although the first French translation of *Die Welt als Wille und Vorstellung* did not appear until 1888. Baudelaire's poem *Correspondances*, published in *Les Fleurs du Mal* in 1857 but possibly written much earlier, linked easily with Wagner's ideal of the *Gesamtkunstwerk*—the work of art which should be a product of all the arts:

> La Nature est un temple où de vivants piliers
> Laissent parfois sortir de confuses paroles;
> L'homme y passe à travers des forêts de symboles
> Qui l'observent avec des regards familiers.
>
> Comme de longs échos qui de loin se confondent
> Dans une ténébreuse et profonde unité,
> Vaste comme la nuit et comme la clarté,
> Les parfums, les couleurs et les sons se répondent.
>
> Il est des parfums frais comme des chairs d'enfants,
> Doux comme les hautbois, verts comme les prairies—
> Et d'autres, corrompus, riches et triomphants,
>
> Ayant l'expansion des choses infinies,
> Comme l'ambre, le musc, le benjoin et l'encens,
> Qui chantent les transports de l'esprit et des sens.

At a deeper level the oriental idealism of Schopenhauer was accepted as the explanation and justification of the flight from 'reality' to the ivory tower, which was the distinguishing mark of the Symbolists or Decadents. In the issue of August 1885 there appeared an article by Mallarmé entitled 'R. Wagner, rêverie d'un poète français' and there, in his mandarinesque prose, Mallarmé expresses his admiration of Wagner's achievements and his divergence from Wagner's aesthetic opinions. He rejects the Myth, but in the interests of a lyrical drama which could only be described as metaphysical—'a theatre without either scenery or actors, where an absolute music might create an ideal life'. In fact, throughout the numbers of the *Revue Wagnérienne* Wagner's ideas are interpreted, and added to, in a preconceived sense. They were discovered, after the event as it were, as an intellectual foundation, a philosophic scheme, which fitted in many ways the nebulous and uncorrelated ideas which had been drifting through French literature ever since Baudelaire's discovery of Poe. It is essential to distinguish, therefore, between the purely musical influence of Wagner, which had passed its peak by the time of Franck's death in 1890, and the more general and more profound influence of Wagner's philosophy and aesthetics represented at first by the *Revue Wagnérienne* and then by its successor, the *Revue Indépendante*.

Throughout the eighteen-nineties this more general influence was strong in all the arts and we shall meet it particularly in the chief operatic productions. Meanwhile, however, with the purely musical side of the Wagnerian crisis over, a reorientation was necessary in the musical world. It came in an improbable way. A young organist who belonged to the Franck circle, Charles Bordes, was appointed in 1890, at the age of twenty-seven, choirmaster at the church of Saint Gervais in Paris. Like Gounod nearly fifty years earlier in the Rue du Bac, Bordes was an enthusiastic worker for the restoration of the music of the fifteenth, sixteenth and seventeenth centuries and for the improvement of the standard in modern ecclesiastical works. In June he gave Franck's three-part Mass at Saint Gervais and this was followed by Schumann's Mass, Palestrina's *Stabat Mater* and Allegri's *Miserere* in 1891. In 1892 he founded a choral society with the name of 'Les Chanteurs de Saint Gervais' and in the same year, with the help of d'Indy, he organized the first of the 'Semaines saintes de Saint Gervais', in which the correct liturgical music for the Holy Week ceremonies of the Church was performed with the greatest care and scholar-

ship. Musicians were amazed and delighted at the revelation of
what had been virtually unknown masterpieces. Gounod, now in
his seventy-fifth year, wrote to Bordes a typically enthusiastic
letter after attending the first Semaine Sainte.

'It is time indeed that the flag of true liturgical art should be raised
in our churches in place of any profane standard and that musical
fresco-work [*la fresque musicale*] should banish the drawing-room ballad
and the saccharine piosities with which our digestions have been
spoiled for so long. Palestrina and Bach *made* the art of music and remain for us the Fathers of the Church. Our concern is to remain their
sons, and I can only thank you for helping us.'

Gounod may not have been successful in his own efforts to restore
'musical fresco' in the *Rédemption* or *Polyeucte*, but his old taste and
enthusiasm never deserted him and it must have been a joy to the
old man to see the works which he had tried in vain to introduce
to the public in the eighteen-forties, receiving recognition, at least
from fellow-musicians.

D'Indy had been at Bordes's right hand in all his productions
and it was these two men, together with the organist Alexandre
Guilmant, who founded in October 1894 the Schola Cantorum,
first as a society for the performance of sacred music and then, two
years later, as a school for the restoration of Church music. Thus
it was that poison and antidote, as it were, flourished on the same
tree; and we find the most intelligent and musically gifted of the
French Wagnerians preparing the ground for the reaction, exactly
as Chabrier had done. Bordes had already shown his enthusiasm
for the folk-music of his native Basque country in a *Trio basque*
(1888) and his *Archives de la tradition basque*, undertaken with the
authority of the Minister of Education (1889–90). His *Anthologie
des maîtres religieux primitifs* made available to other musicians the
fruits of his own study and research, and before the end of the century the Schola Cantorum appears as the conscious rival of the
Conservatoire, a centre of scholarship and a training ground for
artists rather than virtuosi, where Wagner's music was accepted as
the natural climax of a musical tradition which had its roots in
plainsong and the polyphonic masters of the late Middle Ages and
the Renaissance. As a composer Bordes was overshadowed by his
more brilliant contemporaries, though his fantasy on a Basque
theme for pianoforte and orchestra and the thirty-three songs
which he left at his early death in 1909 are the works of a genuinely

creative nature, moulded by his studies, certainly, but personal in the use of his material.

Franck's pupils were the most important body of musicians in France at the beginning of the eighteen-nineties. An extraordinarily intense and, to foreigners, most un-French atmosphere reigned among these disciples. D'Indy in his biography of Franck (1906) and Charles Oulmont in his *Musique de l'amour* (1935) describe a world of tremulous emotion, in which the nobility and purity of master and disciples seems to have been permanently—and one cannot help feeling, rather self-consciously—in evidence. 'There was such an atmosphere of love', d'Indy writes, 'surrounding this pure figure that his pupils loved each other in him and for his sake.' 'To love', Franck would say, 'is to forget oneself only in order to rise higher.' And an anecdote told by Oulmont would certainly explain the violence of the reaction which was to come.

'The daughter of one of Franck's pupils told me that her mother used to listen almost every evening, unknown to him, while her dear master played, several times running, the soft and intimate opening of Beethoven's *Moonlight Sonata*. In summer, when the window was open, she could often catch the words *j'aime, j'aime!*'

In the same way Madame Chausson says that during meal-times Franck would often burst into the dining-room 'urged by the affectionate necessity of seeing the beloved disciple'. Windy grandiloquence we know from the late works of Victor Hugo; the haze of emotion surrounds the figures of Eugène Carrière's pictures, and pretty-pretty sentimentalities abound in all the arts, in France as in England, during the eighteen-eighties and nineties. Franck and his pupils differ from all these by the profoundly and consciously *moral* complexion of their emotion. At times it seems as though they must be choked by their own idealism; and this did indeed happen to some of the less robust members. D'Indy was safe, preserved by a hard core of intense intellectuality, by his breeding and fastidiousness; but Chausson and Lekeu, even perhaps Duparc, suffered intensely. Chausson wrote to his young friend Debussy, in one of those moods of frustration induced, more likely than not, by this perpetual generation of too much emotional heat:

'If only one could find oneself, really blossom, free oneself of a whole heap of opinions which one adopted without really knowing why (because they fascinated one once or because they were expressed by people one loves or admires), opinions which do not really correspond at all to one's own nature!'

Even allowing for Lekeu's youth, his description of his Trio in a letter to his mother, with its plan of the last movement as 'the radiant development of Goodness', seems to tell the same story of an emotionalism which threatens to deform and ultimately to strangle musical expression.

The music itself is the best, and the only permanently important, witness to the good and evil effects of this background. It would be unfair to explain Henri Duparc's disappearance from the musical scene after 1885 (when he was thirty-seven) and his subsequent forty-eight years of silence until his death in 1933, simply by this over-driving of the emotional system; but a real nervous malady may well have been aggravated by the atmosphere of the Franck circle. Duparc was the first to discover Franck as a teacher and he was already working with him before 1870. He met d'Indy in 1869 and took him to visit Franck during the war, in the early months of 1871. From those early years date a 'cello sonata, a *Poème nocturne*, *Ländler* and *Roussalka*, all of which the composer destroyed because they did not satisfy his standard of excellence, though the *Ländler* was performed at the Société Nationale in 1874. A tone-poem *Lénore* was still strongly Lisztian in idiom and *Feuilles volantes* for pianoforte is very closely modelled on Schumann, not always the best Schumann. It is in the fifteen songs, written between 1868–85, that Duparc reveals, almost casually, a lyrical gift which is comparable on occasions with the best of Schubert or Wolf, and in every case immeasurably superior to all other songs which appeared in France during those years, with the single exception of Fauré, who worked in an entirely different idiom. Duparc's lyrical and dramatic style came from the fertilization by Wagner of a natural lyrical gift, such as appears (to take one example only) in the opening of *Chanson triste*—the contemporary drawing-room romance at its very best. What that lyrical gift could become when enriched and made more subtle by a thorough assimilation of Wagnerian harmony can be seen in a single passage later in the same song: 'Tu prendras ma tête malade, Oh! quelquefois sur tes genoux,' the wonderful modulation from G flat to D pivoting round the enharmonic D flat = C sharp; or in a whole song like *L'Invitation au voyage*, *Extase* or

Soupir. Enharmony is at the root of Duparc's style, but enharmony in the Lisztian sense (as in the second and third bars of *Phidylé*) or, even more frequent, in the manner of *Tristan* (*Soupir* and *Extase*) and not in the manner of Franck. Duparc hardly ever uses a chromatically slipping bass. His basses tend to be static, to move very little, while the complicated harmonic web is built up on firm and solid foundations (*Chanson triste*, *Extase*, *Au Pays où l'on fait la guerre*). This is possible in song-writing, where the danger of monotony is small owing to the smallness of the form. It is not possible in larger works, but Duparc either did not write or else destroyed his larger works, and for him it was a solution. It is significant that the songs planned on a larger scale—*La Vague et la Cloche*, *Testament* and *La Vie Antérieure*—are the least successful and they seem to suffer from the typically Franckian failing of elaboration for its own sake. Broken chords and tremolandos fill in the spaces which had better have been left empty, while the work takes on a grandiose, quasi-orchestral air. These are the passages which 'date' in Duparc's songs. Thus the last verse of *Lamento* is a declension from the first, for just this reason; and *Le Manoir de Rosamonde* gets its biting, Wolf-like quality from the complete absence of 'filling' of any kind.

Nearly all Chausson's music bears this date-mark. Ernest Chausson came late to music and he was never a professional musician, in the sense that he never had to write in order to make a livelihood. Both these circumstances influenced his development. He went first to Massenet to study composition in 1880, when he was already twenty-five; but Massenet's urbane and voluble sensuousness said less than nothing to this gauche and melancholy young idealist. In the course of the same year he left Massenet for Franck and almost at once his real latent gifts began to blossom in the sympathetic atmosphere of 'L'amour de la musique, musique de l'amour'. The early songs, op. 2 (1882), contain some of the best Chausson ever wrote. *Papillons* and *Le Colibri* (with its unusual 5/4 rhythm) are famous, but the *Sérénade italienne* too shows both a dramatic sense and a real feeling for the voice, which was often to be obscured by the over-intricate accompaniments in Chausson's later songs. Already during the eighteen-eighties, in his opp. 8 and 13, *Printemps triste*, *Sérénade* and *L'Aveu* the pianoforte accompaniments are becoming thick with arpeggio figures, cross rhythms and forced modulations; and with his settings of Maeterlinck's *Serres chaudes* (1893–6) and *La chanson bien*

douce the atmosphere, like the texture, becomes unbearably thick
and heavy—the 'unrelieved elegiac atmosphere', as one critic im-
patiently describes it. Even so, there are moments when the
'lassitude' and the 'ennui', the cosmic questionings and the sense
of frustrated emotion are forgotten, and in the *Trois Lieder* Chausson returns to a happier, clearer emotional world and a correspondingly cleaner palette (*Les Couronnes, Ballade*). His chamber
music suffers from the same defects as his songs, though in instrumental music these defects are less immediately fatal. Both the
concerto for pianoforte, violin and string quartet and the pianoforte quartet contain beautiful passages (the slow movement of the
quartet, for example) and if Chausson had been able to leave well
alone, to refrain from repetition and chromatic complication,
doubling of parts and filling in with trills, tremolos and arpeggios,
the ideas and even their treatment are fine in themselves. The
young Debussy, whom Chausson befriended and adopted, to use
Debussy's own unexpected phrase, as a 'big, elder brother', put
his finger exactly on his failing.

'You bring such heavy pressure to bear on your musical ideas that
they dare not present themselves to you in their natural guise for fear of
not being suitably dressed. . . . A thing I should like to see you lose is
your preoccupation with the inner parts [*les dessous*].'

Chausson himself was never happy about his own musical development and as early as 1889 he could write of his own songs: 'The
mere cream of music! harmonic clashes that may well be pretty
but are intoxicating and enervating and lead to impotence.'
His restless, melancholy and idealistic character was no doubt
largely to blame, and Franck's circle only fostered the emotionalism of a nature already too much inclined to sentimental brooding. What might have cleared Chausson's emotional atmosphere
and cleaned his musical style, as a strong north-east wind clears
and cleans a heavy grey sky, was a breath of hardship, an acquaintance with the grimmer side of the professional musician's
life. He was a rich (and an exceedingly generous) man and never
knew the necessity of writing to earn his living, of making pianoforte scores of third-rate operas or potpourris for dance orchestras
in order to pay the rent. Every work he wrote could be pondered
over, tinkered at, re-written again and again until he himself lost
all sense of perspective. For the very reason that he only composed
what and when he felt inclined, he never achieved the ease and

versatility, the fluency and variety, of the real professional. His late start was a further handicap; and so his music is always haunted by the spectre of amateurishness. On the other hand—for there is no defect which does not carry with it at least a potential compensation—no music is more personal, more intimate or a better reflection of the composer's character, freer from all concessions to public taste or more possessed of a certain nobility.

'These perpetually intertwining modulations, which come and go, writhe and seem to be either fortuitous or merely clumsy, do nevertheless end by creating a web of sound which . . . taken all in all, lends itself better than any other to the expression of melancholy and meditation.'

Only in two works did Chausson rise superior to his limitations—in the Symphony in B flat and the *Poème* for violin and orchestra. In the *Poème* he epitomized his own style, shortcomings and all, and created a wholly successful work by sheer vitality, the very quality which seems lacking in his songs. There is a richness of invention and an uninhibited emotional sensuousness in his exploitation of the technical and expressive powers of the violin, which may offend our modern canons of taste on occasion but cannot be discounted. In the symphony, on the other hand, Chausson to a great extent escapes from the heavily lyrical style —the rather too plangent melodiousness which we associate with the A string of the violoncello—and achieves a more vigorous and looser style. It is partly owing to the strongly rhythmic character of his material, especially in the first movement, where both subjects keep the composer on the move and do not allow him to get clogged in his own processes. The opening chorale inevitably suggests Franck, but it is not until the last movement that Chausson's music becomes simply reminiscent. There the whole lay-out of the movement and the nature of the material is so like that of the last movement (also the weakest) of Franck's symphony that it seems as though the imitation must have been conscious. It is worth while quoting the first subject, since it exemplifies many of the faults of a typically Franckian melody:

Ex. 18

The repeated opening phrase, with its jaunty shift of stress in bars
two and four, is stiff and jerky; and the second half of the eight-
bar phrase gets bogged almost before it starts, pivots weakly round
on its own axis and comes to a halt. After that it is a question of
repetition and sequences, while the emotional temperature rises;
and this is the interesting point. On nearly every occasion where
Chausson's musical invention flags, the emotional pulse of the
music is artificially quickened and the emotional climaxes (and
this is particularly true of the chamber music) are the scenes of the
most shameless filling. It is almost as though the merest breath of
emotional excitement set Chausson's hands to semiquaver arpeggios and broken chords in nervous reaction, as a man in a dentist's
waiting-room drums on the window-pane.

Harmonically, Chausson was more adventurous in his early
songs than in his later works. After his early student days he
settled down, uneasily at first but then resignedly, within the
Francko-Wagnerian harmonic framework, and his darling work
which caused him so much heart-burning, the opera *Le Roi Arthus*,
is, alas! impeccably Wagnerian from beginning to end.

A more powerful, intellectual current which influenced Franck
himself and, through him, d'Indy was that which flowed from the
works of Beethoven's last manner. Chausson was only touched indirectly, but the young Belgian pupil of Franck, Guillaume Lekeu,
was swept off his feet. Coming to Paris at the age of eighteen, in
1888, he studied first with Franck and then with d'Indy; and in
the six years before his tragic death from typhoid fever in 1894 he
produced a remarkable series of works. He was intensely emotional
(we have already met him fainting during a performance of *Tristan*

at Bayreuth in 1889) and acknowledged no other criterion of excellence in music. Lekeu's 'Je n'aime pas la musique jolie et non sentie', and 'Pour moi l'art est infiniment sentimental, d'où mon admiration pour *Tristan et Yseult*' match Duparc's 'Je veux être ému.' Wagner's music was his natural ideal, and it was probably only his admiration for Beethoven that prevented him from wasting his energies in writing music-dramas before he was twenty and made him turn his interest to chamber music instead. He finished a pianoforte trio, sonatas for pianoforte and for violin and left unfinished a violoncello sonata and a pianoforte quartet; while for the orchestra he wrote two *Études symphoniques*, *Hamlet and Ophelia* and *Chant de triomphale délivrance*, an Adagio for strings and the *Fantasie sur deux airs populaires angevins*. In all these works, as was only to be expected at Lekeu's age, moments of genuine inspiration alternate with passages in which the influences of Beethoven and Wagner have been insufficiently digested and assimilated. Sometimes the very material makes this almost inevitable, as in the case of the grandiose 'question' around which the first movement of the trio is built:

Ex. 19

It is startling to find a boy hardly out of his teens imitating a manner partly forced on Beethoven himself by his deafness. Lekeu was in love with all that was powerful and knotty, violent and rugged, in Beethoven's music, and the rough fugato passages, the sudden sforzando and the explosive fortissimo followed by pianissimo, which abound in the trio, recall the same enthusiasm in another young and promising composer who, like Lekeu, died before he achieved artistic maturity—Alexis de Castillon. Lekeu's violin sonata, which he dedicated to Ysaÿe, is more influenced by Wagner than by Beethoven and contains stretches of music such as were fatally common at this time, where the composer seems to be transcribing for a chamber music medium the ecstasies of the *Liebestod*. The 7/8 rhythm of the slow movement and the long-drawn-out cantilena of the violin part, on the other hand, show a genuinely original melodic gift and an inquiring, experimental mentality which might well have developed a personal idiom if Lekeu had lived. The texture of the trio is predominantly contrapuntal, but in the violin sonata (and the unfinished pianoforte quartet) we find the same faults which spoil Chausson's chamber music—the use of broken chords, arpeggios and tremolando to fill out and give the movement a spurious grandeur and breadth. Sequences can be used for the same effect:

Ex. 20

Oddly enough Lekeu's orchestral music is cleaner and less turgid. The *Fantaisie sur deux airs populaires angevins* was based on two tunes that Lekeu heard whistled when he was dining with the bank manager at Angers. From a letter dated 17 January 1893, written to his mother, it seems as though the *Fantaisie* has a programme. He is describing d'Indy's enthusiasm for the work:

'It is marvellously written, d'Indy says, neither too long nor too short, and its proportions are excellent [*ordonné très harmonieusement*]. He finds the *fête populaire* at the beginning most infectiously gay, the impression of night on the plain at the end "exquisite" and the love scene "charming". The whole bag of tricks, in fact! He says the instrumentation is as good as the music and that the whole work is simple, though modern and original. . . .'

Neither of the Angevin folk-songs used in the *Fantaisie* is particularly attractive in itself; and that is probably an advantage rather than otherwise. The fully-fledged, evocative, haunting melody is usually unsuited to symphonic treatment. The more modest melody, of a less pronounced character but with one or two outstanding rhythmic or melodic traits, is a far better generator of musical thought. Lekeu, for instance, takes the last phrase of his second melody and plays about with it, naïvely but pleasantly, until he gets it into a rhythmic shape which will combine with his first tune. This is a purely musical activity and one that would seem almost an indignity if applied to a more grandiose and emotionally fertile theme. He then tries transferring the rhythm of the second theme to the notes of the first, returns to what had originally been merely a bridge between themes 1 and 2 and varies his own variations—all with a skill which is not that of a master but of a gifted apprentice who is already at his ease in handling musical ideas of a simple order. Youth quite rightly has a passion for the magnificent; it was a very young poet who wrote: 'I think continually of those who are truly great.' But Shakespeare, Beethoven and Michelangelo are not good models for young artists. In the *Fantaisie* Lekeu was content to take two tunes and allow his musical imagination to play with them, unconcerned by cosmic questionings and 'the radiant development of goodness'. His interest seems to have been more musical than emotional and the music is correspondingly better.

The pianoforte is always a dangerous stand-by for the composer whose conceptions are greater than his power of expression. The sheer ability to make so much noise with arpeggios in various positions, repeated chords, octave passages and tremolos, all with the minimum of musical thought and the maximum of 'expressiveness', goes to the head of many composers. Sometimes there is a definite reason. Franck's pupils were overwhelmingly aware of their ideals—the noble, vigorous art robustly constructed on a foundation of solid learning, pure and idealistic in its emotional inspiration and disdaining all concessions to popular taste. This was a very high ideal: so high, in fact, that none but the most exceptionally gifted composer could live up to it all the time. But exceptions were not provided for; there was no hierarchy of values officially permitted. The only solution for men without the inspiration of Franck, the enormous vitality of d'Indy or the purely technical apparatus of either was, on occasion, to cheat—to inflate artificially what was not of its own nature grand, noble and moving enough to satisfy the exacting canons of taste which they had accepted—and the pianoforte can make an admirable wind-bag. It was not conscious hypocrisy, though it was the homage that weakness paid to a forbidding form of virtue; nor was it confined in its essence to a single period or group of people, for it is little else than a form—actually one of the more reputable forms—of that slavery to fashion called snobbery. Grandeur and nobility were the fashion then, just as 'interesting' counterpoint has been in our day; and fashion too eagerly followed will make an unconscious hypocrite—or at least a wind-bag—of anyone.

No one could accuse the young Lekeu of conscious hypocrisy. He was heart and soul in sympathy with Franck's ideals, and even more with their austerer and more intransigent expression in d'Indy's works and character. In a letter to the Belgian violinist, Ysaÿe, who was an enthusiastic admirer of his music and played the violin sonata of this unknown fellow-countryman at his recitals, Lekeu confesses (not without pride, being very young) that in his pianoforte quartet he has 'given himself an emotional programme desperately difficult to follow in detail, at any rate for me. Let us hope that the listener will not find the same difficulty!' We have already seen that the last movement, which he never lived to write, was to be 'the radiant development of goodness'. How he conceived the first movement is recorded in a letter to his mother, dated 2 February 1893. It is worth quoting for its own sake and also because it is typical of the world in which Franck's pupils lived. The flavour of the original French hardly survives translation.

'La première partie de mon quatuor est pour moi le cadre de tout un poème de coeur où mille sentiments se heurtent, où aux cris de souffrance succèdent de longs appels au bonheur, où des caresses se glissent, s'insinuent, cherchant à calmer les plus sombres pensées, où des cris d'amour succèdent au plus sombre désespoir, cherchant à le dominer, comme à côté l'éternelle douleur s'efforce d'écraser la joie de vivre. . . . Je me tue à mettre dans ma musique toute mon âme . . . c'est non seulement une oeuvre terrible à écrire par la difficulté des transitions mais surtout écrasante pour en saisir la structure totale.'

'Je me tue à mettre dans ma musique toute mon âme'—that is the key to so much of this music, to its touching (but often slightly cloying) emotional quality, to the 'difficulty of the bridge passages' and the unsatisfactoriness of the 'total structure'. Lekeu's ideal was to make every note *alive*, not merely well placed in a pattern, but emotionally *speaking*. In the same way he wished, he said, to abolish all 'accompaniment', just as in the modern play the role of confidant has been abolished. It was a dream of idealistic egalitarianism—each part, each voice, each instrument contributing equally to the grand emotional effect. Now this, like all egalitarian dreams, is against nature and therefore against the fundamental principles which govern any art. Order and degree are of the very nature of human existence and there will always be moments of stress and relaxation in a musical composition, an ebb and flow of emotional interest. The whole conception of musical form rests on the assumption that the most inspired composer cannot be inspired the whole time and that hard work and ingenuity, conscious inventiveness, must fill in long stretches of any work. Any attempt to make a whole movement sound equally 'inspired' and lyrical throughout is not only doomed to failure in itself; it also ensures that the moments of real lyrical inspiration pass unnoticed. What are in reality the more humdrum moments sound pretentious and inflated, because the composer will not accept any diminishing of the emotional tension—the machine is driven at full pressure the whole time in the hope of concealing from the passengers the rougher parts of the track.

Chausson and Lekeu, the most emotional of Franck's pupils, both died young—Chausson at forty-four, Lekeu at twenty-four—and they might have learned wisdom and moderation with years, it is true. D'Indy was more intellectual by nature, a theorist where Franck was a mystic, a precise French imagination where Franck and Lekeu were Northern dreamers; hard-headed and matter-of-fact in comparison with Chausson's noble but too-luxuriant melancholy. D'Indy's influence on Lekeu was wholly good. He had started to give the young man lessons not long after Franck's death and in his letters he is always firm and sensible, understanding and never condescending. In a letter dated 26 June 1893, he answers a complaint from Lekeu that he was depressed and felt that he was no good as a composer. Typically enough, d'Indy answers with a prescription for artist's depression, tabulated under three headings:

1. Get to know yourself and your own capabilities and deficiencies.
2. Read and get to know a lot [? of music or in general: it is not clear from the context].
3. Have one or more dependable friends who will give you their honest opinion of your work.

Pseudo-impotence—the feeling of insufficiency and failure—is a regular mark of the artist in any case, says d'Indy. He often feels it himself but does not give way to it; and then he gives his reasons, logical and quite unpriggish.

He was forty-two when he wrote to Lekeu and already a mature composer, with a growing reputation. With Franck's death in 1890 and the foundation of the Schola Cantorum four years later d'Indy's position as *chef d'école* was first privately and then publicly acknowledged. He was ideally suited to the task of championing and doing propaganda for a new conception of music—learned in his art, intensely enthusiastic and a capable writer, who enjoyed controversy and was not afraid of giving or receiving hard thrusts. That there was also something of the schoolmaster in him was perhaps a disadvantage to him as a creative artist, but it helped him at the Schola. He had behind him a formidable record of works, in which the musical development is as regular and consistent as might be expected from so well-regulated and logical a character. The big orchestral works of the eighteen-seventies (the *Wallenstein* trilogy, *Jean Hunyade* and *La Forêt Enchantée*) were continued in the eighteen-eighties with *Saugefleurie* and the *Chant de la Cloche*, a 'dramatic legend' which gained the prize in the City of Paris competition in 1885. All d'Indy's big orchestral works hitherto had borne the heavy imprint first of Liszt, whom he visited in 1873, and then of Wagner. In *Le Chant de la Cloche* this was carried to its furthest extremes. It is in fact a French model of *Die Meistersinger*, based on Schiller's *Lied von der Glocke*, with a full complement of guilds (tanners, tailors, etc.), a Beckmesser with the glorious name of Dietrich Leerschwulst, a misunderstood and noble artist, Wilhelm, instead of Wagner's Walther, and a perfect counterpart to Eva in Lénore. The orchestration is heavy, the harmony rich, and a considerable part is played by large choral sections, which are ably and even powerfully written. It is an impressive work, but more for its technical mastery than for its originality.

Certainly the gulf between *Le Chant de la Cloche*, written between 1879–83 and d'Indy's next orchestral work, the *Symphonie sur un chant montagnard français* or *Symphonie cévenole* was enormous. Here d'Indy, having relieved his system of a vast weight of learning and emotion in *Le Chant de la Cloche*, turned away from Schiller and the German Romantics to an entirely different source of inspiration, the folk music of his own Vivarais country. The orchestration is lighter, the pace of development quicker and the learning better digested than in any previous work. The use of the pianoforte with the orchestra, but not strictly speaking *concertante* in the nineteenth-century sense, may have been suggested to him by Fauré's *Ballade* as well as by Franck's *Variations symphoniques*, which were written at the same time as his own work. The ingenuity by which the theme of the first movement

Ex. 21a

is converted into what appears something completely different in the second

Ex. 21b

is an early example of that process of theme-transformation which d'Indy had learned from Liszt and Franck, though by an excess of loyalty he would admit indebtedness to Franck only. From now onward he applied this principle with increasing skill and sophistication. The pianoforte part of the symphony uses a wide range of purely pianistic devices without ever suggesting the virtuoso either in style or in sentiment. (Virtuoso and opera-composer were terms of almost unqualified abuse in the Franck circle, though Franck himself had started as a virtuoso pianist.) The folk-tunes are a great contrast to the noble, heroic four-square themes which d'Indy had used in his large Wagnerian orchestral works, and this contrast—the chorale and the gay folk-tune—was to become something like a formula for his later works. The use of folk-song brought into d'Indy's work just the breath of fresh air which is so much needed in the music of Chausson and Lekeu, whose *Fantaisie angevine* was almost certainly inspired by d'Indy's *Symphonie cévenole*. To the end of his life d'Indy never ceased to return regularly for recreation and inspiration to his *domaine*, Les Faugs, high in the mountains of the Vivarais. In spite of his conscious professionalism, one side of him remained a patriarchal countryman, with something of the air of a visitor to Paris and a background of health and earthiness which were quite lacking in Franck himself and in his other pupils, most of whom were town-bred men of the middle class. This countryman side of d'Indy found further expression in a *Fantaisie* for orchestra and oboe solo written just after the *Symphonie cévenole*—an excellently written work based entirely on French folk-songs and inexplicably neglected by modern orchestras. It was this countryman who dared, when the Decadents set the aesthetic fashion and the Combes Ministry was in political power, to preach to his pupils at the Schola the intimate connection between art and religion—and not a vague pantheism or fashionable theosophy but a full-blooded Catholicism. We find him inculcating the three theological virtues—Faith, Hope and Charity —as an indispensable introduction to the study of counterpoint.

'Before all else the artist must have *Faith*—faith in God, faith in his art: because it is faith which spurs him on to knowledge and it is by means of this knowledge that he can mount ever higher in the scale of being, to the term of his whole nature, God.

'The artist must practise the virtue of *Hope*, because he expects nothing from the present. He knows that his mission is one of service, that his part is to contribute by his works to the teaching and the life of the generations which are to come after him.

'The artist must be fired by the sublime, the sovereign *Charity*. To love is his goal, because the one principle of all creation is Love, the great, the divine, the charitable Love.'

This is indeed a different atmosphere from the simple effusions of Franck, the Pater Seraphicus. But it is the same faith, only expressed with intellectual passion. The artist must have faith, says d'Indy *because it is faith which spurs him on to knowledge. Credo ut intelligam.* And he was never content until he could see clearly and find a solid intellectual basis for his musical, as well as his religious, faith. In his desire for clarity at all costs, for facts black and white, he inevitably narrowed his sympathies. Even his erudition was marred by prejudice (he could never really persuade himself that J. S. Bach was not a Catholic) and by a tendency to over-simplification. Thus he acknowledged three *types* of music only—'the decorative art of the Gregorian chant, the architectural art of the age of Palestrina, and the expressive art of the Italian eighteenth century'. His anti-Semitism, his contempt for fashion-snobbery and his quality as a fighting journalist are all summed up in his infinitely contemptuous—'the "modern style", this latest metamorphosis of the Jewish School' (Meyerbeer, Halévy, Offenbach). The drier and more didactic side of his nature delighted in scholastic analyses, which he never failed to make alive by including some outrageously tendentious point with an air of greatest innocence. Thus at a time when the divorce between art and morality was fashionably considered to be complete and permanent, d'Indy stated as a self-evident fact, in need of no discussion or proof:

'In artistic creation seven faculties are employed by the soul: the imagination, the heart, the spirit, the intelligence, the memory, the will and the conscience.'

No wonder that the effect of d'Indy's music is almost uniformly tonic on the listener. He was perfectly clear as to the sources of his own inspiration—plainsong, Palestrina and the Netherlands masters, folk music, Bach, late Beethoven; and only with the last of his heroes, Liszt and Wagner, did he come to terms with the morbid and the 'atmospheric', whose cultivation by some of his contemporaries he so deplored. Romain Rolland showed his understanding of the nature of the man and his music when he said that 'd'Indy's music displays qualities that go to the making of a military leader: a clear knowledge of the goal, a patient determination to reach it, a perfect knowledge of the means available, a spirit of order and a thorough mastery of his craft and himself!'

It was this austere, but passionate and inventive character which found expression in d'Indy's chamber music. After the early pianoforte quartet of 1878 he wrote no chamber music for nearly ten years; but after the *Symphonie cévenole*, the exorcising of the spirit of Wagner in *Le Chant de la Cloche* and the cleaning of his orchestral as well as his mental palette, d'Indy wrote five chamber works in little more than ten years—the trumpet septet, the trio for pianoforte, clarinet and violoncello, two string quartets and the *Chansons et Danses* for a wind septet. There was no chamber music in France, apart from the quintet and quartet of Franck or

Fauré's two pianoforte quartets, to match this output either in
quality or quantity. The two quartets owe much to Beethoven in
their conception and to some extent in their idiom. Both are built
round a motto theme, mutations of which provide much of the
thematic material. The texture of the first movements of both
quartets is predominantly contrapuntal, and in the first d'Indy
makes use of ingenious canonic imitations in the development
section. The short dramatic phrases, pregnant with emotion,
which characterize the introductory passages and recur at all
points of stress, are strongly reminiscent of the late quartets of
Beethoven; and the chromatic sweetness of Franck is almost
wholly absent, though the rather laboured emotion of the slow
movement of the second quartet, with its repetitions and heavy
instrumentation, obviously belongs to the Franckian world. The
folk-tunes which appear in the third movement of the first and the
last movement of the second quartet are unexpected and perhaps
a little out of character; but they do lighten an otherwise heavy
atmosphere.

The two septets and the trio are easier going and show d'Indy's
excellent feeling for the nature and timbre of each instrument.
Not for nothing had he assimilated Berlioz's treatise and studied
Berlioz's own music, when acting as choirmaster for big Berlioz
productions between 1875–8. He was a hornplayer himself (the
fanfares of *Saugefleurie* spring perhaps equally from Siegfried and
the naïve delight in his own instrument) and his blending of
horn tone with that of the woodwind—flute, oboe, two clarinets,
and two bassoons—in the *Chansons et Danses* is masterly. The
folk-song element is strong in the *Danses* and again in the *Divertissement* of the trio, where it stands in strong contrast to the 'noble'
Franckian lyricism of the *Chant élégiaque*, one of d'Indy's rare
spontaneously lyrical effusions. Spontaneity is what all this music
lacks. It is solid, vigorous, high-minded and uncompromising. Of
Le Chant de la Cloche he had written to Chausson:

'No concessions: nothing for the ladies or Members of the Institute—
so it will be very boring for the general public, for which I don't care
a damn.'

Nobody asks for concessions, but there is a difference between
being intransigent about conceding and having nothing to con-
cede. D'Indy wrote after the Paris première of *Aida* in April 1876,
of 'this Meyerbeerian-Wagneroid bore with its tendency to Ber-

liozian orchestration, which is only a pale imitation . . . of the aforementioned masters'. If d'Indy had it in him to write the last act of *Aida* and refrained from doing so by a self-denying ordinance, we might admire at least his moral power. But the *Chant élégiaque* of the trio is a poor substitute for a complete opera of the most potent and dramatic melody; and even that single movement is an exception in d'Indy's works, in which the costive lyricism of the slow movement from the second string quartet is typical, and liturgical and folk-song melodies are repeatedly called in to supply what was a basic deficiency of his musical nature.

In *Istar*, a set of symphonic variations, again based on a motto theme, d'Indy's orchestral skill, his fine workmanship and intellectual power, to a large extent cover this deficiency. This work appeared in 1897, the same year as the second string quartet in the last movement of which there is a passage (second subject on page 47 of the score) which is almost identical, even down to the key (F sharp major), with the second variation of *Istar*. The idea of placing the variations first and only allowing the theme to appear at the end of the work was suggested by the programme of the work—the mystical initiation of a fabulous princess, who passes from chamber to chamber and is stripped of jewels, veil and garments until the theme appears as she stands naked before the shrine. It also concentrates attention on the musical processes— which are admirable—rather than on the comparatively uninteresting melodic skeleton. The possibilities of theme-transformation and the building of a whole work from a few cells (which is what the 'mottos' are) suited d'Indy's powerful musical intelligence, his capacity for pure hard work and his poverty of melodic invention. It was typical of the man that he should erect into a general principle what was in reality an alternative—even a *pis-aller*—for those who, like himself, were not gifted with fertility in the creation of the stuff of music. It was thus that the Schola Cantorum, whose instruction was wholly planned and directed by d'Indy, besides doing great service to French music, also served as a school where, by sheer determination and hard work, the least musically gifted could learn to 'compose'—a more doubtful blessing and one which, as we shall see, was to influence the future development of music in France.

IV

AMID the conflicting parties with their various allegiances, followers
of Franck or Wagner, pupils of Massenet or Prix de Rome scholars,
there was a Gallio who seemed to care for none of these things and
was consequently suspect to all parties. Gabriel Fauré was born in
1845 and he was thus six years older than d'Indy and roughly a
contemporary of Massenet. He never studied at the Conservatoire,
and this was a hindrance in his official career until he was well
into middle age. Instead, he spent the years from 1854 to 1865 at
the École Niedermeyer, which had been founded primarily to
train organists and choirmasters and provided an excellent musical education, in many ways superior to that of the Conservatoire.
In the first place the study of the ecclesiastical modes was obliga-
tory and in the second Saint-Saëns was, from 1861 onwards, the
professor of pianoforte. Through him Fauré became acquainted
with music which he would hardly have encountered at the Conservatoire—Liszt, Wagner, Schumann, Beethoven and Bach. The
friendship with Saint-Saëns was valuable for practical purposes
also. After several posts as organist in and out of Paris, Fauré was
appointed in 1877 as choirmaster at the Madeleine, and in the
same year he and Saint-Saëns visited Liszt at Weimar for the performance of Saint-Saëns's *Samson et Dalila*. Fauré's earliest compositions are songs, dating roughly from 1865, his last year at the
École Niedermeyer and his four years as organist at Rennes (1866–
70). While Fauré was teaching at the École Niedermeyer as well
as working at the Madeleine and Saint Sulpice, besides visiting
Weimar in 1877, he went to Cologne in 1878 to hear *Rheingold* and
Walküre and to Munich the next year, where he heard the whole
of *The Ring*. In 1883 he visited Bayreuth. These pilgrimages were
normal among the younger musicians, but what was unusual in
Fauré's case was that his musical development seemed hardly
affected by them.

Unlike the large majority of his contemporaries, he kept instinctively to the smaller forms. The early songs were followed by
chamber music—violin sonata in A (1876), two pianoforte quartets (1879 and 1886), a *Ballade* for pianoforte and orchestra

(originally for pianoforte solo), 1881; and, increasingly as the eighteen-eighties went on, pianoforte music in the small forms developed by the Romantics—impromptus, nocturnes, mazurkas and barcarolles. It is significant that a violin concerto and a symphony, written in 1878 and 1884 respectively, were never published. What is it that distinguishes Fauré's violin sonata and the pianoforte quartets from any contemporary chamber music—Brahms (whose work was unknown to Fauré) in Germany and certainly any of the still rare French composers? What makes even the first volume of songs, with its frequent echoes of Gounod, remarkable?

Fauré was content, like Mozart, with the forms that he found already in existence. He was no revolutionary, no theorist, but that *rara avis* in the musical history of the second half of the nineteenth century, a musician pure and simple, with no gospel, no *Weltanschauung*, no carefully formulated aesthetic. Bizet, dead in 1875 and a completely different nature from Fauré, had resembled him in this and had suffered recurrent pangs of conscience about it. Not so Fauré. When he came to write a song he used quite naturally the sort of text and the musical idiom with which he was familiar; it probably never occurred to him to do otherwise.

The first volume of songs contains five poems by Victor Hugo, four by Théophile Gautier, three by Baudelaire, two by Sully-Prudhomme and one by Leconte de Lisle. The Hugo songs are strongly reminiscent of Gounod. *Le Papillon et la Fleur* and *Mai* are conventional drawing-room romances and *Dans les ruines d'une abbaye* is only slightly more subtle in an occasional point of chromatic colour. All three have accompaniments well within the technical powers of the amateur. The Baudelaire songs quite fail to give musical expression to the grandeur and originality of the poems. *Automne* misses Baudelaire's macabre imagination and *A la très chère* is turned into a conventional love-song with rippling semiquaver accompaniment. Sully-Prudhomme's *Au bord de l'eau* is probably the best song in the book, with the *Lydia* of Leconte de Lisle, *Après un rêve* by Romain Bussine and, in its arch and facile way, Paul de Choudens's *Sylvie*. In fact, literary merit was not in itself an inspiration to Fauré. The atmosphere of a poem appealed to him far more than verbal felicity; he was always in complete contrast to song-writers like Wolf or Debussy, with their strong verbal, almost linguistic sense. In *Au bord de l'eau* Fauré takes a conventional form, the floating and elegant 6/8, and by the simplest means—tying the last quaver of a group of three to the first of the next—he diversifies the rhythm without breaking it. He allows the pianoforte to interrupt and echo the phrases of the voice, not merely to accompany; and he composes the poem right through, not verse by verse. Harmonically, both *Au bord de l'eau* and *Après un rêve* are built round sequences of dominant sevenths, slightly sophisticated but unmistakable. Like Mozart's early works, these early songs of Fauré's are completely of their date and the genius of both composers shows itself in the fluent management of a given idiom. An increasingly personal turn is given to conventional forms, but there is no hint of revolutionary methods. Yet a revolution was what Fauré was imperceptibly accomplishing, both in his songs and his chamber music.

The songs published in the second volume of Hamelle's *Recueils* cover roughly Fauré's production during the eighteen-eighties (actually the first six of Volume III were probably composed during 1889, which makes twenty-five songs, omitting the *Barcarolle* at the end of Volume II, which was much earlier and has strayed from Volume I). In the fifteen to twenty years which separate these songs from those of Volume I Fauré had developed a completely personal style. The violin sonata op. 13 and the first pianoforte quartet were both written before *Nell*, the first song of Volume II; and the first five nocturnes, three impromptus and four barcarolles, the Requiem, the second pianoforte quartet and the *Ballade* are Fauré's other productions during the eighteen-eighties. There is hardly a song in the second volume in which Fauré does not demand a far higher standard of musicianship, and generally of technique, from both singer and pianist than anywhere in Volume I. The 'salon accompaniment' hardly appears at all, or if so, complicated (as in *La Fée aux Chansons* or *Chanson d'amour*) by harmonic subtleties which are more than mere surface effects and take, for example, the most innocent-looking vocal line beginning and ending in G major on an excursion into F major; so that the specifically drawing-room quality of easy and deliberately superficial elegance is wholly absent. Some of the most simple-looking songs are the most subtle. *Aurore*, for example, is a perfect aria in form; a middle section in G minor separates the opening G major section from its slightly ornamented repetition. The originality lies in rhythmic details, such as the ending of a phrase on the weak fourth beat of the bar, the counter-stresses in the pianoforte part in the middle section, and in the rapidly shifting harmony, different from Franck's chromaticism and never leaving nearly related keys but moving unexpectedly within that range. *Le Secret* and *Les Roses d'Ispahan* both follow fundamentally the same pattern. *Les Berceaux* and *Automne* may be regarded as richer and more extended drawing-room romances in the same vein as *Au bord de l'eau* in Volume I. Both are built round a similar rocking figure, above which the voice part rises almost naked at first, as in a Chopin Nocturne, and the same rhythmic pattern persists from beginning to end. Leconte de Lisle is represented in this volume by *Nell* and *Les Roses d'Ispahan*, but the majority of the poems are by Armand Silvestre, a poetaster beloved of song-writers in the eighteen-eighties and able to furnish verses which suggest a mood and call up simple images, which is all that was needed by Fauré.

Only with *Clair de Lune* (1887) do we come for the first time on the name of Paul Verlaine in connection with Fauré. Verlaine's poetry was to be Fauré's chief inspiration as a song-writer for the next few years. *Il pleure dans mon coeur*, the five so-called 'Venice' songs (*Mandoline, En sourdine, Green, A Clymène* and *C'est l'extase*), and the nine songs of *La Bonne Chanson* all appeared between 1889–91, followed by the isolated *En Prison* published in 1900 but probably written earlier. Fauré was forty-five in 1890, and at the height of his powers; for the next ten years after *La Bonne Chanson* he was to compose very little—a handful of songs and pianoforte pieces and the music for *Prométhée*—and it was not until 1904–5 that another period of creative activity began. Only then it is in a sense a new Fauré and a new style, which we shall have to examine in its place. The settings of Verlaine dating from the early eighteen-nineties represent the very best of Fauré's middle period, the perfection of a style which he had been forming in his pianoforte works as well as in the songs of the eighteen-eighties; and before we examine that style it will be as well to bring our review of Fauré's music up to date and say something of the early pianoforte and chamber works.

The three *Romances sans paroles*, op. 17, were almost certainly composed long before their publication in 1883—twenty years earlier according to Norman Suckling, which would make them contemporary with the earliest songs. Their model was frankly Mendelssohn, but in No. 1 Fauré already reveals himself in a typical pianistic device, by which an imitation or echo of the melody played by the right hand appears off the beat in the left. Chopin, Schumann and Mendelssohn between them formed

Fauré's pianoforte style until the break in his whole manner about 1900. The Nocturnes up to and including the sixth naturally owe most to Chopin, especially the second, though Fauré's type of melody is quite unlike Chopin's—purely instrumental where Chopin's was rooted (certainly in the Nocturnes) in the *bel canto* of Italian opera. The actual pianoforte figuration owes more to Schumann, especially in the spreading of a melody between the two hands and concealing it with arpeggio passages, as in the middle section of the fifth Nocturne or the *Ballade*. But Fauré avoids instinctively Schumann's four-square rhythm, just as he very early avoids unambiguous definitions or affirmations of tonality. What was later to become a real extension of the tonal system began in Fauré's case with a natural preference for an iridescent or kaleidoscopic surface, a perpetually dissolving tonal structure which is a continuation of one of Chopin's most original characteristics.

The *Ballade*, op. 17, is the most accomplished of Fauré's earlier pianoforte works and a good compendium of his typical pianistic idioms. He had heard *The Ring* at Munich in 1879 and the *Ballade* is said to have been written 'under the impression of the forest scene in *Siegfried*'. If this is so, Fauré was unique in 1880 in his ability to digest and assimilate Wagner's music into his own musical system. The opening cantilena, with its chromatic bridge-passages, obviously suggests Chopin, though the cut of the melody is unlike his. The canonic imitation in the second half has an obvious parallel in Chopin's F minor Ballade. The actual similarity to the *Waldweben* only starts in the Allegro section in B major, though any of his audience who knew Wagner's music would recognize the Wagnerian character of such a passage as this, with its sequences of dominant sevenths:

Ex. 22

Was it this, certainly unique in pianoforte music in 1880, which made Liszt return the *Ballade* to Fauré with the comment that it was 'too difficult'? or was Liszt, for once, blind to a talent which was in almost every way the antithesis of his own? (If the *Ballade* was shown to Liszt in 1877, when Fauré accompanied Saint-Saëns to Weimar for the first production of *Samson et Dalila*, this makes Joseph de Marliave's statement that it was written 'under the impression of the forest scene in *Siegfried*' difficult to understand, for Fauré did not hear *Siegfried* until his journey to Munich in 1879. It is, of course, possible that he knew the score and that the *Ballade* was written after reading or playing the *Waldweben* at the piano.) Liszt certainly saw the original version of the *Ballade* for pianoforte solo, afterwards arranged by Fauré himself for pianoforte and orchestra.

It is in his chamber music for pianoforte and strings that Fauré's pianoforte writing of this period has become most widely known—the violin sonata and the two pianoforte quartets. The sonata was played at the Trocadéro during the 1878 Exhibition and published by Breitkopf and Härtel, though Fauré made no money by it. It was dedicated to Paul Viardot, the son of Turgenev's friend Pauline and brother of Marianne, to whom Fauré was at that time engaged. It is an attractive work, conventional in its main outlines and original in details, like most of Fauré's compositions at this time. There is a recurring D sharp, for example, in the A major of the first movement; the slow movement is built on an unusual form of 9/8 rhythm; the Scherzo contains a beautiful D flat major intermezzo section and the theme of the last movement circles round a C sharp that might be the dominant of F sharp minor or the mediant of A major—ambiguities typical of the composer. The quartets are probably Fauré's most popular instrumental works outside France. They are similar in general structure and even in some points of detail. In both, the opening theme of the first Allegro appears in the recapitulation in a new light, not restated so much as remembered. In each case the finale is the weakest movement, not in any lack of musical interest so much as a failure to sum up, to clinch, or crown the whole work. *Finis non coronat opus*. Fauré instinctively fought shy of the rhetorical and dramatic and his harmonic idiom did not permit of 'glorious affirmations', of tonality or anything else. The slow movements and the scherzos are the most successful, as might be expected of a composer whose main characteristics were still lyricism and a gift for the unexpected turn of phrase, the enharmonic pun or the melodic quirk.

This last characteristic might, in a different character, have
led to an exclusive interest in colour effects or to subtleties indulged in for their own sake. In Fauré's case it led to an entirely
different result. Surface effects did not satisfy him and, master
of them as he was, he was too thoughtful, too interior an artist
to continue the elaboration of an inessential. In the five 'Venice'
songs and the *Bonne Chanson* cycle Fauré boldly and successfully applied his revolutionary harmonic processes to the melody;
and it is in these songs that we have the first adumbration of
what was ten years later, and in a different mood, to become
something like a new style. He was not acutely sensitive to literary
quality but in Verlaine he found a fellow feeling of dislike for the
emphatic and rhetorical. He could echo the feeling that Verlaine
expressed in his *Art Poétique*, twisting the neck of eloquence and
proclaiming the all-importance of nuance.

If we compare the idiom of the *Requiem*, written in 1887–8, with
that of the songs of the next three or four years, it is difficult to
believe that the difference can be explained simply by the difference between a religious and a secular text—which Fauré did not
in any case feel strongly. The *Requiem* was written by Fauré on the
death of his parents and is simple and straightforward in every
respect. Each composer in writing a *Requiem* naturally emphasizes
one aspect of death, and this fact can be used more profitably to
discover the composer's temperament rather than his theological
complexion. Fauré was not an orthodox Catholic in his beliefs; but
neither was Berlioz nor Verdi, nor perhaps was Mozart by the time
he wrote his *Requiem*. Their unorthodoxy is, however, not to be
gathered from their music. Piety—in the original Latin sense of
pietas, dutifulness—and resignation are the chief characteristics of
Fauré's *Requiem*; but they are not his only response to death, and
the unbiassed listener will detect no false note in the specifically
Christian devotion of the *Pie Jesu*, in the fear of the creature faced
by his Creator expressed in the Offertory and the *Libera me*, or the
anticipation of the Beatific Vision in the final *In Paradisum*. The
whole work is within the Christian framework and the absence of
the *Dies Irae* is as easily explained on aesthetic as on religious
grounds. Fauré, with his knowledge of plainsong, may well have
realized that it was difficult to improve on the original sequence
and that in any case he was not the man to write what in every
modern *Requiem* is a highly dramatic setting. Melodically the music

is simple to the verge of bareness. The *Sanctus*, for example, hardly moves beyond the repetition of the opening phrase and the vocal line of the whole movement lies within the span of a fifth. The same is true of the tenor solo passages in the *Agnus Dei*, and this deliberate limitation of effect wonderfully expresses the feeling of resignation, an undemonstrative grief shot through with the feeling of completion and fulfilment proper to the death of the old.

The *Requiem*, then, is in a sense the end of Fauré's youth, that protracted youth which comes to an end suddenly with some people when their parents die. From now onwards the surface of his music will slowly begin to lose its sheen, as the artist turns inward; but first come the Verlaine songs. Even in the 'Venice' songs the feeling is autumnal. *Mandoline* and *A Clymène* are the fading eighteenth century seen through romantic eyes, *En Sourdine* and *C'est l'extase* the very full bloom of maturity, Verlaine's emotion held like a fly in the purest amber. The pianoforte parts have quite ceased to be accompaniments and are as integral parts of the whole song as those in Wolf's *Spanisches Liederbuch*, which was completed at the same time. The arpeggio figuration of the earlier songs and pianoforte music appears in *En Sourdine* and *A Clymène*, the repeated chords in *Green* and *C'est l'extase*; but both are laden with harmonic implications and are far from being simply filling. The chromaticism of *Green* is no longer decorative and only Fauré's extreme, instinctive elegance and ease of writing can persuade the voice to follow the beat-to-beat modulations without giving a feeling of restlessness or cloying, which the same effect produces in the music of Franck.

Ex. 23

Voi-ci des fruits, des fleurs, des feuilles et des branches _____ Et

puis voi-ci mon cœur qui ne bat que pour vous

The listener is hardly aware of the counterpoint in *En Sourdine* and *C'est l'extase*, as it rises above the rich harmonic web provided by the lower parts of the pianoforte; and this is typical of Fauré, to conceal his skill beneath what still appears to the ordinary listener a drawing-room exterior.

If the 'Venice' songs are autumnal, *La Bonne Chanson* is the music of late spring and early summer. The nine poems all date from the time immediately before Verlaine's marriage and they are radiant with the anticipation of happiness and an almost hysterical hope, which carried the seeds of its own disappointment. Fauré's music matches the poet's joy. The last song of the cycle, *L'hiver a cessé*, is one of the great spring songs and *Donc, ce sera par un clair jour d'été* one of the greatest prothalamiums. But the nagging doubt of *N'est-ce pas* with its child's desire to be reassured—'isolés dans l'amour ainsi qu'en un bois noir'—he does not understand; and it is the ecstatic end of *J'ai presque peur, en verité*, rather than the anxious opening, that corresponds to the poet's mood. Musically *La Bonne Chanson* was never surpassed by Fauré. None of the songs have the purely sensuous appeal of, say, *Après un rêve* or *Au bord de l'eau*. That was already a thing of the past, in the songs as in the pianoforte music, where the Sixth Nocturne (1894) holds the same place as *La Bonne Chanson*. But the purely musical interest, the actual composition, has gained in intensity. *Une Sainte en son auréole* contains minute points of illustration such as Fauré normally shunned by instinct—the suggestion of horn tone, for example, in his setting of

> La note d'or que fait entendre
> Le cor dans le lointain des bois,

—or the warmth and grace of the slight variation of the opening phrase (with its faint suggestion of Fenton and Nannetta in Verdi's *Falstaff*) with which Fauré underlines the words

> De grâce et d'amour.

There are examples of musical illustration all through the cycle. *J'allais par des chemins perfides* is full of them, restless chromaticism giving way to the calm F sharp major triumph of 'l'amour délicieux vainqueur' and the ascending triplets on the final 'joie'. Certainly he had never wedded his music so indissolubly to any text before, and if it was not conscious literary taste, it was something vaguer and possibly profounder—artistic instinct.

Fauré was regarded by intransigent musical conservatives as a subversive force, although he had no symphonic poem or Wagnerian music-drama to his name. It was not until 1897 that he was given a class of composition at the Conservatoire, on Ambroise Thomas's death. He had let it be known earlier that he would be glad to be on the teaching staff of the Conservatoire, but when his name was mentioned Thomas was indignant. 'Fauré? Never. If he is nominated, I resign.' Apart from his instinct, which rightly told him that Fauré's music was moving steadily out of the orbit of the musical world which he knew, Ambroise Thomas was certainly influenced by the fact that Fauré was not a Prix de Rome winner and had not even studied at the Conservatoire. And yet it was the Conservatoire that bred the most subversive of all figures in the French musical world of the eighteen-nineties.

Claude Achille Debussy was born in 1862, studied at the Conservatoire, where he was in Marmontel's class for pianoforte and Guiraud's and Massenet's for composition, and won the Prix de Rome in 1884. At the Conservatoire he was regularly recalcitrant, credited by the more far-seeing of his masters with originality but an unsatisfactory student all the same. In 1879 he spent the summer as private musician to Tchaikovsky's Nadezhda von Meck, whom he accompanied to Italy and Vienna (where he heard *Tristan*) and back to Russia. What Russian music, besides that of Tchaikovsky, he actually heard we do not know, but he certainly became acquainted with some of Borodin's songs, an acquaintance which bore fruit in the songs which he himself composed on his return to Paris in 1880, and in the years immediately following. *Paysage sentimental*, *Voici que le printemps* and *La belle au bois dormant* were all composed before 1884, the year in which he won the Prix de Rome with his cantata *L'Enfant Prodigue*. In them, as in the famous 'air de Lia' from the cantata, Borodin's influence (sequences of major thirds and of ninths, suggestion of the Dorian mode) contends with the pull of the fashionable Massenet. In 1880 Bourgault-Ducoudray was already illustrating his course of musical history at the Conservatoire with examples from Rimsky-Korsakov's *Pskovityanka* and Mussorgky's *Boris Godunov*, so that Debussy had an opportunity of becoming acquainted with Russian music in Paris. Another Russian experience which he was able to renew was that of gypsy music, which he had enjoyed in Moscow restaurants and night-clubs and heard again at the Concert Besselièvre in Paris.

Debussy was primarily attracted by the exotic, by anything which took him from the humdrum routine of the Conservatoire, with its harping on academic correctness and its exclusively operatic bias. When he returned from Rome early in 1887 he had another exotic interest, quite unlike the purely musical concern with Russia, and one which was shared by painters and writers rather than by musicians. This natural affinity with practitioners of the other arts was a remarkable characteristic of Debussy, partly genuine and partly a form of snobbery. Nothing annoyed him more than to be considered as a professional musician, just as nothing gave d'Indy more pleasure; and the painting and poetry of the Pre-Raphaelite Brotherhood, which now interested Debussy, was an enthusiasm which hardly any contemporary musician, except perhaps the young Paul Dukas, could share with him. It was not long before Debussy counted among his friends poets and painters of the *avant-garde*—Henri de Régnier, André Gide, Viélé-Griffin, Whistler and Jacques-Émile Blanche; and in 1892 Pierre Louÿs. The work he was now engaged on was a setting of Gabriel Sarrazin's translation of Rossetti's *Blessed Damozel*. This was to be the third and last of his *envois* as Prix de Rome, the other two being *Printemps* and the *Fantaisie* for pianoforte and orchestra.

Meanwhile he was not content to stay in France. In 1887 he paid a visit to Vienna with the express intention of visiting Brahms. He was more successful than d'Indy had been ten years earlier and Brahms gave him dinner and took him to a performance of *Carmen*. (The picture of Brahms and Debussy sitting together at *Carmen* is one of those historical tableaux which not even the most daring journalist would think of inventing, though doubt has been cast on the whole episode.) He also went to England, possibly on business connected with the copyright of Rossetti's poem, during 1887. But far more important to his musical development were the two pilgrimages, in 1888 and 1889, to Bayreuth. He heard *Parsifal* and *Die Meistersinger* in both years and *Tristan* as well in 1889; but whereas in 1888 he was almost uncritical in his admiration, by the next year he was already uneasy; and, though he was fascinated by *Tristan*, which he knew well but had only once heard performed, he was critical of Wagner's dramatic method and was reaching out in his own mind to a quite different musical ideal.

In October 1889 his friend Maurice Emmanuel quotes him as saying, 'I am not tempted to imitate what I admire in Wagner. I conceive dramatic form differently; music begins where words are powerless to express. Music is made for the inexpressible and I should like it to seem to rise from the shadows and indeed sometimes to return to them.' He compared Wagner to Hugo and saw both of them as the end of a great tradition rather than as pioneers of a new art. He even distrusted the splendour of the Wagnerian orchestra and saw clearly—almost alone in 1889—the danger of musicians arraying in the most magnificent of orchestral garments 'ideas comparable to twopenny-ha'penny dolls'. To his friend Chausson he wrote that his own ideal was 'to discover the perfect shape of a musical idea and to allow it just the right amount of ornamentation'. Later, after his own experience of operatic composition, he was to give an even clearer statement of the principles which guided him, though whether these were present to his mind clearly at the time of composition is not certain. It seems from his letters that he had only a vague idea of the new aesthetic principles which were to determine the nature of his opera and that details were all worked out empirically as he went along. What is certain is that he returned from his second visit to Bayreuth largely disillusioned in Wagner as a guide for his own development, though still profoundly influenced by his music.

It was in this state of mind that, in 1889, he renewed his acquaintance with Russian music at the Universal Exhibition. In the June of that year a Russian orchestra, conducted by Rimsky-Korsakov, gave two Saturday afternoon concerts at the Exhibition. The programme of the first, on 22 June, was:

Overture to *Russlan and Ludmilla*	Glinka
In the steppes of Central Asia	Borodin
Allegro from Pianoforte Concerto No. 1	Tchaikovsky
Antar	Rimsky-Korsakov
Overture on Russian themes	Balakirev
Marche solennelle	Cui
Pianoforte pieces	Lyadov
Fantasy on Finnish airs	Dargomyzhsky
Stenka Razin	Glazunov

and a week later—

Second Symphony	Glazunov
Pianoforte Concerto	Rimsky-Korsakov
Kamarinskaya	Glinka
Polovtsian march and dances	Borodin
A Night on the Bald Mountain	Mussorgsky
Pianoforte pieces	Balakirev, Tchaikovsky
	and Blumenfeld
First Scherzo for orchestra	Lyadov
Capriccio espagnol	Rimsky-Korsakov

It is known that about this time Debussy had in his possession the score of Mussorgsky's *Boris Godunov*—the original, that is to say, and not the doctored version by Rimsky-Korsakov. This had been brought back from Moscow by Saint-Saëns in 1874 and lent by him to Jules de Brayer, one of the writers in the *Revue Wagnérienne*, who lent the score to Debussy. He certainly worked through it in 1893, when staying with Chausson at Lugano. Still more radical in their influence were the concerts given by the Javanese *gamelang* orchestras at the Exhibition, where Debussy heard for the first time the pentatonic Oriental scale and sonorities from which string tone was completely absent and the whole musical effect was produced by instruments of percussion. New rhythmic and melodic ideas and, generally, a new approach to musical structure and feeling, were revealed to him by these concerts which left a permanent mark on his writing for the pianoforte and the development of his musical ideals.

The *Cinq Poèmes* of Baudelaire, which were published in 1890, dated from the years of his greatest Wagnerian enthusiasm and were contemporary with the music of the *Damoiselle Élue*. The musical language of these songs is Wagnerian, though the aesthetic behind them is already tentatively new, Pre-Raphaelite and hieratic in the *Damoiselle Élue*, genuinely personal and original in some of the songs, particularly *Le Jet d'eau* and the magnificent close of *Recueillement* where tonality is already uncertain. Fauré was one of the first admirers of these songs (proving thereby the rightness of Ambroise Thomas's instinct), but he could not persuade any publisher to accept them. The early pianoforte works, *Deux Arabesques* and *Petite Suite*, reveal a quite different Debussy still touched by the popular favourites of the day—Benjamin Godard, Massenet, Saint-Saëns and, above all, Grieg, whose influence appears also in the *Suite bergamasque*, much of which also dates from this period of Debussy's production.

In the evolution of Debussy's mature style it is impossible to discount the influence of a strange figure whose objective importance has been hotly debated. Erik Satie was born in 1866 at Honfleur and inherited English blood from his mother. He spent a year, 1879–80, at the Paris Conservatoire, where he was a contemporary of Debussy, and this was, in fact, the year during which another contemporary, Maurice Emmanuel, noted down some of the daring harmonies and harmonic progressions with which Debussy used to shock his class-mates when—as often happened, apparently—he filled in the time spent waiting for the tardy Guiraud improvising at the piano. These included 'chains of fifths and parallel octaves, false relations of all kinds, unresolved chords of the ninth, eleventh and thirteenth'. No doubt there was as much exhibitionism as genuine music in these displays; but it was an original form of exhibitionism. Did the piano pieces published by Satie a few years later owe something to reminiscences of Conservatoire gossip about Debussy's antics? In the *Sarabandes* Satie plays with chords of the ninth. *Gymnopédies* are apparently three slow valses of the most simple kind, though they contain certain subtleties of rhythm and display an unusual preference for chains of fourths. In *Gnossiennes* bar-lines are dispensed with and the Lewis Carroll-like instructions to the player, for which Satie was to become famous, make their first appearance. (*Ouvrez la tête, Postulez en vous-même.*) The fact that Debussy himself orchestrated the first and third of the Gnossiennes makes it improbable that he regarded Satie as a plagiarist. Satie, on the other hand, allowed it to be understood that the idea of setting Maeterlinck's *Pelléas et Mélisande* was originally his and that Debussy appropriated it without telling him. There can be no question of much musical indebtedness on the part of Debussy, for Satie was not primarily so much a musician as an eccentric and an original. He was the enemy of all convention and a solitary. There was an aesthetic asceticism in his character and this found expression in the deliberate bareness and directness of expression in his music. He almost certainly gave Debussy general ideas which were important in his work on *Pelléas et Mélisande*. The two most often quoted are the suggestion that 'one should use a certain Puvis de Chavannes atmosphere' and the famous quip on the role of the orchestra: 'The orchestra should not grimace when a character comes on to

the stage. Look! Do the trees in the scenery grimace?' To compare
the orchestra with the backcloth was indeed revolutionary in the
days of the Wagnerian ascendancy; but Satie himself paid his
tribute to the Wagnerian cult, when he collaborated with the
egregious Sar Péladan and wrote a parody of Wagnerian liturgical
music for *Le Fils des Étoiles*.

Satie seems to have possessed something of that innocence of
character, which never fails to affect the ordinary world; and to
have combined it with a vein of genuine aesthetic originality, not
primarily creative. These two characteristics, rare enough when
combined in the same person, were dramatically offset by the
temperament of an English eccentric, expressed with an unmistakably Parisian gift for intellectual salesmanship.

The year 1892 was decisive in Debussy's development, not by
reason of purely musical experience but, typically enough, for his
discovery of two new writers. It was in 1892 that he met Pierre
Louÿs and in the summer of the same year that he bought a copy
of Maeterlinck's *Pelléas et Mélisande*, published in Brussels that May.
He was engaged on a wholly unsuitable libretto given him by the
ardent Wagnerian Catulle Mendès, but a single reading of Maeterlinck's play decided him to abandon what had always been a half-
hearted undertaking. It was not until he had seen the play, which
was given in Paris in May 1893, that he determined to try to set it
as an opera, but musical ideas seem to have suggested themselves
to him even as he read the text for the first time. The *Damoiselle
Élue* was given in April 1893, and this was followed in December
by the string quartet, and just one year later by the *Prélude à
l'après-midi d'un faune*. Of the songs, three settings of Verlaine (*La
mer est plus belle*, *Le son du cor s'afflige* and *L'Échelonnement des haies*)
date from 1891, *Fêtes galantes* from 1892 and *Proses lyriques* from
1892 and 1893. Debussy was already working hard at the first
draft of *Pelléas* and he had finished the first draft of Act IV, Scene
4, as early as September 1893.

The *Damoiselle Élue* was already old when the public heard it,
and Debussy himself had moved on to fresh pastures. The very
personal combination of Pre-Raphaelite preciosity and the 'chaste'
sensuality of the aesthetes with a rich Wagnerian orchestra and
something of the semi-mystical manner of *Parsifal* impressed
d'Indy, who was temperamentally Debussy's antithesis, and it can
still impress a modern audience. With the string quartet Debussy
produced the first work of his maturity. The ingredients that had

gone into that style were indeed extraordinary—the church modes, Borodin, Grieg, a dash of Massenet and a dash of Franck, the music of the gypsy orchestras and the Javanese *gamelang* are all traceable. The opening of the first movement suggests the Phrygian mode plainly enough, but the two episodes which occur before the appearance of the second subject both have the exquisite facility and charm of Massenet phrases, though their treatment is subtle and harmonically bold beyond Massenet's. The second movement with its pizzicato and the repetition of the ambiguous melodic snatch, which circles on itself in a kind of pirouette, is probably of gypsy inspiration, though the composite rhythms and the ostinato effects may have been remotely suggested by the Javanese orchestra. The slow movement closely resembles the more languorous and exotic Borodin (compare the Nocturne of the Petite Suite for pianoforte), though the middle section is a whole world distant and already calls up the absolutely personal style of *Pelléas*. The last is the weakest of the four movements, with its transformed thematic material from earlier movements and more than a passing nod to Grieg's G minor string quartet. Debussy spent only a very short while in Franck's organ class at the Conservatoire and was to refer irreverently to Franck as 'the modulation-machine'. But in the string quartet he followed Franck's principle of 'cyclic' form, possibly under the influence of Paul Dukas with whom he had been friendly since 1885. The first subject of the first movement is transformed into the melodic pirouette which dominates the second, where it appears in two different forms, and further transformations from the introduction dominate the last movement. The method was as unsuited to Debussy as it was suited to d'Indy. The 'treatment' and 'development' of a melodic cell were but the modern equivalents of sonata writing, to which Liszt had added the literary ideas of the Romantics. Franck and d'Indy were the inheritors of Liszt in this matter, while Debussy in 1893 was set on a path of musical development which quickly led him to the rejection of music conceived as a rhetorical discourse. How far he had already gone is shown by the *Prélude à l'après-midi d'un faune*.

Debussy's original plan was for a *Prélude, Interlude et Paraphrase finale* founded on Mallarmé's poem, a triptych of which he eventually only completed the one panel. He made quite clear the relationship between his music and the poem, speaking of it as 'a very free illustration . . . a succession of *décors* through which the Faun's desires and dreams move in the afternoon heat'. The *Pré-*

lude à l'après-midi d'un faune is thus not programme music, strictly speaking, but rather a series of evocations. Only the scenes evoked by Debussy are purely imaginary instead of being places with human and historical associations. Debussy explicitly denied that the music was designed as a synthesis of the whole poem; it is decoration, not narrative. Unlike most revolutionary works, the *Prélude* had an immediate success. The form is simple and the material consists virtually of two main themes. The sense of freedom, at which Debussy was aiming all his life and achieved for the first time in this work, comes from the asymmetrical character of the music, the perpetual tonal ambiguity and the breaking up of all the traditional melodic and rhythmic formulae into irregular fragments. The public recognized an entirely new atmosphere. This was modern music with the vaunted French qualities of grace, charm and colour, with all the lightness of touch and transparency of texture which they thought Wagner had banished from any music that could be called modern. For the first time Debussy had achieved a wholly individual idiom; but neither he nor his audience can have realized how completely novel and original.

Ortega y Gasset, writing nearly thirty years later, tried to go to the root of the matter when he distinguished between the music of the nineteenth century and that of Debussy by the difference of response demanded in the listener. In *El Espectador*, Vol. III (1921), he wrote:

'I should be inclined to say that we hear Beethoven's Romance in F major, but what we actually listen to is our own personal song . . . whereas the music of Debussy . . . demands of us a quite different activity. Instead of concentrating on the emotional echo which the music sets up within us, we give our whole attention (aural and otherwise) to the sounds themselves, to the fascinating sequence of events actually taking place in the orchestra.'

This is virtually to call Debussy a pioneer of the objective, and Ortega y Gasset confirms this by calling the listener's state of mind 'outward concentration' when he listens to Debussy and 'inward concentration' for the classics of the nineteenth century. And yet for the musician himself every external object is only valid or useful for the emotion it arouses in him. 'En musique, le paysage est un sentiment.' Nothing can enter music except through the composer's sensibility, and Debussy's originality lay in his finding musical expression for new forms of sensibility, not in his banishing music's power to set up echoes in the listener's consciousness. It would be more accurate to say that Debussy, like Mallarmé, regarded as the true stuff of art the echoes which any object—a landscape, a poem or a person—start reverberating in the artist. All the rest he regarded as rhetoric—the formal periods, the prepared cadences, the developments and, above all, the repetitions which are the foundation of the accepted classical ideas of form. His ideal was a music that should sound like an improvisation, and in a sense he achieved it better in the *Prélude à l'après-midi d'un faune* than anywhere else. What unconsciously disturbed the first audiences more than the unconventional structure and harmony was the fact that the reverberations that his music set up—the echoes in the composer's sensibility which he transferred to theirs—were of a wholly sensual nature. No hint of a noble idealism or conventional lyricism appears in the desires and dreams of the Faun; Debussy's was the language of sense-impressions refined to their utmost point, the patterns that crowd the mind on the threshold of sleep made audible. It was the first impression in music of the revolt against the discursive intellect, the turning away from reason; and it found its natural outlet in a style from which as many traces as possible of the rationalized eighteenth-century manner had been banished. This rejection of reason explains Debussy's instinctive attraction to Russian music. In Borodin's songs and in Balakirev's tone-poem *Thamar* he found not only novel effects of harmony and orchestral colour but an immediacy and a purity of sense-impressions such as, in the West, we normally find only in children. In Mussorgsky still more the classical ideal was not so much flouted as ignored; formal symmetry, beautiful line-drawing and all the rhetorical devices are completely absent. It did not matter that the Russians were essentially *naïfs*, whereas Debussy's approach was the last refinement of sophistication. They served his purpose and he used them for a time and then, like all original artists, outgrew them.

In September 1894 Debussy wrote to the violinist Ysaÿe that he was writing three Nocturnes for solo violin and orchestra and added that they were based on 'an experiment in the different arrangements of a single colour, what would be in painting "a study in grey" '. Debussy knew and admired Whistler's Nocturnes and when his own were finished, though there was no part for solo violin, the impression was nevertheless of three colour-studies corresponding in manner and atmosphere to those of Whistler. Two of the three had a comparatively prosaic origin which Debussy was not anxious to divulge to the general public. Mystery he believed to be an integral element in any work of art, and mystery is easily dispelled. A Parisian audience, recognising that the clouds of *Nuages* had drifted over the Seine and been watched from the Pont de la Concorde, and that the *cor anglais* phrase was a stylization, however subtle and successful, of a tug's hooter, might have easily ridiculed the whole piece. *Fêtes*, too, might have been disturbed if it could be situated in the Bois and the three muted trumpets would lose their swagger if they had been connected in the listener's mind with the Garde Républicaine sounding the final round-up for the closing of the park. *Sirènes* proved the most difficult of the three, because the women's wordless vocalizations were too often out of tune. In the *Nocturnes* Debussy's indebtedness to the Russians is more noticeable than in the *Prélude à l'après-midi d'un faune*. The resemblance of the opening bars to a passage in Mussorgsky's song-cycle *Sunless* is not in itself important, but Debussy developed here a habit of thinking in two-bar cells, in which the second was often a slight variant of the first, and this was to become a mannerism with him. He learned it from the Russian nationalist composers, who had incorporated this folksong trait into their style and had in so doing given Debussy an excuse for returning to one of the practices which he rejected most violently in the classical tradition—that of repetition. It was not, of course, the same form of repetition as occurs in the actual form of the sonata; it was often more a form of impromptu variation, a 'dispersive eloquence' in the words of Léon Vallas.

The singing of the Sirens was wordless and as instrumental as possible; for the singing, *cantabile* element in music, which was predominant in the classical style of the eighteenth century from its Italian origins, was foreign to Debussy's aesthetic ideals.

'Melody, one may say, is almost anti-lyrical. It is powerless to express the mobility of the human soul and of life. Its essential place is in the song, the expression of one definite emotion.'

In the *Prélude à l'après-midi d'un faune* and the *Nocturnes*, melody is fragmentary and vague; it can be nothing else without becoming formal, if it is only the formality of a folk-song. Even in his *Cinq Poèmes*, written in the late eighteen-eighties, much of the vocal writing is nearer to a Wagnerian form of recitative than to any formal melody, and this tendency increased in the *Trois Mélodies*

(1891), *Fêtes Galantes* (1892) and *Proses Lyriques* (1892–3), and cul-
minated in the *Chansons de Bilitis* (1897). In the *Trois Mélodies* and
Fêtes Galantes Debussy had gone to Verlaine for his texts, but the
Proses Lyriques are his own poems, in the manner of Mallarmé but
without more than an amateur's skill. The *Chansons de Bilitis* were
imitations of the Greek anthology by Debussy's intimate friend
Pierre Louÿs. More than the orchestral works of these years all
these songs have dated. Some of them—*De grève* and *La Chevelure*,
for instance—are perfect realizations of Debussy's method, subtle
dramatic and poetic unities. But a modern listener is struck by the
poverty, the over-discretion, of the writing for the voice. In *Pelléas
et Mélisande* Debussy was developing a musical-dramatic idiom in
which the voice has its own quite distinct and original role,
limited but perfectly in accordance with its nature. In the songs
there is a strong hint of the French tendency to treat singing as a
form of heightened declamation, as Lully and Rameau treat it.
Reynaldo Hahn expressed the extreme of this position when he
wrote that 'the role of music in a song should never be greater
than that of the footlights in a play'. A song like *De rêve* from the
Proses Lyriques is virtually a piano solo with obbligato voice. A
beautiful voice is not the first requirement of a singer of Debussy's
songs; but good diction and poetic sensibility are indispensable.
For this reason the songs are very difficult to translate. The words
and the instrument are the primary conveyers of the emotion and
pure singing tone is at a discount. The effect is beautiful and
original but too often bloodless and precious, quite unlike Debussy's
orchestral or piano music. The human voice is not a tracer of
beautiful lines and patterns nor in any sense discreet; it is warm
and vibrant and essentially emotional in quality. Debussy may in
theory have admitted the presence of 'melody' in the song, but his
instinct for the nature of the French language and the character of
his musical inspiration prevented him from exploiting anything
but a minute fraction of the potentialities of the human voice. He
wrote at the end of a period of great singers, when it was easy to
feel that nothing new could be accomplished along the old lines.
Half a century later, with the art of singing in manifest decline
partly owing to the very movement inaugurated by Debussy, the
picture is very different and his deliberate rejection of the specific
beauties of the human voice seems a gratuitous refusal of qualities
which have been seen to be fundamental to music itself.

His literary sense, on the other hand, was excellent. His feeling for Verlaine's poetry is uncannily sensitive, and to compare his settings of the poet with Fauré's is an interesting study in two entirely different approaches to the same problem. Debussy is a faithful follower of Verlaine's own principles. *Rien que la nuance.* He only allows music's natural eloquence to appear for an occasional phrase at the climax of a song. Normally his writing for the voice is a kind of heightened recitative intimately bound up with a piano part that follows the minutest shades of emotional variation in the text and provides by far the larger part of the purely musical interest. *Colloque sentimental* is probably the most successful of Debussy's songs in this species of recitative, for there the piano part is more modest and the voice is the vehicle of the poem's emotion. Compared with Fauré's settings of the same poems, both *Green* and *Il pleure dans mon coeur* are probably nearer to Verlaine's literary ideal, but musically they are impoverished by excessive restraint. Fauré establishes the atmosphere by musical means and his song develops along those musical lines, carrying the poem with it rather than being dictated by the poem. In fact, Debussy was unconsciously influenced in his song-writing during the eighteen-nineties by the Wagnerian theories which he had professed so ardently until a few years before.

V

FRENCH music had been so exclusively operatic for the first half of the nineteenth century, that at first the young composers, who wished to break the tradition against which Berlioz had struggled in vain, turned away from the stage. Gounod had succumbed under pressure during the eighteen-fifties, and the success of *Faust* had won him to operatic composition until his flight to England in 1870 and the return to his earlier ideals, which was made possible by the English public's taste for oratorio. Saint-Saëns started writing operas in the eighteen-seventies and, though his only success in the genre was not performed in France until 1890, he continued producing operas until 1911. César Franck was the least operatically-minded of musicians but even he wrote two operas, *Hulda* and *Ghisèle*, which were given a few performances after his death. Of his pupils and circle nearly all succumbed at last to the temptation, though Duparc and Lekeu were prevented by chronic illness in the one case and an early death in the other. It was impossible to make anything like a financial success of composition without writing for the theatre and even high-minded men with money of their own, like d'Indy and Chausson, were not in the last resort indifferent to the kind of success which only an opera can give. Opera alone enabled a composer to get a large hearing, and possibly a large fee, both orchestral and chamber music remaining the taste of a comparatively small public and producing correspondingly small financial results. A strong additional incentive in the case of the more advanced musicians was, of course, provided by the example of Wagner. There was a natural desire to reproduce in France and with French material the kind of music-drama that united the symphonic ideal with the operatic tradition.

After Bizet's premature death in 1875 Massenet had virtually no rival and in 1884 *Manon* achieved a success that placed him unequivocally at the head of French operatic composers for something like a decade, though he did not repeat his outstanding success with any of his productions until *Werther* (1892) and *Thaïs* (1894). *Werther* is in some ways his masterpiece, one of the very few of his works with a male protagonist, though *Werther* is an hysterical boy rather than an adult. The structure of the work is conventional but the muscal language has points of interest. There were already hints of a semi-Wagnerian use of the orchestra in *Manon*, as we have seen, and in *Werther* Massenet went further along the same path. Charlotte's soliloquy in Act III, for example, might also come from the *Meistersinger*, as far as the orchestral part is concerned, though the vocal line, with its tendency to mono-tone, is in the direct line from Gounod's recitative:

Ex 24.

Melodically Massenet was moving away, with the fashion, from the enclosed and self-sufficient air, towards a freer and more frag-mentary melody of the kind foreshadowed by Meyerbeer in Act IV of *Les Huguenots*. Thus Werther's monologue starts informally, as it were:

Ex. 25

The final cadence is still purely traditional in the Gounod manner and this 'tame' ending is even more noticeable in the theme which accompanies Werther's hopeless love throughout the opera. On the other hand, the orchestral music which introduces the scene of Werther's suicide in Act IV has an hysterical violence most apt in the circumstances, and closely resembles the music of Tchaikovsky.

Thaïs relies much more than *Werther* on external effect and on the popularity, even so late in the day, of the theme of the 'good prostitute'. Massenet obviously hoped to repeat the success of *Hérodiade* and to exploit once again, in the relationship between Thaïs and Athanaël, the 'érotisme discret et quasi-religieux' which d'Indy had considered to be the distinguishing mark of *Marie Magdeleine* twenty years earlier. The whole work is more old-fashioned than *Werther*, and it was already anachronistic in 1894 to make the climax of the ballet a ball-room waltz danced by La Perdition. Like Puccini after him, Massenet was an adept at gleaning ideas from the methods of the modernists of the day; and so we find, separating the first two scenes of Act II, a small symphonic poem describing the loves of Venus and Adonis, while the famous *Méditation* is a transformation (in the Lisztian and Franckian sense) of the main theme from this orchestral interlude. It is interesting, too, to observe the naïve rhythmic associations—traceable to the *opéra comique* of the eighteenth century—which make Massenet employ the voluptuous 12/8 or 9/8 rhythm for Thaïs before her conversion, whereas afterwards she sings in a simple 4/4 time or at most an occasional and chaste 6/8 (*L'amour est une vertu rare*). The famous song to her looking-glass (*Dis-moi que je suis belle*) is a direct descendant of the *N'est-ce plus ma main* in *Manon*.

In the same year as *Thaïs* (1894) Massenet produced two other works. *Le Portrait de Manon* is a one-act *opéra comique* dealing with an imaginary episode in the old age of des Grieux, who finds himself on the point of thwarting a budding love-affair between his nephew and a girl who turns out to be a daughter of Manon. It is a nostalgic trifle, only appealing to those for whom *Manon* itself is a classic (as it was to the opera-goers of the eighteen-nineties), but it had its importance historically as a break-away, by an otherwise traditionalist composer, from the grand operatic tradition towards something like chamber opera. This example was not lost, as we shall see, upon one of Massenet's most gifted pupils, Reynaldo Hahn, who developed the intimate, miniaturist side of his master's gift in his *Mozart*. Massenet's third work in 1894 was very different and to understand the circumstances that led him to write *La Navarraise* we shall have to turn to the work of one of his pupils.

Alfred Bruneau was nineteen when he entered Massenet's composition class in 1876. He had already written several orchestral works (*Léda, La Belle au bois dormant, Penthésilée*) before he produced his first opera, *Kérim*, in 1887. This was an Oriental piece, slight in matter but well written, without showing remarkable originality, though some of Bruneau's harmonic experiments attracted attention. Bruneau's great desire was to obtain from Zola permission to use his story, *La Faute de l'Abbé Mouret*, for an operatic book; but when he discovered that his master, Massenet, had already entered into negotiations with Zola with the same object, he contented himself with another Zola story, *Le Rêve*, from which Louis Gallet constructed a libretto. *Le Rêve* was given at the Opéra-Comique on 18 June 1891 and had an immediate success, even those who were shocked by its revolutionary elements admitting the power and originality of the music. Gounod murmured: 'C'est une partition parfumée,' which was non-committal but presumably laudatory—and Chabrier wrote to the author of his 'début de maître', while the *Echo de Paris* gave Bruneau a dinner at which Edmond de Goncourt, Maupassant, Alphonse Daudet, Mendès and Banville were present.

It was in the last resort the human qualities of Bruneau's music which made the success of *Le Rêve*. He was a passionate believer in Zola's humanism and 'vitalism', in the beauty and value of the great fundamental simplicities of human life. Directness, sincerity and intensity of feeling—*une mâle et saine vigueur*—were rare qualities in the French operatic world of the day, and there was a large and intelligent section of the public who were tiring of Massenet's erotic subjects and the complex and obviously derivative lucubrations of the Wagnerian enthusiasts. Chabrier himself wrote to Bruneau: 'You have appeared at the very moment when that is what is needed and demanded'—aware that his own *Gwendoline* was too blindly Wagnerian and that *Le Roi malgré lui* suffered from its old-fashioned form and its too tortuous harmonic style. Bruneau had learned from Wagner a more dramatic use of the orchestra and the effectiveness of the leitmotiv as a simple dramatic aid, without bothering his head with the symphonic development of his themes. From Bizet and like the new Italian 'verists' (Mascagni's *Cavalleria Rusticana* appeared in 1890) he had learned the power of going straight to the point, of facing his audience with a direct statement, and the possibility of putting on to the lyrical stage realistic fragments of life as lived by ordinary human beings, without gorgeous historical or mythological settings. 'Je veux faire du théâtre vivant, humain et bref' was his motto, and in pursuit of that object he was ready to sacrifice all the conventions, musical as well as dramatic.

It is a mistake to think of Bruneau as a conscious, theoretical innovator; his aim was that of Gluck, only in nineteenth-century terms, and his musical irregularities have dramatic, not musical, explanations. It is interesting to find in his music effects which are usually associated with Puccini—the predilection for strong unison passages, for example, and sequences of common chords. For all their difference of temperament and background, both Puccini and Bruneau were working for the same realistic effect in an idiom based on that of Massenet. In *Le Rêve* Massenet's pupil still appears occasionally, but what struck contemporary listeners was Bruneau's dramatic use of dissonance, if dissonance served his dramatic purpose, and in this he was bolder than Puccini or any of the Italian verists. A passage such as:

Ex. 26

which has been claimed as an early example of bitonality, is actually to be understood as an extreme use of passing-notes and suspensions, and its effect in performance is simply of dramatic tension, which is what Bruneau wished, and not of harmonic experiment, with which he was not concerned. Occasionally the combination of a simple, conventional vocal line with sophisticated harmonic accompaniment defeats Bruneau's own end, especially if it occurs in a passage which an earlier or later composer would have written as plain recitative.

After *Le Rêve* Bruneau's partnership with Zola became the main inspiration of his music and was cemented by a close personal friendship which lasted until Zola's death in 1902. During that time (which included the period of the Dreyfus trial, when Bruneau whole-heartedly supported his friend and found his music for a time proscribed), three new operas appeared—*L'Attaque du Moulin* (1893), *Messidor* (1897) and *L'Ouragan* (1901). In *L'Attaque du Moulin* Bruneau chose one of the stories from Zola's *Soirées de Medan*, a perfect 'veristic' subject dealing with an incident from the Franco-Prussian War, though the setting was changed to the Revolutionary period at the Paris production, for political reasons. Bruneau's lyrical gift, which found expression in his *Dix Lieds* (1891) and *Six Chansons à danser* (1894) was at its strongest in *L'Attaque du moulin* and *Messidor*, although the latter was set to a prose libretto taken verbatim from Zola's book. But in *Messidor* he deserts pure realism. There is a vein of symbolism running through the story and the Legend of the Gold, whose evil influence is contrasted with the beneficent influence of Water, dominates the whole work and lifts it from the purely naturalistic world of *L'Attaque du Moulin*. In *L'Ouragan* the weather and the scenery are used, in a naïve but effective way, to symbolize the passions of the characters; and the sea, the storm, the quiet secluded bay and the evocation of distant tropical countries each corresponds to the nature of one of the protagonists.

Bruneau's music is so conceived that it suffers badly when removed from its context in the theatre and divorced from stage action. At the same time his melodic gift is not striking enough to make such quotations a fair sample of his power as an operatic writer, and his whole musical idiom—French, and not without traits of Massenet's influence, but solid, forthright and Wagnerian in the strength and texture of the orchestral writing— is not original enough to have preserved his operas in the repertory, at least outside France. Like all enthusiastic apostles of a new artistic creed, Bruneau has paid for his temporary success with a swift falling into comparative oblivion. Zola's writing was the whole inspiration of his mature work, and as Zola's realism or naturalism has dated and proved its insufficiency as a creed, so Bruneau's music has lost its appeal. Zola's gifts as a writer and Bruneau's as a composer may well come up for reassessment in due time. Certainly no one can deny the breadth and vigour, the real poetry and the high-minded idealism which lie behind the brutal and squalid scenes that take up a large part, though by no means the whole, of a great canvas like *Germinal*. What was modern and bold when such a book was written is now out of date and comparatively tame, while the setting and method of presentation is still too nearly contemporary to be interesting historically. The same applies to

Bruneau's music, and for that reason many moving and beautiful scenes, which cannot by their nature be divorced from their context, are lost as far as modern listeners are concerned.

Massenet's music, too, has suffered from its fashionableness. No composer has been more whole-heartedly despised by one section of his contemporaries nor more popular with the general public. Massenet's whole nature was centred in the desire to please, and this has been enough to damn him in the eyes of intellectuals who, in every generation, provide a strong—and generally wholesome—puritan element in matters of taste. The desire to please creates prettiness, that facile and doubtfully-bred poor relation of beauty. The appeal of the pretty is directly to the untrained senses and, through them, to the surface emotions. Massenet's music resembles the pretty, superficial and sentimental type of woman who relies on her charm, her feminine instinct, her dressmaker and her hairdresser, to carry her through life. It is an eternal feminine type and, like all such types, it has its biological and social justification; not certainly as the highest nor—as misogynists would say—as the basic type of woman, but simply as *a* type, despised by intellectuals and adored by the public, which has an unreasoning instinct for what *is* and remains indifferent to what ought to be. Massenet's operas, something like twenty of them, are a portrait-gallery of women, most of whom conform to this type. Each new work after *Hérodiade* (1881) is a variation on the same theme—the feminine character in the most striking points in which it differs from the masculine. Manon, Esclarmonde, Thaïs, La Navarraise, Sapho, Cinderella, Griselda, Ariadne, Thérèse are all *grandes amoureuses* and they all, in different ways, conform to the feminine type, accepted in Latin countries until recently, for whom sexual love provides the central, and often only meaning of existence. Long before Massenet died in 1912 this type had fallen into disrepute in England (largely owing to the violent protests of women themselves), and since then the reaction has spread over the whole world. Beneath a new form of puritanism the love-obsessed woman has been progressively degraded. We find her in Strauss's *Salomé* and again in *Elektra*, where Chrysothemis is the mere woman and the foil to her virile sister; and she has sunk as low as it is possible to sink in Alban Berg's *Lulu*. In *Turandot*, again, a woman's obsession with love has turned sour and taken the form of cruelty and a craving for power: the wheel has gone full circle from the healthy, instinctive passion of Massenet's heroines with their clinging caresses and their simple philosophy of the world well lost for love. Love has been stripped of its idealistic glamour and reduced to sex alone.

No wonder that Massenet's operas have lost their popularity. What of their musical value? Massenet was an opportunist, as any purveyor of the pretty, the immediately catching, must be; for prettiness varies with the fashion while beauty, to the trained and discerning eye, is eternal. Alcestis, appealing only incidentally to the eye, is immortal; but Manon must watch the fashions, in music as in anything else. After *Thaïs* Massenet was aware of the storm of realism which blew up from Italy with the appearance of *Cavalleria Rusticana* and had already caused a minor disturbance in France with Bruneau's *Le Rêve*. *La Navarraise* (1894) was an essay in the veristic manner—short, sharp, brutal and designed to work by direct action on the spectators, to galvanize instead of to charm. This was not Massenet's true gift, but for a short time the opera had a success; and in his next, *Sapho* (based on Alphonse Daudet's novel), he tried again, in a full-length work—*La Navarraise* had only two acts—to portray the woman to whom love brings simply tragedy. The theme associated with the heroine, Fanny, is a direct descendant of the tragic theme in *Carmen* and Act III, in which Fanny tries to get her lover back from his family, is the nearest that Massenet ever approached to genuine tragedy. In the first two acts, on the other hand, he expressed better even than in *Manon* the precarious bliss of the clandestine love-affair, a Bohemianism with the perpetual hint of tragedy. The conflict between his mistress and his family in the young man's emotions, so natural and moving to a nineteenth-century Latin audience, would probably seem as unreal and exaggerated to a sophisticated modern audience as does the parallel situation in *Carmen*. The moral feeling on which the convention was based has, temporarily at least, been so weakened that the dramatic point is lost. Even so, the pleading of Fanny with Jean is irresistible, (Ex. 27) and the touching variation which follows is typical of Massenet at his best (Ex. 28).

Cendrillon (1899) is treated frankly as a fairy story, with some excellent writing in the Italian buffo style for Pandolfe. The music is largely decorative, written to entertain and only touching the sentimental here and there (the farewell to the old armchair in Act III, for example, in the same vein as Manon's farewell to the furniture in the room she had shared with des Grieux).

Ex. 27

Pen – dant ___ un an ___ je fus ___ ta femme ___

___ et j'entends res – ter à toi pour tou – jours

Ex. 28

Vieus, m'ami ___ je ser – ai si douce et si bon – ne pour toi

que ton cœur ___ s'ouv – ri – ra

In *Grisélidis* (1901) and *Le Jongleur de Notre Dame* (1902) Massenet attempted a new field, medieval legend. The opening scene of *Grisélidis*, in which a beautiful, passive girl is found in a wood by a nobleman out hunting and taken home to be his wife, was to be repeated with much greater effect in the next year, when Debussy's *Pelléas et Mélisande* appeared; but this was coincidence. 'Patient Grizel' was certainly a new type of figure in Massenet's gallery of *grandes amoureuses* and the lyrical part of Alain and the *opéra-comique* music of the Devil provide the most successful parts of the opera. *Le Jongleur de Notre Dame*, on the other hand, is one of Massenet's best works—paradoxically, because there is not a single feminine character in the original version. It is the story of a wandering player turned monk, ashamed of his ignorance and lack of talent in the monastery and finally singing and dancing before the statue of Our Lady, who rewards his humility with a miracle. It was first published by Gaston Paris twenty-five years before, as *Le Tombeur de Notre Dame*, and was treated again later by Anatole France in *L'Étui de Nacre*. Massenet obtains the contrast, necessary to a work in which only male voices are used, by the underlining of the two elements which were at war in the Jongleur himself—the secular and the religious. The crowd scenes in Act I and the blasphemous 'Alléluia du vin' are followed in Act II by the rehearsing of a new motet in the cloister, brilliantly done, and by the rival claims of the various monks for the supremacy of their various arts —sculpture, painting, poetry and music. Boniface, the cook, a half-comic character and the only one who understands the Jongleur, is one of Massenet's best minor roles; and the musical quality of the whole work, in which there is no hint of a love-interest, shows that Massenet's lyre was not really one-stringed, and that circumstances and his own taste account to a large extent for the repetitiveness of his other libretti.

In *Chérubin* (1905) he repeated the experiment of *Portrait de Manon* and wrote a sequel to Mozart's *Figaro*, in which Cherubino's amorous career at the age of seventeen provides opportunities for love-music at different levels and for Spanish pastiche of the same kind as he had attempted in the ballet music of *Le Cid* twenty years before. There is no attempt in any way to imitate Mozart. Both *Chérubin* and *Ariane*, which followed in the next year, show signs of Massenet's age. He had always been industrious, and industry combined with a great natural facility had led him to exploit to the full for over thirty years a never very rich vein. After

Le Jongleur de Notre Dame he became simply repetitive and *Thérèse* (1907) was his last success. This is an intimate, two-act opera based on a story of the French Revolution and the conflict of two allegiances—love and duty—in the heart of the heroine. The old régime is characterized by a *menuet d'amour*, which is a charming piece of pastiche in the same style as Reynaldo Hahn's *Mozart*, and the Revolution by a simple march-theme. Massenet had been able to adapt himself to the first minor operatic revolution which threatened his popularity—the appearance of Bruneau and lyrical realism. That school reached the zenith of its popularity in 1900 when Charpentier, another of his pupils, produced his *Louise*, written in a skilfully modernized version of Massenet's own style. After that he was too old to compete any more, and apart from his final success with *Don Quichotte* (1910) the remaining operas written before his death in 1912 (*Bacchus*, *Roma* and the posthumously performed *Panurge* and *Cléopatre*) added nothing to his reputation.

Both Massenet and his contemporary Saint-Saëns were out of sympathy with the developments of French music after 1890, but whereas Saint-Saëns became personally embittered and intransigently hostile to the younger generation, Massenet was both more generous and by nature more easy-going. The testimonies of his pupils—they range from Debussy, Bruneau and Koechlin to Charpentier and Laparra—bear witness to his purely musical gifts, his keen dramatic sense and his personal charm and affability. If he was not much more than the *homme moyen sensuel* writing for his spiritual peers, he was a good craftsman and an excellent man of the theatre. His detractors have mostly been men of higher ideals and sometimes of greater potentialities, but few of them have in practice achieved anything so near perfection in any genre, however humble, as Massenet achieved in his best works. He was one of the last of the purely operatic composers in France, certainly overrated by the contemporary public but as certainly underrated by his detractors and their modern descendants.

Saint-Saëns, a man of the same generation as Massenet, was temperamentally his opposite. Possessed of the same facility and industry, he devoted only a small part of his energy to the stage but, in such a prolific composer, that fraction amounted in the end to eleven operas. The earlier ones, including his only real success, *Samson et Dalila*, have already been discussed in an earlier chapter. None of the remaining seven achieved any such success. *Proserpine*

(1887) and *Ascanio* (1890) are large romantic historical operas. *Proserpine* deals with the figure of the by now conventional romantic prostitute redeemed by love, and the music falls on too many occasions into the styles favoured by the operatic public of the day —Massenet's in the lyrical passages and Verdi's in the dramatic. *Ascanio* is based on an imaginary incident in the life of Benvenuto Cellini and is probably the only opera of Saint-Saëns, except *Samson et Dalila*, which would be worth a modern performance. The musical characterization of the three women—Colombe, Scozzone and the Duchesse d'Étampes—is more genuinely dramatic than in the majority of Saint-Saëns's stage works, where the natural symphonist too often loses the dramatic thread of the music. There is some delightful music in the ballet organized by François I for the Emperor Charles V and plenty of interest and action in the story throughout. *Phryné* (1893) and *Hélène* (1904) are slight works in Saint-Saëns's Hellenistic vein, deliberately restrained in scope and manner of presentation. 'The artist who does not feel thoroughly satisfied with elegant lines, harmonious colours or a fine series of chords does not understand art,' he was to write. Certainly the comedy of *Phryné* and the lyrical poetry of *Hélène* are expressed with impeccable elegance and harmoniousness. Craft is never lacking nor, within narrow and academic limits, taste; there is even a mild sensuous appeal and some wit. But in the theatre more is required, and even the slightest comedy needs warmth of feeling and personality to make it live. In *L'Ancêtre* (1907), which represents Saint-Saëns's belated bow to the realists, he never rises beyond the conventional. He was at heart an eclectic, a connoisseur of styles, and Ravel was right in proclaiming him a kindred spirit. This is the temperament least suited to the stage. Operatic music must be more than mellifluous and correctly written, ingenious and apt. Saint-Saëns was handicapped by his eighteenth-century rationalism when he came to write for the theatre, and the majority of his operatic music suffers from the same neat and tasteful desiccation as the philosophy of the Encyclopaedists. Personal vitality is the first necessity for operatic music. Taste and intellectual distinction are lost in the theatre unless backed up by more solid and earthy qualities.

Gustave Charpentier, the composer of *Louise* (1900), had neither taste nor distinction, but he had a certain sort of personality. His own statement of his aims in writing *Louise* gives a fair idea of his calibre.

'I wished to give on the stage . . . the lyric impression of the sensations that I reap in our beautiful, fairy-like modern life. Perhaps I see this as in a fever but that is my right, for the street intoxicates me. The essential point of the drama is the coming together, the clashing, of two feelings in Louise's heart—love, which binds her to her family, to her father, the fear of leaving suffering behind her and, on the other hand, the irresistible longing for liberty, pleasure, happiness, love, the cry of her being which demands to live as she wishes. Passion will conquer because it is served by a prodigious and mysterious auxiliary, which has little by little breathed its dream into her young soul—Paris, the voluptuous city, the great city of light, pleasure and joy which calls her irresistibly towards an undaunted future.'

Charpentier was a Prix de Rome scholar and had already, when he wrote the book and music of *Louise*, composed a 'symphony-drama', *La Vie du Poète*, which he remodelled and added to in the sequel to *Louise*, *Julien* (1913). The story of *Louise* is a cross between the middle-class *comédie larmoyante* of the eighteenth century and a sentimental defence of the gospel of Free Love, set against a pretentious mystical background of Paris, envisaged as a kind of idol to whom Louise is sacrificed. This crossing of the realistic with the mystical was exactly in the spirit of Bruneau's *Messidor* and *L'Ouragan*, as we have seen, and the enormously greater success of *Louise* is largely due to the qualities which make it inferior to either of Bruneau's operas as a work of art—the catchiness of Louise's 'Depuis le jour', the bold modernity (in 1900) of the scenes in Louise's workshop and, above all, the theme, the 'message' of the work expressed in Julien's 'Tout être a le droit d'être libre: tout être a le devoir d'aimer.' There was something original and titillating in 1900 to hear from the stage of the Opéra-Comique such lines as:

JULIEN: Au souffle du désir Louise s'éveille! Hosanna! Ton cher corps me désire?
LOUISE: Je veux du plaisir!

whose real place was in one of the more pretentious numbers in a revue at the Casino de Paris or the Folies-Bergère.

The figure of Louise represents the first stage in the descent from Massenet's romantic heroines. The conflict between right and wrong, which still forms the basis of all Massenet's operas, changes its character in *Louise* and appears as a conflict between two rights or, at its most extreme, is completely reversed. Charpentier would persuade his audience that Louise was right to

leave her family for her lover. Massenet could never have conceived such a drama; but once Charpentier had attempted it
successfully, Massenet's heroines began to date and in the years
between 1900 and his death in 1912 Massenet saw his works
gradually lose their popularity and become old-fashioned.

Symbolism in one shape or another had become, thanks to the
spreading and widening influence of Wagner's ideas, an almost
essential ingredient for an opera in France during the last decade
of the nineteenth and the first of the present century. The older
generation of Wagnerians had been content to enrich their
orchestral palettes, to readjust the relationship between voice and
orchestra, to borrow superficial effects of musical characterization and at least to compromise between the old and the new in
their treatment of recitative. These were the composers so bitterly
attacked in the *Revue Wagnérienne* of April 1885 (cf. pages 57–8), but
as yet France had not produced any truly Wagnerian music, any
music which sprang from an understanding of Wagner's own
philosophy. The type of Wagnerian opera represented by Chabrier's *Gwendoline* (1886) was continued during the eighteen-nineties
with Reyer's *Salammbô* (1890), Bourgault-Ducoudray's *Thamara*
(1891), Camille Erlanger's *Julien l'Hospitalier* (1896) and, incidentally, in the two posthumously produced operas by César
Franck, *Hulda* and *Ghisèle*. In all these works the influence of
Wagner the musician is overwhelming, but they remain operas
in the old-fashioned sense, with their ballets, lyrical interludes,
conventional love-scenes (almost always in D flat or G flat
major), their thinly disguised recitatives and independent numbers. The libretti are the legitimate descendants of *Euryanthe*,
Rienzi, *Tannhäuser* and *Lohengrin*, with a dash of *Les Huguenots* or
Tristan; they never touch the philosophical world of *The Ring*. It
was to spread the knowledge of Wagnerian philosophy and
aesthetics that the *Revue Wagnérienne* was founded and it was not
long before the full Wagnerian faith found expression in a lyrical
drama. The distinction of writing such a work, which demanded
philosophical intelligence as well as solid musical gifts, fell to
Vincent d'Indy. We have seen him in the eighteen-eighties react-
ing, after his *Le Chant de la Cloche*, against the excessively German
character of a superficial Wagnerism towards a new and purely
French ideal, as in the *Symphonie cévenole*. But the ardent idealism
of his nature, combined with a strong taste for the imposing and
magnificent, his religious faith and his passion for rich and solid

musical structure made it inevitable that Wagner should be his inspiration when he came to write for the theatre.

His *Fervaal* appeared in 1897. The setting of the story, the struggle between the Saracen south and the vague Celtic Cravann, was familiar. *Gwendoline* and *Hulda* were stories of racial struggles between the Scandinavian tribes, *Salammbô* depicted a conflict half racial and half religious, *Thamara* a war between Persians and Kurds; but in none of these works were the protagonists conceived as anything but ordinary human beings. None of them were symbols like d'Indy's Fervaal-Humanity, Guilhen-Love and Arfagard-Error. *Fervaal* is the French *Parsifal*, 'un long cri d'amour que spiritualise une Foi peu définie mais manifeste'. The wound of Fervaal cured in the magic gardens of Guilhen, the oath of chastity which binds him until he sees that 'purity is more than chastity', and the vague apotheosis, in which the hero disappears on the mountainside to the theme of the *Pange lingua*, announcing the new religion of love—the whole story suggests numerous parallels with *Parsifal*. Arfagard's initiation of his pupil into the mythology of the old Celtic religion (Act I) recalls Wotan. Even the key signatures are made to serve as symbols. Thus F sharp major is the key of divine love (as it was for Franck), the enharmonically identical G flat major that of human love; A flat major represents false love; G minor the obsolete religion of the Druids; and so forth. But the pace of the work is slow and the orchestra again and again interrupts the simplest conversation or narration with a pointed comment or reference, to drive home the full significance to the listener. In the last act the action puts a great strain on any but the most sympathetic audience. Guilhen rejoins Fervaal but dies as the moon goes behind a cloud. He picks her up in a thunderstorm and starts to climb the mystical mountain, intoning a metrical version of the *Pange lingua*, which is taken up by the invisible chorus, while Fervaal executes what can only be described as a form of yodelling to punctuate their phrases. It is only too easy to make fun of this intensely serious work. *Fervaal* is a poor music-drama and we can now only accept the very best music-dramas, those in fact written by the inventor of the genre, who proved to have inaugurated an aesthetic theory of which he alone is the successful exponent. Like Bruneau's operas, *Fervaal* suffers from the fact that in 1897 it was the extreme of modernity, written absolutely in accordance with Wagner's ideals, which seemed destined to make the older opera obsolete in a comparatively short time. The nobility, the strength of feeling, the musical skill and the occasional power of characterization, which no one could deny to d'Indy's music, are wasted in practice, because they are all scrupulously subordinated to a preconceived theory.

One of the reasons for the success of the single operatic masterpiece produced in France between 1890–1910—*Pelléas et Mélisande*—was precisely this, that Debussy discovered his theories as he composed and was able to formulate them only after his score was finished, thus reversing the process which led to the composition of *Fervaal*. Debussy had started as an ardent Wagnerian, and like many original characters he had reacted against his former idol. Of the relation between music and words he wrote:

'One should sing when there is something to sing about, and keep the emotional power of the voice in reserve. There must be variations in vigour and expression. In places one must use monochrome and be content with grisaille. Any musical development not called for by the words is a mistake.'

He had digested many of Wagner's dramatic theories and in Maeterlinck's play he found a poem which itself contributed a great deal to his theory of opera. In his introduction to the three volumes of his plays Maeterlinck characterizes the evolution of thought during the nineteenth century as a general tendency to replace certainties by uncertainties; and his whole poetic approach is founded on the belief in the fundamental mysteriousness of all, and particularly of human, existence. There was in this a reaction against the insufferable claims of the so-called scientific realism, which had been fashionable, and Maeterlinck and the French Symbolists represented the rights of the non-intellectual elements against the exaggerated claims of the intellect. This was parallel to Debussy's position in the sister art of music, but how far it was Maeterlinck who helped him to crystallize his own ideas, and so to find his own style, is difficult to say. In any case it was only after he had bought his copy of *Pelléas et Mélisande*, during the summer of 1892, that he achieved a mature style of his own. Maeterlinck himself was at first hostile to the idea of his setting the poem to music, although he had expressly said that two at least of his plays were written for music. He himself was no musician, but Debussy could without difficulty set the complete poem of *Pelléas et Mélisande* except for a few unimportant lines.

No man creates a new style from nothing, and the elements which went to make up Debussy's idiom in *Pelléas* can be traced fairly clearly, without any reflexion on the extraordinary originality of the whole work. Charles Bordes spoke of the work as 'Boris Godunov's grandson' and Mussorgsky's is probably the strongest single external influence in the whole work. But it was a similarity of ideals rather than of actual musical language. Debussy rediscovered French musical prosody. Largely under the influence of foreign models—Gluck, Rossini and Meyerbeer—French composers had come to set their own language as though it were as strongly accented as German or Italian. Debussy modelled his prosody, as Mussorgsky had modelled his, on the natural spoken language, with the result that the whole of his opera is written in a *quasi parlando* idiom, in which rhetorical emphasis is scrupulously avoided and the easy-moving flow of spoken French is imitated. Take any phrase at random—Pelléas's speaking to himself before he meets Mélisande for the last time, for example (Act IV, Scene 4):

Ex. 29.

Il faut que je lui di-se tout ce que je n'ai pas dit

This fluidity and lightness in the treatment of the text gives the work a large part of its character and is often lost in translation. The familiar tribrach with a slight emphasis on the first beat ($\smallsmile \smile \smile$), which corresponds to a common Russian speech-rhythm and complicates the translation of Russian operatic texts, is based on exactly the same principle as Debussy's—the closest possible following of the rhythm of the spoken language. French seems a light-weight or feminine language to nations whose own idioms are strongly accented. Englishmen and Germans are used to weighty concentrations of consonants and Italians to rich sonorities of vowels in strongly accented positions, and both these forms of strength are foreign to the French. Romain Rolland's Jean-Christophe, a German musician very much of an exile in Paris, complained of the 'lack of will-power' and the 'Franco-Belgian sickliness' in *Pelléas et Mélisande*, and Debussy's treatment of the language was partly responsible for this impression. Maeterlinck was not concerned with the will in any case and any drama in which the active human qualities—intellect and will—are hardly taken into account easily assumes a certain flaccidity or preciousness. Golaud is the one completely human character in the whole play and he moves in a nightmare, always bound to stumble 'like a blind man', as he says to himself, between two passive innocents who never seem guilty because they have no wills to be engaged. The clearest reminiscences of Mussorgsky are generally in music connected with Golaud and are most frequent in Act I. The stifled broken rhythms, which almost always accompany Golaud and even intrude on the stillness of Act V are taken unmistakably from *Boris Godunov*:

Ex. 30.

Mélisande is also characterized by nervous, hesitant rhythms in all her dealings with Golaud and only achieves rhythmical stability when she is alone or with Pelléas. In Act II, Scene 2, for example, where Golaud and Mélisande have their first quarrel, Mélisande's guilty conscience over the lost ring is expressed by such rhythms

as ♪♩ ♪♩ or ♩ ♪♫♫ . The scene in the subterranean grotto

where Golaud is on the point of murdering Pelléas is, by contrast, entirely in quadruple time, and Golaud's warning to his brother is rhythmically the simplest passage in the whole work; he has regained control of himself and is deliberately prosaic and almost nonchalant. It is by rhythmic variations of this kind rather than by elaborate harmonic subtleties that Debussy characterizes both scenes and states of mind. Weight and consistency are as important in his orchestration as instrumental colours. The division of the strings for short passages; the omission of the violins altogether in the scene between Golaud and Pelléas in the subterranean grotto; the punctuation of Golaud's brusque recitative by a widespread pizzicato triad instead of the more obvious brass or conventionally sinister low register of the wood-wind—these were typical of the general colour scheme at which Debussy was aiming.

In the harmonic field he tends to replace the diminished seventh, with its emotional associations, by the dominant ninth. Whole-tone passages are still exceptional and expressive of nervous tension rather than normal, as they were to become in the piano works that follow. Occasionally, as Jean-Christophe complained, 'the Massenet that slumbers at the heart of every Frenchman awakes and waxes lyrical'. Arkel, the one character in the play who is conceived with a touch of sentimentality, is generally associated with these movements of a slightly facile emotionalism (Act IV, Scene 2, the melody in octaves at the words 'Je ne t'ai embrassée qu'une seule fois jusqu' ici' and in Act IV at 'Il ne faut plus l'inquiéter'). The child Yniold is used only as an instrument of Golaud's jealousy, except in Act IV, Scene 3 (generally omitted), which may have been suggested to Debussy by the nursery scene in *Boris Godunov*. Act III, Scene 4, is one of the most moving in the whole work and a heartrending expression of jealousy. Golaud knows that he can only frighten his wife and that she has found all that he cannot give her; but with that unbearable passion for tangible proof which is typical of jealousy, he must know everything and even employ his own child as a spy. Debussy builds up the child's growing terror and the man's agonized exasperation into a climax which shows that he was capable of more than the merely veiled, discreet and anaemic drama which is often attributed to him.

Pelléas et Mélisande seemed to its first hearers thin and inconclusive. They were used to the Wagnerian orchestra and to the rich, powerful and emphatic manner of Wagner's mature style, by the side of which Debussy's idiom seemed meagre, his colours faint and his character-drawing insipid. The musical world, always ready in France for a journalistic war, was immediately divided into champions and enemies of the new work, with most of the younger men enthusiastically favourable after the first few performances. Soon a new artistic religion had formed among the initiates and, much to Debussy's disgust, his work became the fashion. Léon Vallas quotes from an article by Jean Lorrain, published in January 1904:

'There is the fair girl—too fragile, too white and too fair, who has evidently got herself up to look like Mary Garden (Mélisande) turning over the pages of the score that lies on the edge of her box. There are the handsome young men (almost all the Debussyites are young, very young), with their long hair carefully brushed on to their foreheads;

with full, flat-toned faces and deep-set eyes, velvet-collared and full-sleeved coats, rather too waisted suits and large satin ties too tight or floating artistically . . . the Pelleasters.'[1]

Debussy was a national figure, but his development after *Pelléas et Mélisande* does not concern us here, for he never wrote another opera, though we shall find his influence in one at least of the works that still remain to be discussed in this chapter.

Not, however, in the new work by Vincent d'Indy, which was given in Brussels on 7 January 1903, and eleven months later at the Paris Opéra. *L'Étranger* represents a further penetration of Wagnerian philosophical ideas into d'Indy's music. D'Indy had expressed great admiration for *La Demoiselle Élue* and his article in *L'Occident* after the first performance of *Pelléas* compared Debussy with Monteverdi. He had no sympathy with the new music, but he was fair to Debussy, and it was only the Debussyites against whom he and the Schola waged war to the death. The setting of *L'Étranger* is neither exotic nor mythical, as in *Fervaal*; but against the comparatively simple and realistic background the familiar symbols stand out even more clearly. D'Indy's Wagnerian passion was wholly different in kind from that of any of his fellow-countrymen who were also composers. The incorrigible realism of the Latin temperament prevented the majority from seeing anything in *Tristan* but a superb poem of voluptuousness, in *The Ring* anything but an involved story of giants and heroes, and in *Parsifal* anything but a German comment on the complex relationship between sex and religion. It is no part of the French tradition to make music a vehicle of philosophical ideas; but in *L'Étranger* d'Indy was doing precisely this. Superficially the music is less Wagnerian than that of *Fervaal*, but in fact the whole work is a transposition into French terms—and at the same time, a baptising—of some of Wagner's most cherished beliefs. The Stranger is a Christian Wotan, with something of the Flying Dutchman and Parsifal added. The key to his character is renunciation of love—the refusal of personal happiness in order to achieve a higher object. 'To help others, to serve others, that is my only joy and my only thought.' Settling as a stranger in a French fishing village, he attracts a girl with the

---

[1] The first performance of *Pelléas* was on 30 April 1902. As a matter of interest I give the dates of the first performances of Wagner's works in Paris. *Tannhäuser*, 1861; *Rienzi*, 1869; *Lohengrin*, 1887; *Die Walküre*, 1893; *Der Fliegende Holländer* and *Die Meistersinger*, 1897; *Tristan und Isolde*, 1899; *Siegfried* and *Götterdämmerung*, 1902; *Das Rheingold*, 1909; *Der Ring des Nibelungen* (complete), 1911; *Parsifal*, 1914.

mystical name of Vita—Life—and when they have confessed their mutual love the Stranger has failed in his vow of renunciation and both he and she die while trying to rescue the crew of a shipwreck. Throughout the work the sea has a mystical significance. The prelude opens with a seascape in the orchestra, Vita apostrophizes the sea in a long and highly dramatic scene at the climax of the work and the two disappear finally in a vast wave which provides a *Liebestod*. D'Indy's music accentuates the contrast between Vita and the Stranger on the one hand and the hostile and misunderstanding villagers (represented chiefly by Vita's mother and betrothed) on the other. On the one hand there is the tortured, emotional and highly chromatic idiom of *Parsifal*, even suggesting the developments of Richard Strauss in a passage such as this, from Act I:

Ex. 31.

On the other there is the folk-song element, as in the chorus *Dimanche, c'est dimanche, vive le vin* in Act II; and the music of the vain, handsome young André, Vita's betrothed, who has a simple sensuousness and lightness that recall Bizet's Don José on several occasions. Certainly d'Indy far surpassed in *L'Étranger* his own achievement in *Fervaal*. The work is shorter (two acts instead of three), the music has more variety and the story more interest. The use of symbolism, though in the opposite sense to d'Indy's, had been a characteristic of Bruneau's *Messidor* in 1897 and again—with the sea in the background, as in *L'Étranger*—in his *L'Ouragan*. Bruneau was less of a musician than d'Indy and his 'message' of the acceptance of life and love was possibly less suitable for musical expression than d'Indy's theme of renunciation.

In any case the purely realistic or 'veristic' type of opera was dead in France. Even Xavier Leroux's *Le Chemineau* (1907), to a

5

text by Richepin, had a poetic quality which raises it above the
level of *verismo*. The harvest-field scene in Act I and the carol-sing-
ing children in Act IV, the Tramp's music with its nostalgia for
the open road and the characterization of Toinette and her love-
child Toinet are effective in the theatre and have an emotional
power and a direct appeal that were quickly going out of fashion in
French music.

In the same year as *Le Chemineau* there appeared the first major
work in which the influence of *Pelléas et Mélisande* can be seen opera-
ting in a distinguished musical intelligence very different from
Debussy's own. Paul Dukas was three years younger than Debussy
and hitherto he had written for the orchestra (including a symphony) and the piano, in a style that was symphonic in the traditional sense. His opera, *Ariane et Barbe-Bleue*, was itself symphonic
in character and thus at the opposite pole to Debussy's work. For
his libretto he chose another of Maeterlinck's plays, *Ariane et Barbe-
Bleue*, which the author described as:

'A short poem, of the genre which goes by the unfortunate name of
opéra-comique, meant to provide musicians . . . with a theme suitable for
musical development. It was not designed as anything more ambitious
and my intentions are entirely mistaken by those who tried to find in
addition some moral or philosophical message.'

Nevertheless, it is impossible to ignore the basic idea of the play:
that women in general prefer marriage and security, even on the
most degrading terms, to freedom. Ariane, Bluebeard's new wife,
succumbs like her predecessors to the temptations of inquisitiveness.
But she alone refuses to be treated as a child or a chattel and suc-
ceeds in liberating her fellow-wives. She is the only one who takes
advantage of her liberty, while the rest prefer to stay as prisoners
in Bluebeard's harem rather than face the world as free agents. In
1907 this appeared as scarcely veiled comment on the feminist
movement, in spite of Maeterlinck's assurance; but the poem was
admirably suited for music. Dukas's manner is broader and the
structure of his scenes is more architectural than Debussy's. The
chorus plays a considerable part and there are also purely decorative, descriptive scenes (the discovery of the jewels in Act I) which
allow for musical developments in which the drama comes to a
standstill. In Act III, Scene 1, Dukas builds up a whole scene
symphonically on a mere phrase; but it is symphonic development in what may be called the Russian manner—by repetition

and variations, that is to say, rather than in the classical. Harmonically Dukas's idiom is more dissonant than Debussy's. His excessive use of the whole-tone scale is a weakness and gives the modern listener an impression of vagueness, that 'impressionism' in the loose sense of the word, which is connected with the music of Debussy's imitators. There are situations very like those in *Pelléas et Mélisande*: the subterranean dungeon, for example, and the women's return to the sunlight and clear air of the country as the clock strikes noon. But Dukas's orchestration alone would be enough to distinguish his music from Debussy's. It is full and brilliant, the brass is used with conventional effectiveness and the colouring is bright and dramatic in contrast (Dukas has a marked preference for extreme sharp tonalities), reminiscent of Rimsky-Korsakov rather than Debussy. The recitative is less fluid than in *Pelléas* and in Ariane's farewell there is an amplitude and a direct emotional appeal which is rhetorical in the best sense. The work as a whole is not only musically interesting and, within limits, original, but also marked by sincerity and depth of feeling. Dukas had not Debussy's personality and he was weak in melodic invention; but musical craftsmanship and nobility of sentiment are characteristic of *Ariane et Barbe-Bleue* as of everything else that he wrote.

It is something of a paradox to mention a musical genre only when it is on the eve of disappearing. Any detailed account of French operetta is impossible owing to the vastness of the field and to its lying on the borders of what, for want of a better word, must be called 'serious' music. The French have shown a unique gift for entertainment music, and they have made an artistic genre of what in most countries has been more than half commercial. The old *opéra comique*, which began as a parody of serious opera, reached its zenith in the generation immediately before the revolution of 1789. The Encyclopaedists admired its naturalness, its simplicity and its power as what would now be called an ideological weapon. Rousseauist sentimentality and social criticism were the chief marks of the genre from 1750 to 1790, and during the Revolution years Cherubini and Méhul so developed both its emotional and musical scope that the distinction between opera proper and *opéra comique* was rapidly diminishing. It was Cherubini's *opéras comiques* that impressed Beethoven and inspired *Fidelio* at a time when French opera proper was moribund and needed a new injection of Italian vitality. Spontini, in fact, did for the opera what Cherubini, another Italian, had done for the *opéra comique*.

In spite of foreign influences—which were to increase rather than otherwise, with the advent first of Rossini and then of Meyerbeer—the *opéra comique* flowered again with Boïeldieu, Hérold, and above all Auber, whose astonishing activities lasted from 1820 to 1869. However, all Auber's best work was done before 1850 and the complaint of a German-Jewish 'cellist, Jacques Lévy, who had risen to the post of conductor at the Théâtre-Français in 1850 was justified. 'It occurred to me', wrote Offenbach—for Lévy assumed the name of his father's birthplace as a surname early in his career —'that *opéra comique* was no longer to be found at the Opéra-Comique; that really funny, gay, witty, live music was gradually being forgotten and that what was being written for the Opéra-Comique was really small-scale grand opera.' In fact, the technical distinction between opera proper and *opéra comique*—the musical recitative of the first and the spoken dialogue of the second—was the only distinction left.

It was to remedy this that on 5 July 1855 Offenbach opened the Bouffes-Parisiens. For the remaining fifteen years of the Second Empire Offenbach's pieces—at least one a year and often more— delighted first Paris and then the whole of Europe. The most famous have become classics—*Orphée aux Enfers* (1858), *La Belle Hélène* (1864), *La Vie Parisienne* (1866) and *La Grande-Duchesse de Gerolstein* (1867). With Meyerbeer's works at the Opéra and Offenbach's at the Bouffes-Parisiens it was no wonder that serious-minded and ardent musical patriots like d'Indy should have spoken bitterly later of the *école judaïque*. Offenbach's *opéras bouffes* returned to an old tradition of the *opéra comique*, that of parody; but now the parody was not so much musical as political, a satire on all institutions, social life and—thinly veiled—on individuals. The wildest and most nonsensical situations were treated with hilarious verve; nothing and nobody was immune. Napoleon III was a faithful admirer of Offenbach, who may be considered the last of the court jesters, an 'all-licensed fool' whose quips attracted a European public and did much to give Paris the reputation which it has not yet lost in the minds of middle-class families from Oslo to Athens. In the same vein as Offenbach, Florimond Ronger (known as Hervé) had enormous success beginning with *L'Oeil Crevé* (1867), *Chilpéric* (1868) and a parody in the old tradition of the *opéra comique*, *Le Petit Faust* (1869).

Offenbach and Hervé continued their activity after the fall of the Second Empire in 1871; but just as the revolution of 1789 had effected a change in the *opéra comique* and Offenbach had created a new type of entertainment for the Second Empire, the advent of the Third Republic saw a still further development in a genre whose very nature it was to reflect the passions and interests of the day. The great success of the year 1872 was not Offenbach's *La Jolie Parfumeuse* but Lecocq's *La Fille de Madame Angot*. In fact the operetta had begun to replace the *opéra bouffe*. Times were harder and more serious and satire was no longer popular; no country which has just received a profound humiliation can be asked to laugh at itself. Charm and surface emotion took the place of the brilliant buffoonery of the *opéra bouffe*. Lecocq and Planquette (*Les Cloches de Corneville*, 1877) were the first masters of the new genre, but it was André Messager who brought sensitive and highly-trained musicianship to a genre whose first concern is the entertainment of the public. Messager had been a pupil of Fauré and of Saint-Saëns at the École Niedermeyer and he was the first conductor of *Pelléas et Mélisande*, which Debussy dedicated to him. He had that first essential of a fine artist, a sense of his own limitations, and he worked by instinct in the style for which all his gifts suited him. An operetta, *La Béarnaise* (1885), had an immediate success and was given the following year in London, and with *La Basoche* (1890) his name was made. He was an extremely fertile composer, and ballets and operettas flowed from his pen during the eighteen-nineties. *Madame Chrysanthème* (1893), *Les P'tites Michu* (1897) and finally *Véronique* (1898) raised French operetta to an entirely new musical level. The elegance and harmonic subtlety of a passage such as the following, from *La Basoche*, only passes unnoticed because, like so many of Fauré's happiest inspirations, it appears so completely natural in its context (Ex. 32).

Ex. 32.

Prom-et - tez, Col-et-te, De res - ter mu-et - te

Or take a progression like the following from *Véronique*, where the modal instruction of the École Niedermeyer has obviously borne fruit (Ex. 33).

Ex. 33.

Such details as these were something entirely new in 'popular' music. But Messager did not despise the tradition he found: he merely ennobled it. Take only one instance—the famous duet *Va petit âne* from *Véronique*, with its captivating rhythm and subtle simplicity (Ex. 34).

Ex. 34.

In Messager the styles of the operetta and the *opéra comique* were inextricably mingled, just as in the works of Audran (*Miss Helyett,* 1890) and Claude Terrasse (*Chonchette, Le Sire de Vergy, Monsieur*

de la Palisse, 1902–4), the old *opéra bouffe* of Offenbach and Hervé lived on side by side with the operetta. But in spite of an apparent vitality the French operetta was living on its capital and apart from Messager no real personality appeared after the eighteen-nineties. Once again there was to be a metamorphosis brought about by foreign influence and the social upheaval of the 1914–18 war. Meanwhile, Lehár's *The Merry Widow* put all native works in the shade, having its first performance in Paris on 28 April 1909 and reaching its one-hundredth less than four years later on 16 January 1914.

VI

'The Parisienne of the two big exhibitions, 1889 and 1900, had France under her skirts. Art went through this phase of half-lights, muslins, enervating charms and scents. From having been solidly built, muscular, clean-cut music, poetry and painting became undulating, soft, hazy.' JEAN COCTEAU.

BY 1905 the Schola Cantorum under d'Indy had developed into a new outpost of orthodoxy and the radicals of music were to be found among the pupils, past and present, of the Conservatoire. This reversal of positions is common and in the nature of things; but the process was particularly swift and noticeable in the case of the Schola. Both Bordes and d'Indy were teachers by temperament, and their realization of the wealth of the musical past, hitherto undreamed of in France or indeed elsewhere, led them to over-emphasize that fundamental rule of all sane artistic progress —that it is only from the art of the past that the art of the future can grow. Antiquarian and musicological interests had played a large part in the foundation of the Schola; and Gregorian music, folk-song, sixteenth-century polyphony, Monteverdi, Bach, Rameau and Gluck—virtually all rediscovered for France by the Schola— these made an obviously impressive but not easily digestible diet for the would-be composer. The revival of French music of the seventeenth and eighteenth centuries was of more antiquarian than practical interest to young composers, and the modern period, starting with Haydn, was made to lead very directly to the music of d'Indy's own master, César Franck.

The solidity and excellence of this course of training were undeniable but, combined with the strongly dogmatic attitude of d'Indy himself and the weaknesses of his own theory of composition, it tended to form priggish and capable, rather than original musicians, strongly biased against any experimenting with what were regarded as the inviolable fundamentals of the art. Like all schools, it catered for the average talent and it did much to raise the general standard of musical knowledge and taste throughout France, especially through the provincial Scholas at Lyons, Toulouse and elsewhere. But no school can cater for the rare genius; and the comparatively negative and tolerant atmosphere of the Conservatoire was a more favourable atmosphere for the development of great originality, which was more likely to be tolerated by Massenet or gently encouraged by Fauré than by the violent and opinionated d'Indy.

If we compare the products of the two institutions—the Schola Cantorum became an École Supérieure de Musique in 1900—we shall find an interesting difference of development. When Ambroise Thomas died in 1896, his obvious successor as Director of the Conservatoire was Massenet, who had been professor of advanced composition there since 1878. But Massenet would only accept the post on the condition that he was elected for life and, when this condition was refused, he resigned from his professorship. Thus two of the chief positions at the Conservatoire became vacant at the same time. A nonentity, Théodore Dubois, was appointed to the directorship, but the far more important composition class was taken by Fauré. Debussy and Bruneau had been pupils of Massenet, and among those who now passed from Massenet to Fauré were Florent Schmitt, Charles Koechlin and Georges Enesco, while Maurice Ravel joined Fauré's composition class in 1897. Paul Dukas had been a pupil of Guiraud (with Debussy) and of Dubois; and Roger Ducasse and Nadia Boulanger were both to be pupils of Fauré and products of the Conservatoire. The majority of the composers who made their names in the first quarter of the twentieth century were, in fact, Conservatoire pupils, however much they may have rebelled against the lack of imagination and the routine of that venerable institution.

If we turn to the Schola we find a different picture. Albéric Magnard, Déodat de Séverac and Pierre de Bréville were composers of talent and a certain vein of originality; but the single product of the Schola who achieved a position comparable with that of the finest Conservatoire pupils is Albert Roussel, a late-comer to music whose mature work bears very few traces of his Schola formation. D'Indy's own early training and sympathies were too exclusively coloured by César Franck to make him patient or understanding of the developments in French music which took place around 1900; and he was so dominated by his own theories that he found it almost impossible to admit alternative answers to his pupils' questions. The stumbling-block in almost every case was the music of Debussy, for at least after *Pelléas et Mélisande* (1902) it was impossible, without living in a perfectly unreal world, to be unaware of what was in many ways a new music.

In the last years of the old century there appeared a new composer who was often to be compared with Debussy, though his mentality was in fact different. This was Maurice Ravel. The son of a Swiss engineer and a mother of Basque origin, Ravel was born in 1875 at Ciboure on the French Basque coast, but his family moved to Paris almost immediately, and in 1889 he entered the Conservatoire. It was the year of the World Exhibition and the visit of the Russian orchestra under Rimsky-Korsakov (see p. 89) and the fourteen-year-old Ravel, like the twenty-seven-year-old Debussy, did not miss the novel musical experience provided by the Javanese orchestra of *gamelangs*. It was not long before very precise tastes declared themselves in this enthusiastic but rather mysterious—and deliberately mystifying—youth. He was an excellent pianist, but his interest in the traditional literature of the piano was largely technical. Schumann, Chopin and Liszt—especially Liszt—provided starting-points for his technical experiments, but his sensibility was wholly modern. Debussy, the Debussy of *Prélude à l'après-midi d'un faune*, with Chabrier, Satie and Borodin contributed to the formation of an idiom which seemed to be mature almost as soon as it was conceived.

In 1895 he published his first works, the *Menuet Antique* and the *Habañera*, and in 1898 he appeared before the public for the first time with his *Sites auriculaires* (the influence of Satie is clear enough in the titles). The first of the *Sites* was the *Habañera*, which was later to be orchestrated and reappear in the *Rapsodie espagnole*; the second an *Entre cloches* which has not been published. The public and the critics were not impressed. Nor was the Conservatoire when Ravel competed in 1901, 1902, 1903 and finally in 1904 for the Prix de Rome. In fact so hostile was the jury at the preliminary competition in 1904 that they excluded him from the final trial. This might have passed unnoticed had Ravel been known simply as the composer of the *Sites auriculaires*, or even of the pretty though slightly mawkish *Pavane pour une infante défunte* (1899). But by 1904 he had already appeared again before the public with two works of a very different calibre—*Jeux d'eau* (1901) for piano and the string quartet (1904), which had won the emphatic approval of Debussy and the more tempered admiration of Ravel's own master, Fauré. There was therefore a scandal, an 'affaire Ravel' which was taken up by *Le Matin* and elicited several eminent protests, among others that of Romain Rolland. Ravel alone was, at least on the surface, unmoved, but the scandal hastened, if it did not actually cause, Dubois's retirement from the Conservatoire.

The piano-writing in *Jeux d'eau* was suggested by Liszt's *Jeux d'eau à la Villa d'Este*, but Ravel wrote something approaching a movement in sonata form. The cascades of fourths, even the sequences of sevenths and ninths, never destroy the sense of tonality, for Ravel's logical mind disliked instinctively the ambiguity, the deliberate effects of haze in which Debussy excelled. In 1901, when *Jeux d'eau* appeared, Debussy had written nothing for the piano in what was to be his mature style. The suite *Pour le piano* (1901) contained a prelude and toccata to which Bach, the clavecinistes and Scarlatti contribute something as well as Chopin and Balakirev, though the final amalgam is distinctly Debussy's own. The Sarabande (which was already written in 1896, when it appeared in *Le Grand Journal*) was a masterly carrying-out of what Satie had adumbrated in his *Sarabandes* ten years earlier. Ravel in his next piano work, *Sonatine* (1905), wrote a minuet which recreates in a wholly modern idiom another eighteenth-century dance form. He had already tried his hand at this type of piece in the *Menuet Antique* (1895) and the *Pavane pour une infante défunte* (1899), for these pavanes, sarabandes and minuets were a fashionable affectation, like the ballades and villanelles of Banville and his English imitators. Debussy soon outgrew this phase, though traces of it remained in his piano works; but in Ravel every kind of artificiality was in a sense natural. ('Has it never occurred to them', Ravel said of his critics, 'that one may be artificial by nature?') A recent critic (M. Goldbeck in *Contrepoints*) has summed up the truth about this particular form of 'insincerity'.

'Insincerity is a legitimate element in art, but only on condition that it is fully recognized as such. This demands a rare sense of irony, a rare degree of self-analysis and self-control. We have only to think of Ravel's heroic scrupulousness, treating every emotion to the end as though it must be insincere.'

This is a dangerous doctrine, an aesthetic casuistry which is only elaborated in the Silver Age of any art. Perhaps, like all true casuistry, it applies only to a single case and has been extended into a general principle by a series of false analogies. Ravel himself was perfectly sincere. But probably for deep psychological reasons he found his inspiration not at first hand, in nature and human emotion, but in what had already passed through the aesthetic consciousness of other men. His art was, technically speaking, parasitic because it fed on predigested food. He sat down in front of a piano concerto by Mozart or Saint-Saëns 'as a landscape painter sets up his easel in front of a clump of trees', and what he produced was not pastiche (oddly enough his piano pieces *A la manière de . . .* are unsuccessful) but original compositions. He was before all else a composer, in the literal sense of the word; the technical problems suggested by other men's music inspired him, whetted his appetite for invention and suggested new schemes and elaborations, in which climaxes and stresses are dictated not so much by emotional impulse as by the aesthetic demands of the music. The result is a fundamental coolness in his music, the deliberate use of emotion as a gambit and that touch of sentimentality which often accompanies excessive emotional self-consciousness.

This characteristic was already visible in the string quartet and was more noticeable still in the *Introduction and Allegro* (1906) for string quartet, harp, flute and clarinet. From this combination Ravel extracts the most poignant beauty, sensational in the literal sense, making virtually no intellectual appeal and ravishing the senses without touching the heart. The use of the harp as a solo instrument and the character of the material give the whole a half exotic, half archaic air and a quality of evocativeness, which is also the main characteristic of the *Rapsodie espagnole* of the following year. This was Ravel's first large orchestral work and, as in his piano music, so here he appears at once as a master of his medium. All his life he was happier orchestrating his own, or even other men's, piano music than writing directly for the orchestra; and the *Rapsodie espagnole* includes an orchestration of his own early *Habañera*. But the unfailing aptness of his orchestral writing—clear, thin, and nervous and quite unlike the warm, veiled manner of Debussy—often suggests the bright, wiry, fundamentally percussive tone of the piano. Ravel's critics were merciless on his small perfection.

'Ravel? Very soft trills in the muted strings, flute, horn, side-drum, wind machine, muted brass and glissandi in the double basses. Crumbs. Brush the cloth, will you, Marie?'

His two sets of piano pieces (*Miroirs*, 1905; *Gaspard de la Nuit*, 1908) are the greatest achievements of these years. They contain eight pieces, five in *Miroirs* and three in *Gaspard de la Nuit*, whose titles reveal the composer's taste for the macabre (*Noctuelles, Oiseaux tristes, Le Gibet, Scarbo*) as well as the decoratively poetic (*Une barque sur l'océan, La Vallée des Cloches* and *Ondine*) and the familiar Spanish interest in *Alborada del gracioso*. In these pieces Ravel further developed the comparatively simple piano style of *Jeux d'éau*. In the earlier set *Alborada del gracioso* carries the piano-writing of Albéniz, Balakirev and Liszt to its logical conclusion. What is ornamentation with them becomes with Ravel the foundation of the music. Where Liszt and Albéniz surrounded a strong melody with *fioriture* of every kind and Balakirev in *Islamey* wrote a kind of symphonic variations, Ravel used the pianistic devices themselves as his subject matter, often entirely separated from melody, which appears at its most potent either unaccompanied or in a very simple form, as in *Ondine*. The *Vallée des Cloches* is an experiment in sonorities (it might be a study in the use of the pedal) and *Une barque sur l'océan* depicts the movement of water, though Ravel is less happy with the free, natural movement of the sea than with the artificially canalized fountains which play in *Jeux d'eau*.

Gaspard de la Nuit consists of three pieces inspired by a Hoffman-nesque poet, Aloysius Bertrand. *Ondine* is a metamorphosis of the Loreley and the Sirens; *Le Gibet* a Gothic fantasy suggested by a gibbet swaying at night in the wind; and *Scarbo* the kind of figure M. R. James might have imagined, an evil dwarf, half ghost and half gargoyle. These are period pieces, musical counter-parts to the works inspired by Mrs. Radcliffe and 'Monk' Lewis or by the architecture of the Gothic revival. Ravel was in fact using, as always, a ready-made artistic genre as his inspiration and deploying all his technical powers of invention within these self-imposed stylistic limits. *Ondine* is perhaps his most perfect work up to this time. The song of the siren is as haunting and as sinuous as anything in the *Introduction and Allegro* and the piano figuration and lay-out are freer and less intricate than in *Miroirs*, without any sacrifice of originality. All three pieces, and especially *Scarbo*, are of the 'transcendentally virtuosic' order. *Le Gibet* relies the least on technical brilliance but demands very subtle interpretation and a complete mastery of tone and rhythm (Gil Marchex has cata-logued twenty-seven kinds of touch necessary in this one work alone—an exaggeration, possibly, but an exaggeration of the truth). In *Ondine* Ravel writes a long, extended melody with an accom-panying piano figure and develops the melody in the Russian manner, by fairly close melodic variation of the component phrases, while he elaborates the pianistic setting into something much more than an accompaniment. The melody itself is asymmetrical, and is formed of a series of irregular phrases which move within the span of the fifth. The logic that marked Ravel's development of figures and harmonic sequences in *Jeux d'eau* and *Sonatine* and the deliberate transparency of texture which he preserves even when the piano decoration is at its most ornate (both in *Ondine* and *Scarbo*) are typically French and are characteristics that distinguish his music from Debussy's. *Le Gibet* is built entirely round the pedal B flat which sounds for the whole fifty-odd bars of the piece. There are marked resemblances to Debussy's *Hommage à Rameau* (*Images* I, No. 2; 1905), but the desolate atmosphere of the piece is entirely different—romantic and descriptive where Debussy's is a free fantasy on an archaic dance rhythm.

Scarbo is one of the very few works by Ravel to open with an introduction, a device beloved and abused by Franck and his school, who learned it from Liszt, but one that was antipathetic to the more fastidious Ravel and Debussy. Harmonically *Scarbo* is the most 'advanced' and dissonant of Ravel's works up to this time. It opens with a variation of the chord with which the early *Habañera* opens (Example 35) and is built on two main subjects

Ex. 35.

or cells. One of these has a Spanish rhythmic suggestion, of which Ravel makes full use in his variations. This he treats as belonging to the whole-tone scale, whose use, unusual in Ravel, was probably suggested by the macabre atmosphere he wished to create. The other is an explosive rhythmic figure which is used in a great variety of harmonic forms but always dissonant (Ex. 36, opposite).

In form *Scarbo* is something like a sonata movement, though the development is pure variation. The reprise is largely taken up by new variations on the second subject and by a cadenza, in which for nearly thirty bars Ravel plays with passages in minor seconds,

From left to right: Schmitt, Séverac, M. D. Calvocoressi, Cipa Godebski (*seated, with his son*), Roussel, Ricardo Viñes (*at the piano*), Ravel

elaborating what had been an accompaniment figure in *Jeux d'eau* into something more substantial, though little else than a series of brilliant sequences.

Ex. 36.

In the same years as *Gaspard de la Nuit* Ravel also published five small pieces for piano duet, written for the children of his friends the Godebskis. *Ma Mère l'Oÿe* is a miniature fairy-tale suite, technically at the opposite extreme to *Gaspard de la Nuit*. The first piece is a Pavane of the Sleeping Beauty; the second, Tom Thumb; the third, Laideronette, Empress of the Pagodas; the fourth, Conversation between Beauty and the Beast; and the fifth, The Magic Garden. In all of them Ravel maintains the naïve prettiness characteristic of the best illustrations of children's books, and the particular atmosphere he wished to re-create musically. Tom Thumb has touching, desolate melody standing out above the wandering thirds with their shifting accents and steady rhythm, and it rises to a climax in a passage that Massenet or Puccini might envy. Is it a reminiscence or a parody of those melodies in octaves which are so effective in *Werther* and *Madame Butterfly*?

Ex. 37.

Ravel had used the device in the string quartet (second subject of the first movement) and the *Introduction and Allegro* and was to use it again in *Daphnis et Chloé*, always with the same bitter-sweet clash of the major 7th accentuated, so that it becomes a recognizable feature of his style. In fact the opening of the *Habañera* (Example 35) is only a more sophisticated form of the same process, the epicure's blending of the excessively sweet with just the right touch of bitterness to flatter the sophisticated palate, in harmony as in gastronomy. In Laideronette, Debussy's pagodas (No. 1 of *Estampes*, 1903) reappear in the form of a musical-box tune on the black notes, alternating with a very Russian version in slow time. Beauty discourses to the Beast in a slow waltz, in the Montmartre manner of Satie, and the Beast answers with tender gruffness, his ugliness suggested by the low register and discreet dissonances. The two voices combine, and a *pianissimo glissando* brings about the transformation. The Fairy Garden, where we should expect glittering arpeggios and magic harmonies in the manner of Rimsky-Korsakov, opens with twenty-one diatonic bars in C major-E minor, as sober as a Fauré offertory. Even the second half, with widely-spaced *arpeggiando* chords in the high register of the piano, is largely diatonic, and the only splash of colour is provided at the very end by the ascending and descending *glissando* scales of C major, which throw a shimmering veil of sound over the miniature fanfares with which the piece ends. The whole set marks the extreme of Ravel's artificiality as shown in his piano works. The children for whom it was written should have been hooped, ruffled and jewelled, *Las Meninas* of Velasquez or Oscar Wilde's Infanta. They do not belong to the same order of creation as the children of Bizet's *Jeux d'Enfants* or Mussorgsky's nursery-songs. Schumann's *Kinderscenen* represent a parallel form of stylization, sentimentally idealized in the German manner instead of aesthetically in the French.

Technically Ravel's piano idiom, which is his most notable contribution to music, was original as a synthesis rather than wholly novel. The finger technique is based on that of Scarlatti and the French harpsichord writers of the eighteenth century, the touch required is not beyond that needed for Chopin, nor is the phrasing unlike Chabrier's; but, like a confectioner or cook of genius, Ravel has made out of familiar ingredients an original, though fundamentally a traditional, style of his own. This basic link with tradition distinguished all Ravel's music from the genuinely revolutionary music of Debussy, and thus whatever indebtedness there was on Debussy's side is quite outweighed by the absolute originality of his contribution not only to piano-writing but to the whole art of music.

Parallel and superficially similar to Ravel's piano works, those of Debussy which followed *Pour le piano* form a new departure in his creative activity. It is worth while comparing the dates of publication of the two composers' piano works during these years:

Ravel	*Debussy*
Jeux d'eau, 1901	Pour le Piano, 1902
Sonatine, 1905	Estampes, 1903
Miroirs, 1905	L'Isle joyeuse, 1904
Gaspard de la Nuit, 1908	Images I, 1905
Ma Mère l'Oye, 1908	Images II, 1908
Valses nobles et senti-	Children's Corner, 1908
mentales, 1911	Préludes I, 1910
	Préludes II, 1913

There is little doubt that Debussy was stimulated in his piano-writing by the appearance of *Jeux d'eau*, and it is acknowledged by his chief biographer, Léon Vallas, that the *Soirée dans Grenade* (No. 2 of *Estampes*) was inspired by Ravel's *Habañera* of 1895 (later No. 3 of the *Rapsodie Espagnole*).

On the other hand, *Pagodes* (*Estampes* No. 1) was inspired by the Javanese *gamelang* orchestra and the third piece, *Jardins sous la pluie*, is in every way unlike Ravel—much less adventurous harmonically and using both the whole-tone scale and fragments of popular songs (*Nous n'irons plus au bois* and *Dodo, l'enfant do*). Neither of these elements was common in Ravel's style. It is possible to trace in the last movement of the *Sonatine* elements borrowed from *Estampes*, but this is a game which can be played *ad infinitum*. Did Ravel's *Vallée des Cloches* give Debussy the idea of his *Cloches à travers les feuilles*, for example? If so, the two works show the differences rather than the points of resemblance between the two composers. Both Debussy's and Ravel's music shared the same literary background and both were exploring the possibilities of piano sonorities. But whereas Debussy had developed from the richness and warmth of the Wagnerian orchestra and his music was colouristic and concerned with emotional as well as sensual impressions, Ravel was first and foremost a pianist—a linear and percussive explorer, a prose-writer and a draughtsman, where Debussy was poet and painter. 'Debussy pense timbres, Ravel instruments', in the words of Roland Manuel; and Ravel's approach to music is summed up in this suggestion of the primacy of the technical data over the poetic possibilities which fascinated Debussy.

Whatever Ravel may have borrowed or learned from Debussy, or vice versa, there can be no comparing their comparative status as original artists. Even in his piano works, and leaving *Pelléas et Mélisande* and the orchestral works on one side, Debussy created a new world of feeling as well as a new technique. Ravel was a great technical innovator, but within the classical tradition as an artistic thinker. In almost all his works the continuous, logical dialogue, which Debussy shattered in his *Prélude à l'après-midi d'un faune* and the *Nocturnes*, is preserved and its logical coherence often stressed by the ruthless repetition of a figure or progression or the aggressive insistence on a pedal point (*Jeux d'eau* and the last movement of the *Sonatine*, *La Vallée des Cloches*, *Le Gibet*). Debussy's manner is determined by the free following of his sensibility, so that his music achieves at its best that effect of improvisation which was his ideal. His technique is wholly at the service of his imagination, whereas Ravel's imagination seems to be stimulated by technical problems—either an unusual combination as in the *Introduction and Allegro* or, more generally, the re-creating of a given style or atmosphere as in *Gaspard de la Nuit* and *Ma Mère l'Oye*.

In an article in the journal of the Société Internationale de Musique, published in 1913, Debussy spoke of the musician's claim to a unique interpretation of nature.

'To musicians only is it given to capture all the poetry of night and day, of the earth and the heavens; to reconstruct their atmosphere and record the rhythm of their heartbeats.'

He quotes *Der Freischütz* as an example of this potentiality realized, and specifically rejects Beethoven's Pastoral Symphony and the music of Berlioz—'leaves that literature has dried and pressed between the pages of its books'.

'Music should humbly seek to please: within these limits great beauty may well be found. Extreme complication is contrary to art. Beauty must appeal to the senses, must provide us with immediate enjoyment, must impress us or insinuate itself into us without any effort on our part. Take Leonardo da Vinci or Mozart! These are the great artists.'

What composers write about music is generally less interesting for its absolute, objective truth than for the light that it throws on their own music. Ideals and ideas, the whole literary inspiration on which music throve during the second half of the nineteenth century, were banished from Debussy's music from the *Prélude à l'après midi d'un faune* onwards, as they were banished from Mallarmé's poetry. But, since music must always be the expression

of something, however remote and abstracted from every-day life,
Debussy made use of sense-impressions as interpreted by his own
sensibility—'an emotional transposition of what remains invisible
in nature'. His piano music from 1903 onwards contains the purest
expression of this ideal. *Estampes*, the two sets of *Images* and the
Préludes amount to about three dozen small piano pieces, some of
them deceptively simple in appearance and very few making such
technical demands as Ravel's *Alborada del gracioso* or *Scarbo*. The
exotic element present in *Estampes* (*Pagodes, Soirée dans Grenade*) is
less strong in the later sets, though it is to be found in *La Sérénade
interrompue* and *La Puerta del vino*. In general Debussy turned rather
to purely poetic titles suggesting the simplest natural phenomena
(*Jardins sous la pluie, Reflets dans l'eau, Le Vent dans la plaine, Brouillards*), or an image that appealed to him (*Les sons et les parfums tour-
nent dans l'air du soir, Les fées sont d'exquises danseuses, La Terrasse des
audiences du clair de lune*). A number of these pieces are in the style
of archaic dances and probably owe this, but very little else, to
Satie. *Hommage à Rameau, Danseuses de Delphes, La Cathédrale engloutie, Les sons et les parfums, La Fille aux cheveux de lin* and *Canope*
are grave and archaic, while *Soirée dans Grenade* and *La Puerta del
vino* are based on the rhythm of the *Habanera*. Dance elements are
frequent in many of the other pieces—the steady *ostinato* of *Mouvement*, the rhythmic fragments of *Les Collines d'Anacapri* and the
obvious affiliations of *La Danse de Puck* and *Minstrels*.

The importance of these titles varies, and Debussy's practice
in the *Préludes*, placing the title at the end of the piece rather
than the beginning, was a warning against taking any literary
suggestion too seriously. The scene or the sense-impression has
passed through the composer's sensibility and emerges in a purely
musical form. Unity of mood is essential in such small pieces,
some of them less than forty bars long; and Debussy always sets
the atmosphere in the first bar—by a rhythmic figure in many
cases or a particular harmonic colour (*Et la lune descend, Voiles*),
but always simple and unmistakable. The majority of these piano
pieces are miniature variations, not on themes but on a few very
simple ideas, occasionally purely melodic (*La Fille aux cheveux de
lin*), more often harmonic (*Ondine, Les fées sont d'exquises danseuses,*)
but generally with a strongly rhythmic interest. In the longer
pieces of *Images* the rhythm tends to be extended uniformly over
considerable periods, and *Jardins sous la pluie* even harks back to
the Prelude of *Pour le piano* in its comparatively conventional

figuration. In the *Préludes* Debussy developed the technique which
he had used in *Poissons d'or* (*Images* II, No. 3). This was an apparently disjointed manner, in which rhythmic figures and fragments of melody succeed each other in widely different registers
and connected by the slightest link. In *Poissons d'or* this darting-
off at a tangent, lightning-quick changes of direction and speed
suggest the movement of the goldfish; but Debussy's own sensibility was almost as mercurial, and in the *Préludes* it is his sensibility he is following rather than any external image. His great art
lay in preserving a sense of continuity and a unity of mood, even
when he was working in a small form and on principle yielding to
every distraction—for that is what his ideal of improvisation
amounts to.

— Harmonically the range of these piano pieces is wide, varying
from diatonic harmonies and triads (*Brouillards, Bruyères, Canope,
La Cathédrale engloutie*) to the thorough-going use of the whole-tone
scale (*Voiles, Mouvement*), experiments with sequences of sevenths
and ninths or the prophetic chains of fourths (Ex. 38a and 38b).

Ex. 38a.

Ex. 38b.

The first of these is from *Ondine*; the second, which is very
close to Scriabin's last piano sonatas, from *Les Fées sont d'exquises
danseuses*. Unlike Ravel, Debussy does not exclude from his exquisite sensations the surprise of a perfectly conventional diatonic

common chord. There is the big E flat major climax after nearly two pages of whole-tone arpeggios in *Reflets dans l'eau*, a parallel passage in the same key in *Poissons d'or*, and the insistent B major tonality at the end of *Les Collines d'Anacapri*. Occasionally a conventional prettiness suggests that a piece was written a good deal earlier and included in the *Préludes* for lack of a better home. *La Fille aux cheveux de lin* and *Bruyères*, from internal evidence, might have been written in the eighteen-nineties.

Debussy's humour was less sardonic and more direct than Ravel's. The popular songs which appear for a moment in *Les Collines d'Anacapri* and *Minstrels* are used evocatively and are deliberately taken up into the body of the piece rather than left, as it were, between quotation marks. The effect Debussy was aiming at was poetry, not wit, and when he tried his *Hommage à S. Pickwick Esq., P.P.M.P.C.*, he failed. *God Save the King* as the bass to an archaic dance in the manner of Satie is simply inept, and Debussy had not the gift for thumb-nail dramatic sketches like Mussorgsky's *Samuel Goldenberg and Schmuyle*. But the conception of many of the *Préludes* owes something to Mussorgsky's *Pictures from an Exhibition*, though Debussy's nature and his way of writing for the piano were totally unlike Mussorgsky's. There are striking parallels in the simple, intimate genre pictures (cf. Mussorgsky's *Il vecchio castello* and Debussy's *Sérénade interrompue* or *Puerta del vino*), fantastic portraits, fairy pieces (Mussorgsky's *Hut on Fowls' Legs* and Debussy's *Ondine* or *Les fées sont d'exquises danseuses*) or mysterious evocations (Mussorgsky's *Catacombs* and Debussy's *La Cathédrale engloutie*). Debussy's scope is wider, and the best of the *Préludes* are inspired by inanimate nature, which did not enter Mussorgsky's range at all. In a few the virtuosity of the piano-writing provides the main interest. *Les Tierces alternées* is a study and *Feux d'artifice* a bravura piece of a kind much more typical of Ravel. There are not many pieces in which virtuosity looms large with the exception of *L'Isle joyeuse* and *Mouvement* from *Images I*. *Ce qu'a vu le vent d'ouest* is one of the few examples in Debussy's piano music of work that seems fundamentally orchestral in conception. *La Cathédrale engloutie*, which is certainly effective in Henri Büsser's orchestration, is nevertheless genuine piano music in which Debussy achieves by pedal effects an atmospheric haze such as no other medium can attain, and sets against it the stark, primitive melody suggesting the vanished cathedral.

Debussy's children's pieces (*Children's Corner*, 1908) are almost

contemporary with Ravel's *Ma Mère l'Oye*, but of less importance
musically. They are not fairy stories but nursery scenes, simple and
unstylized; and they show a deliberately simplified side of Debussy's
normal self rather than any attempt to enter the child mind.

With the single exception of Ravel's *Sonatine* all these piano
pieces by Debussy and Ravel are in the small, salon forms adopted
by Chopin and Schumann and transferred to the concert-hall by
Liszt, who enlarged them and added brilliant decoration without
altering their fundamental character. If *Jeux d'eau* and *Scarbo* are
cast in a kind of sonata form, it is irrelevant to their character, and
their harmonic audacities make nonsense of the key-relationships
which are fundamental to the form. Both Debussy and Ravel
transformed the spirit of the salon-piece, following the example of
Balakirev, Liszt, Chabrier and Mussorgsky; but Fauré continued
to write unperturbed the nocturnes, barcarolles, impromptus and
valses-caprices which he had inherited from Chopin. Superficially
his piano music remains salon-music in a stricter sense than that
of Debussy or Ravel; but in musical quality it became increasingly
austere. Apart from his Theme and Variations (1897) Fauré composed nothing for the piano in the more academic forms. In the
seventh Nocturne, written in the following year, the opening
rhythm suggests a rather broader melodic flow, but the lay-out
for the piano is familiar and a continuation of his earlier style—
frequent arpeggio passages and accompaniments, exploitation of
contrasting binary and ternary rhythms, scale-passages passing from
hand to hand as accompaniment to the main melody, use of extreme
keys both flat and sharp. If anything it is more conventional than the
stormy fifth Barcarolle (1895) in which his use of harmonic appoggi-
aturas reaches its height in such a passage as the following:

Ex. 39.

which is typical of the whole work. In the eighth Barcarolle (1908)
Fauré experimented again, only this time much more radically,
with the broken rhythm which he had used in the opening of the
seventh Nocturne. The division of a nine-eight bar thus ♪ ♩ ♩. ♩.
dominates the whole piece and in spite of the lush D flat major
tonality the texture is noticeably thinner, though there is one
climax on a dominant ninth which suggests that Debussy's idiom
was infiltrating even into so personal a style as Fauré's. In the
ninth Nocturne (1908) and the ninth Barcarolle (1910) the break-
away from the ornate, flowing style of piano-writing is very noticeable, particularly in the Nocturne, where the shifting harmonies
give an impression of unrest and almost crabbedness when combined with the austere piano-writing. Fauré was experimenting
with the new style which he perfected in *Pénélope* (1913), where his
harmonies are intensely elliptical, and in the Nocturne he seems
to be feeling his way through the progressions which were to be
eliminated later. A series of sequences, for example:

Ex. 40.

seems experimental and quite unlike the effortlessly finished
manner of Fauré's earlier work. There is a certain amount of
whole-tone harmony which increases the impression of unrest, and
it is only at the very end that a short singing melody in B major,
rising by thirds in a manner very typical of the composer, gives
the listener the familiar feeling of lyrical expansion and complete
ease. The ninth Barcarolle is a contrast, in that it is almost entirely
diatonic; the piano-writing is more flowing and chromatic ornamentation had disappeared. The result is a line-drawing with a

wash of A minor over it, and a lyrical resignation takes the place of the warmer emotions.

In his songs Fauré was moving in the same direction. After the Verlaine settings he wrote only isolated songs, including the magnificent *Le Parfum impérissable* and *Dans la Forêt de Septembre*, until the cycle entitled *La Chanson d'Eve*. With this cycle of ten songs written between 1907–10 begins Fauré's old age. The quintet of 1906 dates partly from an earlier period—it was planned in 1890. There belong to this final period of Fauré's creative activity four song cycles; *Pénélope;* about twenty piano pieces; the Fantaisie for piano and orchestra; and six chamber works—a second quintet, a trio, two violoncello sonatas, the second violin sonata and the string quartet. In 1905 Fauré succeeded Dubois as Director of the Conservatoire, and his new administrative duties encroached on his creative activity. The works from 1907 onwards virtually forgo colour, and even the ornamental writing for the piano, so typical of the composer, is progressively modified. The intellectual content becomes correspondingly denser; harmonies are increasingly elliptical, lines are severer and notes fewer. In fact Fauré was one of the first to lead the way towards that stripping of the inessential (*dépouillement*) that became the battle-cry of the young composers during and immediately after the war of 1914–18.

Paradoxically enough, it was in his two works for the stage that Fauré developed this ascetic tendency. *Prométhée*, written for performance in the outdoor theatre at Béziers in 1900, is not strictly speaking an opera and has never held the stage when transplanted from the setting for which it was designed. The music reveals a side of Fauré unfamiliar to most people, more austere and more obviously virile, working with large choral masses and not afraid of the orchestral brass, whose effect was well calculated for the open air. There are the more familiar moments of elegiac beauty, as in the funeral music for Pandora; but in the gods Kratos, Bia and Hephaistos, Fauré naturally saw figures parallel to the supernatural characters of *The Ring* and, without imitating Wagner, he found a breadth and magnificence of utterance which hardly has a parallel in the rest of his music. *Pénélope*, which was first performed at Monte Carlo in 1913, is Fauré's single adventure in the conventional operatic form. His genius for understatement and his increasing tendency to a dry and elliptical musical idiom made a popular success—and perhaps even a first-rate opera, as such—impossible. But in *Pénélope* the much-vaunted affinity of the

French and the Hellenic genius does appear and finds what may
be its classic expression. Generally the affinity has been with a
decadent Hellenism—the nostalgic charms of the Anthology or
Daphnis and Chloe as re-created by Pierre Louÿs, Anatole France,
Saint-Saëns (*Phryné* and *Hélène*), Gounod (*Sapho* and *Philémon et
Baucis*); the Alexandria of Massenet's *Thaïs*; or Debussy's Faun
and the Bilitis songs. Fauré pays his tribute to this tradition in
Pénélope, in the spinning chorus and the dances in Acts I and III;
but the main body of the work, if it can be called an expression
of Hellenic ideals, is an expression of something more noble and
heroic than the graces of the Anthology. Penelope herself, from
her first entrance, has a grandeur and gravity that she never loses,
even in the more lyrical second act. Musically she is characterized
by Fauré with great skill, and she alone of all the characters is
never sacrificed to purely musical considerations. Her humanity,
her combination of dignity and tenderness, colours the whole
work and her self-control and imperturbable sense of fitness find reflection in the music. Again, the hot noon of Act I, the evening
falling on the cliff above the sea in Act II, and the early morning
of Act III, all have that dry, luminous quality which we associate
with the Greek mind as well as the Greek climate; and Fauré's
suggestion of this quality by musical means is wonderfully vivid.
On many occasions he builds a whole scene around a musical
phrase or rhythm. These are not leitmotivs, of which there are
several, but more in the nature of symphonic themes. Act II is
particularly rich in them.

Ex. 41*a* and 41*b*.

Like Debussy in *Pelléas et Mélisande*, Fauré uses rhythm as a means of expression, with the greatest effect. The dotted rhythms connected with the bow of Ulysses and the combination of the same rhythm with whole-tone harmony for the suitors are the most obvious examples; but Eumaeus's breathless and over-zealous loyalty always finds expression in a free-moving delivery which is soon syncopated and broken by his quick indignation and enthusiasm. What is wanting in *Pénélope* as an opera, is simplicity and broad lyrical sweep. Fauré's great lyrical days were over and though his chastened and partly intellectualized art was still to produce works of great beauty, his inclinations were even less theatrical than when, as a young man, he refused to write an opera for Pauline Viardot.

Debussy himself was developing in the same direction. *La Mer* (1905), though still opulent by later standards, is tonic and astringent compared with the *Nocturnes* and *Pelléas*; and the orchestral *Images* and *Le Martyre de Saint Sébastien* were further steps along the path that closed with the three sonatas written at the end of his life. Ravel came later to the same process, as was natural to a younger man, and the *Valses nobles et sentimentales* (1911) are the first example in his work of this deliberate simplification of manner.

Of the three orchestral *Images* by Debussy *Ibéria*, in three movements, was finished first. The first volume of Albéniz's *Ibéria* appeared in 1906 and Ravel's *Rapsodie espagnole* was first performed in March 1908; while the complete rough copy of Debussy's three movements bears the date '25 December 1908'. The similarity to Ravel's work is largely superficial. Ravel's *Prélude à la Nuit* is a counterpart to Debussy's *Les Parfums de la Nuit* and both composers tried in their last movements to find musical expression for the atmosphere and bustle of a Spanish *fiesta*. But in Charles Malherbe's programme-note there is a suggestion that Debussy was concerned in *Ibéria* more than ever before with sensations, visual as well as auditory.

'These are real pictures, in which the musician is bent on translating for the ear impressions made on the eyes. To make them more intense he tries to combine the two forms of sensation. As the painter delights in contrasting tonalities, in the play of light and shade, so the composer enjoys the clash of unforeseen dissonances and the blending of rare sonorities.'

This, without the strongly personal element of poetry which had hitherto characterized all Debussy's music, was very near Ravel's ideal. It is the exact reverse of Beethoven's description of his Pastoral Symphony; it is, in fact, *mehr Malerei als Empfindung*—more scene-painting than sensibility. None of the movements of *Ibéria* have the personal poetry of the *Nocturnes* or *La Mer*; it is as though Debussy had lost the strongly personal quality of his earlier works and had retained only his skill, taste and sensibility. The *Rondes de Printemps*, constructed with a certain academic formality, is a masterpiece of orchestral writing. But what had he in mind when he wrote to Durand of the *Images* which he could not finish (8 August 1906)?

'The music is well written but with the conventional means [*le coutumier métier*] that is so difficult to overcome and so boring. Now I think I have a glimpse of what is needed instead of this academic labour [*travail de mandarin*] which is certainly not my line.'

Here we see once again Debussy's ideal of music as improvisation —perhaps his greatest contribution to musical aesthetics. But he never quite achieves it in the *Images*. There is a melancholy personal note in the *Gigues*; but Debussy's best work at this time was in his piano pieces. The music of *Le Martyre de Saint Sébastien* is too well wedded to the romantic decadence of d'Annunzio's text, and it has never survived transplantation to the concert hall. It was only too true that Debussy, in his own words, 'had no great effort to make in order to rise to the heights of mysticism reached by the poet's drama'. He protested that he had written the work as he would have done for a church, and by this he understood '. . . decorative music . . . the illustration in sounds and rhythms of a noble text'. The modern reader of Debussy's score is faced with a kind of hieratic affectation, admirably suited to d'Annunzio's text and effective apparently in the theatre. But the combination of extreme, if veiled, carnality and theatrical religiosity is no longer as tempting as it was in 1911, and not even the beauties of Debussy's choral writing can reconcile us to the character of the work.

Le Martyre de Saint Sébastien was a notable stage on the path towards the simplification, the *dépouillement* of musical style. It even had its parallel in *Polyeucte* and the later works of Gounod. Fauré's *La Chanson d'Eve* has the spareness and the dry luminosity of old age; both there and in the piano works lyrical warmth is not banished—it has naturally withdrawn. Ornamentation, too, is reduced not according to any theory but simply because Fauré, after the age of sixty, was concerned with the essentials of his music and his ideas no longer had the physical ardour of youth which finds its natural expression in ornament and sensuous gesture. With Debussy, and later Ravel, it was different. The years immediately before 1914 were the last of the era of harmonic research and refinement indulged for its own sake, the last years of music conceived as the succession of ingenious and elaborate chords. Within a few years the tide was to turn and a horizontal conception of music was for a time to replace this vertical conception. The reason was simple: harmonic refinements had been carried to the extreme limit possible within the borders of tonality, and there was no further development possible in that direction.

While the first stirrings of this fundamental change were beginning to make themselves felt beneath the surface or in isolated works, the general impression given by French music between 1900 and 1914 was still one of great harmonic opulence and ever-increasing refinement. Ravel's *Histoires naturelles* (1906) represent a further sophistication of Debussy's methods of song writing. Debussy's declamation was a heightening and stylization of normal speech; and the critics who heard in Ravel's songs 'the unmistakable echo of Debussy's music' certainly had this justification—that no other French composer except Debussy had ever treated his text with more passionate respect and consideration. As always, Ravel's music is illustrative, visual in its suggestions (*The Peacock* and *The Guinea Hen* are the obvious examples) and Jules Renard's dry, sardonic wit is matched by the music. Ravel's unusually careful modelling of his melody on the natural line and rhythm of the spoken word and his sharp etching of character in a few bars bring the *Histoires naturelles*, wholly French though they are, within the orbit of Mussorgsky's influence. The neatest of French composers had, in fact, a great admiration for the most clumsy of Russians, as he was to show later when he orchestrated the *Pictures from an Exhibition*. But if there is a monstrous-seeming cross of La Fontaine and Mussorgsky in the *Histoires Naturelles*, the result is wholly personal, small and perfectly calculated. This same tendency was continued in Ravel's opera, *L'Heure Espagnole*, in which all the parts except that of Gonzalve (in which lyricism is parodied) are to be sung, according to the composer, in the *quasi parlando* of the Italian comic opera. This opera, begun in 1907 but not produced until 1911, is the acme of artificiality and successful because it never pretends to be anything else. The clocks and mechanical toys of Torquemada's shop provide the lyrical element, while the characters are the automatons. Parody is the essence of the work—parody of the accepted notions of Spanish life, character and dances, and parody of the conventional figures of the lyrical drama, comic or tragic.

The appearance of Diaghilev and the Russian Ballet in Paris in 1908–9 diverted the attentions of musicians to a form of music which had been very little favoured by serious French composers, with the exception of Delibes, since the days of Rameau. For Diaghilev Ravel wrote his *Daphnis et Chloé* and Debussy's ballet *Jeux* (1913), a fine and sensitive work, was spoiled by a poor scenario and weak choreography (as was the ballet constructed around the *Prélude à l'après-midi d'un faune*). But Diaghilev was not the only figure in the world of ballet ready to commission works from composers. Ida Rubinstein had asked Debussy to collaborate with d'Annunzio in *Le Martyre de Saint Sébastien* in 1911 and Maud Allan had obtained a short work from him, *Khamma*, at about the same time. A Russian dancer at the Opéra, Truhanova, had persuaded Ravel to make a ballet out of his *Valses Nobles et Sentimentales* and asked Paul Dukas for *La Péri*, and these works were given on a single evening in April 1912, with d'Indy's *Istar* and Schmitt's *Tragédie de Salomé*. Both Schmitt and Dukas were products of the Conservatoire, and though the music of neither has ever achieved international status comparable with that of Ravel and Debussy, both were in their different ways typical of their generation and gifted and original artists.

Florent Schmitt was Ravel's senior by five years and therefore an older contemporary of his at the Conservatoire. He was a pupil first of Massenet and then of Fauré, and in 1900 he won the Prix de Rome at the age of thirty. A Lorrainer by birth, like Hérold and Ambroise Thomas, his early sympathies as shown in his first pianoforte pieces (*Soirs*, 1890–96 and the *Musiques Intimes*, 1890–1900) were with the mawkish French imitators of Schumann. But this affinity with German music was to declare itself very differently in his first major work, the fruit of what should properly have been his period of study in Rome, though in fact he spent most of the time travelling from one end of Europe to the other. His setting of *Psalm 47* for soprano solo, chorus, organ and orchestra is an essay in the *kolossal* and is in the sharpest possible contrast to the advanced French music of the period—to the mature Debussy and the budding Ravel. It has closer affinity

with the music of Richard Strauss, in the contrapuntal texture and
the exploitation of large masses of sound. Harmonically there is a
deliberate ruthlessness such as is seldom found in French music,
and a savage pleasure in dissonance that was new and perhaps
prophetic. The conception of a psalm as a poem of bloodthirsty
rejoicing celebrating the victory of a savage oriental tribe was
new in 1904, and after Saint-Saëns's suave orientalism these
clashing fanfares and passionate languors seemed an approach to
genuine Eastern music, of which earlier imitations had been mere
drawing-room essays. The violin and bassoon which answer each
other in the orchestral introduction to the middle section:

Ex. 42.

are given real *melismata* and create an atmosphere not unworthy
of the ecstatic sensuality of the Song of Solomon. But what
impressed the first audiences (the work was first performed in
1906) were the energy and violence which unleashed such
volumes of sheer noise. There were understanding and admiring
critics—among them the poet and wit Léon-Paul Fargue, who
was delighted with 'cet orchestre de triphtongues, de saxotartes,
de trimbalets, de tromboches, de pangibles et de fusils à derrière
prêtés par ces dames'. But the majority were put out by Schmitt's
incisive rhythm, which commands attention with jerky and dotted
phrases and was in strong contrast to the deliberate subtlety and
discretion of Fauré and Debussy.

His critics expressed astonishment that after such a work, and indeed for many years to come, Schmitt could be content to return to
such colourless and comparatively conventional writing as appears
in his *Pièces Romantiques* for the piano. But Schmitt's interest in the
piano was never whole-hearted and he has always tended to regard
his piano music as sketches for orchestral transcription. 'This con-
venient but disappointing instrument', he calls it, 'which is, when
all is said and done, no more than a *pis-aller*, admirable no doubt
but a *pis-aller* just the same'. His orchestral music—*Musiques de*

plein air, Danses des Dévadasis, Le Palais Hanté—shows an increasing mastery of writing and a progressive refinement of taste, but the fundamental character of Schmitt's music remains unchanged. There is a romantic violence and search for unusual effects, as in the Psalm, and a gradual departure from the deliberately emotional. As the descriptive element in Schmitt's music grows, the manner becomes increasingly a cross between that of Debussy and Rimsky-Korsakov. The Russian element predominates in the conventional orientalism of the *Danse des Dévadasis*, a scene for orchestra and women's voices; and in *La Tragédie de Salomé* Schmitt produced something like a masterpiece in this Franco-Russian style.

This work was originally commissioned by the dancer Loie Fuller and in its original version, for small orchestra, it was first performed in 1907. Schmitt then made a symphonic arrangement for a large orchestra and this, the universally known version, was not given until 1911. Richard Strauss's *Salomé* had its first Paris performance in May 1907, six months before the appearance of Schmitt's first version, but the two works have nothing in common except the general outline of the story; and Maurice Barrès's 'Du sang, de la volupté, de la mort' was a fashionable commonplace of the period, exploited by d'Annunzio in Italy and Ibañez in Spain. The music of *La Tragédie de Salomé* may after forty years sound unoriginal, the work of a period rather than an individual and it is easy to overlook some genuinely original features. Certainly both Scheherazade and Mélisande make frequent appearances in the score, but in one respect, at least, Schmitt revealed new possibilities which were to be exploited by the young Stravinsky, who arrived in Paris in 1910 and was soon a friend of Schmitt's. This was the ingenious combination of deliberate dissonances in the form of superimposed chords, orthodox in themselves but belonging to different keys, moving in blocks and in an unusual rhythm, generally continued *ostinato* for a considerable period with varying degrees of violence. The *Danse de l'Effroi* from *Salomé*, for example, was not without its effect on Stravinsky when he wrote *Le Sacre du Printemps* two years later (Ex. 43, on next page).

Stravinsky's influence on Schmitt, on the other hand, was to become very strong in the years to come.

The piano quintet, which bears the next opus number to *La Tragédie de Salomé* in the catalogue of Schmitt's works, was written earlier, although it was not finished until a year after the first version of *Salomé*, in 1908, and was later revised. Schmitt was not at this time happy unless working on a very large scale. All his effects are minutely calculated, there is no question of rough work, impressionistic in the sense of loose in structure or careless in detail. In Octave Ferroud's words, 'he is precise as a clockmaker but one who thinks it beneath him to make watches and prefers to build the astronomical clock of Strasbourg cathedral'. This is hardly the temperament for chamber music, and in fact the Quintet gives the impression of an orchestral work reduced.

Ex. 43.

Paul Dukas was five years older than Schmitt, born in 1865. At the Conservatoire he was a pupil of Ernest Guiraud and Théodore Dubois and a friend of Debussy, with whom he shared the wider cultural interests which most musicians lacked. In fact Dukas, like Debussy, developed something of an anti-musical snobbery, an unreasoning preference for the company and conversation of sculptors, painters or writers rather than of musicians. He had won a second Prix de Rome with his cantata *Velléda* and written a considerable amount of music of all descriptions before his overture to *Polyeucte* was given a public performance, in 1892. Like everything he wrote—he was already an accomplished critic in the Revue Hebdomadaire—or composed, *Polyeucte* is distinguished, solidly written but clearly conceived and neatly executed. The influence of Wagner is naturally strong and there are

Lisztian characteristics such as had been adopted by the Franck-ists, with whom Dukas had a good deal in common. Thus two themes, the one sacred and the other profane, are contrasted and there are certain rhetorical gestures in the music which recall Liszt's tone-poems, as does the final apotheosis with harp and divided strings. The symphony which followed in 1896 is more original. It was bold to open a symphony in those days with an un-equivocal chord of C major and though some of the symphonic development is prolix, the music never loses its vigorous rhythm, and its bold structure remains clear even beneath the ornamenta-tion in the second movement. Dukas had, in fact, digested Wag-ner's music, which had enriched his palette but otherwise left him fundamentally unchanged—the typical French reaction. His lines are delicate and precise, his colouring clear and bright, his archi-tecture solid. In spite of his admiration for Debussy there is no hint of the deliberate haze of impressionism and very little exotic colouring. In fact Dukas's approach to music is largely intellectual, and this makes both its strength and its weakness.

His next work, and that which alone has made him famous out-side France, was the tone-poem *L'Apprenti Sorcier* (1897). Like all Dukas's music, but very unlike many tone-poems, this was care-fully and successfully designed from the formal point of view, as a set of variations; and the orchestration is as deft and glittering as anything that had been produced in France. But this only partly accounts for the success of the work. What was lacking in both *Polyeucte* and the symphony and was never really to be achieved in Dukas's later works, was musical individuality, the essential characteristic of any work which is to be a popular success. Both the themes and their presentation in *L'Apprenti Sorcier* call up a definite picture and have an unmistakable character of their own. It is ironical that this cultivated and intellectual composer should achieve his unique popular success with a comic work, a refined and Gallic version of Richard Strauss. His admirers naturally find much more of his individual style and personality in the opera *Ariane et Barbe-Bleue* (already discussed on pp. 120–121), or the two large works for piano written in 1901 and 1903, the sonata and the Variations on a theme by Rameau. If the influence of Debussy is strong in the opera, that of Franck and the Schola is overwhelming in the sonata, a large work in four movements which plays for an hour. Chromatic harmony and a very full, rich piano style often requiring three staves carries with it a corresponding emotional ardour and an earnestness which Dukas nowhere else reveals in so open a manner. There are passages, especially in the second movement, which are modelled on Beethoven; and the opening of that movement, as well as the disastrous B major theme in the last, unfortunately recall Franck at his weakest. The sonata cannot fail to impress by its obvious sincerity and grandiose intentions; but it is not the best of Dukas. The Variations, Interlude and Finale on a theme by Rameau are both more interesting pianistically and also more in accord with Dukas's own character as shown in his other works.

Although he lived until 1935 he published only one work of importance after *Ariane et Barbe-Bleue* in 1907. This was *La Péri*, a cross between ballet and tone-poem, written for Truhanova and performed in 1912. Like Schmitt's *La Tragédie de Salomé*, *La Péri* combines in a charming and individual way the brilliant colouring and something of the melodic and harmonic traits of Rimsky-Korsakov, with the extreme delicacy and grace, the dramatic poetry and the fine sense of composition (in the painter's sense) which are typical of French music of this period. In fact Dukas and Schmitt are interesting examples of a process only possible in France, where the problem of presentation which we call 'style' is traditionally the chief preoccupation of the artist.

Franck and Debussy were strong musical personalities. Their methods were adapted to their individual range of sentiment and sensibility and each created a style of his own, idiosyncratic and easy to recognize. To composers such as Schmitt and Dukas, gifted and intelligent musicians without very strong musical personalities, these two styles and their variants were merely the latest additions to the stock vocabulary of music; and they borrowed from both or either in order to form their own, individual if not highly original, manner. The sense of continuity, always strong in French art, had not been shattered and it was natural that by the side of two great original figures there should spring up lesser men, fine artists and excellent craftsmen, for whom nobody would claim honours of the first rank. France is in this sense less individualist than England, where artists of even the third class generally consider originality to be an essential characteristic of any art worth noticing. In France, and to some extent in Italy, there has persisted the Latin tradition of working in a given medium and accepting the content of a work of art as given, in order to concentrate on the form or style. Thus there have appeared numbers of works in all the arts whose interest is chiefly stylistic. Compare *La Tragédie de Salomé* and *La Péri* with Debussy's *Martyre de St. Sébastien* or d'Indy's *Istar*. However these particular works of Debussy and d'Indy are rated, they are original; they are not essays in an already given style or a combination of two given styles, but wholly new creations. This quick formation of a contemporary 'classical' idiom has been typical of French music, which has not generally been dominated by single giant figures. Berlioz, the exception to every rule, is the obvious exception to this; but even dominant figures such as Franck, Fauré or Debussy do not enjoy unquestioned ascendancy such as Richard Strauss or Puccini enjoyed in Germany and Italy. The high plateau rather than the mountain range has been the typical conformation of the French artistic world, and there has been a comparative homogeneity of style and purpose. The subtle, though real, distinction between the music of Debussy and Ravel—music which the grosser, uneducated ear can hardly distinguish apart—presents a typically French point of interest. A composer of Debussy's originality would, in Germany, have overawed and overshadowed a Dukas or a Schmitt, who would never have developed his own individual contribution to music. In France there may be less genius and more talent; certainly more independence and a greater sense of equality in the musical world. Distinctions tend to be fine and, compared with similarities, small; but in the arts the distinction between work of the first and second or even third ranks is always a matter of what seem to the layman small points.

This strongly developed aesthetic sense has at times tended to make French art—music between 1900–10 and painting rather later—an unduly professional affair. The more highly wrought, elliptical and exquisite an art becomes, the narrower its appeal. There are signs of excessive inbreeding here and there in Debussy's music—in *Le Martyre de Saint Sébastien*, for example, as in Ravel's songs. And it was one side of this over-professionalism that d'Indy and the Schola Cantorum existed to combat, the too thorough divorce of music from the rest of the human personality and that isolation of the aesthetic sense which always ends in sterility.

VII

'WHY are we so attached to the Schola?' asked Michel d'Argoeuves in an essay included in the anniversary volume published in 1925. 'Because we see in it an idea, we find in it a fructifying thought, an aesthetic necessary to the future of the art of music, a safeguard against the eccentricity and exaggeration which have spoilt so many generous natures.' The moral appeal was strong, the appeal to a strenuous, almost Puritanical idealism with a strong intellectual bias, which are features of the French as opposed to the Parisian character, features which are often overlooked by foreigners and intellectuals, who tend to identify Paris with France.

It would be an exaggeration to describe the Schola Cantorum as provincial, in our modern supercilious sense; but it had from the beginning a strong vein of regionalism and some of its most distinguished members—d'Indy himself, Charles Bordes and Déodat de Séverac—chose to give to much of their music a regional character. In d'Indy's pigeon-holed mind extremes were nicely balanced: the universalism of the fervent Catholic and musical traditionalist was offset by the local fervour of the amateur of folk-songs, just as the country gentleman was offset by the horn-player and consciously professional musician. There was nothing amateur about the composers of the Schola in the sense of their being ill-trained; but the most distinguished were late starters, with an idealistic passion for music as an art of expression and they were only secondarily craftsmen or 'career' musicians. Albert Roussel was nearing forty before he gave up the Navy in favour of music. Albéric Magnard, a pupil of d'Indy rather than of the Schola itself, was in violent revolt against the world of his father, editor of *Le Figaro*, and against what he regarded as its musical equivalent at the Conservatoire. His reaction made him something of a musical Puritan, detesting and suspecting grace, charm and suavity as so many genteel disguises for stupidity and self-interest. Déodat de Séverac, the most conscious regionalist composer of the Schola, was in love with his own countryside of Provence and Roussillon, with its life and its people, their qualities moral as well

Seated, left to right: Roussel, Bréville, d'Indy, Poujeaud, Labey.
Standing, left to right: Sérieyx, Castérac, Coindreau, Alquier, Estienne

as aesthetic; and to find an expression for this emotion, half moral as well as half aesthetic, he deserted the Conservatoire for the Schola.

In fact idealism of one kind or another was the hall-mark of all the Schola products, and the disinterested musical missionary work of d'Indy and, above all, of Bordes spread their ideas and ideals all over France and in a remarkably short time from Rumania to Chile. The anniversary volume of 1925 records the work of the Schola at Lyons, Montpellier, Saint Jean de Luz, Nantes, Avignon, Marseilles, Pau, Caen, Le Havre, Nancy, Reims, Besançon, Arles, Privas, Valence, Moulins, Auxerre, Fontainebleau, Orléans, Bordeaux, Brest, Rennes, Cherbourg, Rouen and a host of smaller towns. There was a considerable South American contingent among the pupils in the first decade of the present century and an influx of Rumanians. Most of these returned to their native countries as professors of various branches of music and thus spread the influence of the Schola far beyond France. Spanish composers were intimately connected with the Schola, either as students or teachers—Albéniz teaching the piano there from 1898–1901 and Nin from 1905–8, and Turina studying composition with d'Indy. Musicology was taught at different times by Pierre Aubry, Michel Brenet, André Pirro and Maurice Emmanuel. In fact it was a gifted as well as an idealistic staff, united and strongly impressed with the personality of d'Indy himself.

The tree must be judged by its fruits. The rediscovery and performance of pre-classical music, the intelligent study of plain-song and the collection and musical valuation of folk-music made the Schola Cantorum a magnificent educational machine; its fruits are to be seen all over France to-day. Composition, on the other hand, cannot really be taught. D'Indy himself, in the first chapter of his *Cours de Composition* admits this.

'No artistic education, however excellent and complete, can bestow genius where it does not exist; but it can bring talent to birth and it must shape taste. Our object here is to provide favourable conditions for genius to bud, by developing talent and taste in the reasoned and critical study of musical masterpieces.'

What can be taught, and what the Schola was accused by its enemies of teaching, are trade tricks. When Déodat de Séverac had finished his studies at the Schola in 1907 he submitted a final thesis, which he called 'Centralization and Musical Cliques' (or in French, to make the point of the following extract clear, *'La Centralisation et les petites chapelles en musique'*). Music, he says, is a temple.

'Let us go in. The ceremony has just started. The faithful are on their knees before the sanctuary where the statue of Pure Disinterested Art is enthroned. All adore this god and hold communion with him. But suddenly in each transept priests' voices can be heard and at once the faithful divide into two groups and crowd into the two side chapels.

'In the right-hand chapel the preacher is a sort of medieval monk: his sermon is well constructed, both firm and gentle. He preaches the great classical tradition and the need for a "severe discipline" in the writing of music. He says that Art can and must progress unceasingly, without moving outside the path traced by the great masters. Some of his young partisans and his detractors seem to me to understand him rather badly for, no sooner has he ceased to speak, than his partisans try to place upon the altar the statue of a strange muse, Horizontal Music. On the base of the statue these words are engraved in Gothic letters: *Unum solum, necessarium contrapunctum*. His detractors understand him no better but think him to be a sectarian reactionary, ready to employ every form of the Inquisition against "innovators".

'Neither party seems to have understood the grandeur and the liberal character of his teaching. They have been struck by the letter rather than the spirit and have interpreted it rather narrowly. They have taken the classical tradition to be equivalent to a few contrapuntal processes, combinations of themes submitted to laws of tonality which are determined and unchangeable. The master has shown them the architectural beauty of classical works and their logical structure, and they have taken classicism to reside entirely in "form" and even a certain definite form which is never to be touched.

'The priest officiating in the left-hand chapel speaks with elegance and charm. His is an informal conversation rather than a dissertation. He displays an Attic wit and the grace of a courtier. His message is "the love of music for music's sake" and the pathos of his delivery is sometimes sublime but always charming and fascinating. His young partisans and his detractors seem to understand him, too, rather badly. The former raise on the altar the statue of a Muse no less strange than that of the opposite chapel, Vertical Music. On the base there gleam, in modern lettering, the words: *Nihil nisi Harmonia prodest*. His detractors go away irritated and proclaim everywhere that he wishes to burn at the stake all the prophets of music and that he is preparing generations of anarchists to carry out his designs.'

Séverac made no claim to being a writer, but his allegory shows the state of music as it appeared to a loyal, but by no means a blind, pupil of the Schola. D'Indy preaches in the right-hand chapel and Debussy in the left, and Séverac stood between the two, aware of the good and bad points of both.

The qualities that strike the listener in the music of those who bear the hall-mark of the Schola training are solidity and seriousness. The four-square structure and the rich, thick texture spoke of Wagner to contemporaries used to Debussy's fugitive rhythms and pointillistic use of colour; and Wagner and Franck were for d'Indy the culmination in modern times of the great European classical tradition. Franck's ardent faith lived on, somewhat attenuated, in the chorales and the symphonic apotheoses of the Good, which became something like a commonplace of the Schola style. The famous cyclic form and the principle of theme-transformation, which were used by Berlioz and Liszt before Franck, were adopted by d'Indy himself, whose intelligence and technical efficiency were stronger than his lyrical gift, as devices admirably suited to his own particular musical temperament. His naturally dogmatic spirit raised these humble processes to fundamental artistic principles, whose confirmation he sought far and wide in the whole field of music. Many of d'Indy's supporters have claimed that this spirit of dogmatism was entirely absent from his teaching; but if this is really so, it is difficult to explain the dogmatic tone of the *Cours de composition* and, still more, the marked family likeness of so much of the music written by his pupils. His teaching, in the words of Michel d'Argoeuves,

'could not fail to give his pupils a high artistic ideal. It issued not only in a complete knowledge of music but a formation in all the domains of thought, a formation of taste and judgement and also an unquestionable elevation of feelings and ideas.'

We may perhaps find a parallel to d'Indy as a teacher in Arnold Schönberg, another primarily intellectual musician capable of inspiring passionate loyalty in his pupils, with a similar tendency to elevate means into ends and to impress his own strong personality on the music of even his most original students. Alban Berg took as long to develop his own musical character apart from Schönberg as Roussel took to grow out of the manner and outlook of d'Indy and the Schola—a good ten years or more in each case.

D'Indy's own music, after *L'Étranger* in 1901, appeared less

frequently. Like Fauré after 1906, he was taken up with the administrative cares of a flourishing institution and, well fitted
though he was to the work, he had less time for composition. Two
chamber works and three full-size pieces for orchestra were
d'Indy's only works of importance between *L'Étranger* and his last
opera, *La Légende de Saint Christophe*, on which he worked from
1908–15. The violin sonata (1904) is a predominantly lyrical,
meditative work, in which the only brilliant passages for the violin
occur in the last movement. Inevitably the shadow of Franck's
violin sonata hovers over the work. The opening 9/8, with
its gentle swaying motion, has many parallels in other French
music, but the resemblance to the opening of the Franck sonata
is immediate and overwhelming. The second movement contains
a passage in 7/4 time of a folk-like character and the slow
movement which follows it, though short, reintroduces material
from the first movement. This binding or identifying of separate
movements, which was to become an obsession with Schönberg
and his pupils, is something more fundamental to d'Indy than
'cyclic form' was to Franck. The cyclic principle, according to
d'Indy, 'subordinates the structure to certain themes, which reappear in various forms in each movement, acting as regulators
and making for unity'. What to Franck was half a convenience and
half a poetic fancy has become a basic principle of composition. In
the piano sonata (1907) the first movement consists of an introduction, theme and variations and so, virtually, does the last. There
is only a short movement dividing the two and, given d'Indy's
piano style based on the monumental Lisztian manner of the
fugue in Franck's *Prelude, chorale and fugue*, the effect is heavy and
indigestible. The piano sonata, admittedly one of his weaker
works, looks very much like d'Indy's reply to Dukas's sonata.
Both works are written in a similar style, though Dukas had a
better understanding of the piano; and in both there are obvious
echoes of the late keyboard style of Beethoven, in the pedal trills
and the figuration, for example, and the use of the extreme
registers of the instrument.

Two of the three orchestral works of this period of d'Indy's life
are among the best music that he ever wrote, the second symphony
(written 1902–3 and performed in 1904) and the *Jour d'été à la
Montagne* (1905). *Souvenirs*, which followed in 1906, is a weaker
work but very characteristic of d'Indy for good and for evil. The
symphony, which is dedicated to Dukas, is one of d'Indy's most

solid and logically constructed works. One of the two motto
themes of the work consists of the four notes, B flat, D flat, C, E:

Ex. 44

These thirds not only reappear in every movement, but form the
base of much of the melodic material. The orchestration is heavier
than anything that d'Indy had written since *Le Chant de la Cloche*
fifteen years earlier. There are still strong reminiscences of Wagner, of *Götterdämmerung* in the development of the first movement
and of *Parsifal* in the slow movement, where the wide intervals and
enharmonic modulations of the main theme are based on the
second of the two 'cell' themes which had supplied the second
subject of the first movement. In the second movement there is a
middle section, in a dotted march rhythm and orchestrated largely
for harp and woodwind, which lightens the atmosphere; and the
folk-like material of the third movement, though treated rather
portentously, provides further variety. The fourth movement
opens with a lengthy introduction, in which themes from the other
movements are passed in review as in Beethoven's ninth symphony. The fugue which forms the main body of the movement
culminates in the usual chorale, the victorious affirmation of positive faith, whose struggles with negation provide the programme of
every large-scale work issuing from Franck's circle. D'Indy's
grasp and organization of his material is nowhere more impressive
than in this symphony. Romain Rolland was right when he said
that 'd'Indy hardly eliminates anything: he organizes.' Some of
his material might well have been eliminated by a composer more
fertile in lyrical inspiration, who could afford to pick and choose
among his ideas. D'Indy, like all cultivators of a poor soil, relies
on skilled and unremitting labour and achieves results that many
composers, naturally more gifted than he, might well envy.

In his *Jour d'été à la Montagne* he treats the kind of subject that
lent itself to what is loosely called the 'impressionist' technique of
Debussy. In fact d'Indy in this work does for the mountains what

Debussy in *La Mer* did for the sea, and in precisely the same year (1905). There the resemblance ends. For whereas there is no human figure in *La Mer*, d'Indy's mountains are the backcloth for the composer's very human meditations and aspirations. The sun rises to light the countryman to his work, it sets that he may rest, and he rests, after reciting his evening prayer, to regain strength for another day's labour. Debussy's enthralled contemplation of the play of light and shadow, the patterns of the waves, the rhythm of the swell and the shifting activity of the winds is replaced by d'Indy's delighted following of the patterns and rhythms of a human existence lived in profound harmony with the changing phases of day and night. D'Indy, intellectual and anthropocentric, is in a direct line with Milton. Debussy's pure sensibility is nearer that of the pantheist mystics and represents a mode of feeling which was still comparatively new in music, though it was to find a very English expression in some of Vaughan Williams's music, noticeably in the Pastoral Symphony.

D'Indy drew the programme for his work from Roger de Pampelonne's *Les Heures de la Montagne*, a work in which there are belated echoes of the voice of Victor Hugo. 'La Vie et la Mort se tiennent par la main pour crier vers le ciel: Providence et Bonté!' 'O Nuit! la vie dévorante s'agite sous le jour dévorant: elle se créé sous le manteau perlé de tes bras étendus. . . .' These poetic commonplaces give no idea of the quality of d'Indy's music. The three movements are Dawn, Day (Afternoon beneath the pine trees) and Evening. In the first the motionless silence before the dawn is gradually broken by the twittering of birds and the sun rises to a B major trumpet theme, which eventually floods the whole orchestra. The second movement has a meditative and lyrical opening, with the strings divided (they were in sixteen parts before sunrise and are still in eight) and muted. The composer's thoughts are interrupted by two folk-songs, which mount to him from the valley and get the upper hand of the movement, though the meditative mood returns at the end. This conflation of slow movement and scherzo is modelled on the middle movement in Franck's symphony. The last movement opens *animé et joyeux*, again in B major; but an antiphon of Our Lady, intoned by the horn and taken up by the orchestra, brings the merrymaking to a close and after the evening prayer the mists and silence return to the mountain. The widely spaced and almost motionless chords of the opening reappear and the work ends with the hoot of an owl, a neat parallel with the bird songs which hailed the sunrise in the first movement. *Jour d'été à la Montagne*, perhaps d'Indy's most successful work, is almost the last of the Lisztian tone-poems by a French composer and is instinct with a poetic feeling which marks the *Symphonie cévenole* alone among the rest of his music.

La Légende de Saint Christophe, the opera which occupied d'Indy from 1908–15, was not performed until 1920. The libretto, written as usual by the composer, is full of polemics. When Christopher before his conversion serves Evil, he witnesses a procession of his master's servants, which includes Freethinkers, Scientists and False Artists. The Freethinkers carry Masonic emblems, and the Scientists sing a hymn to 'sinus, cosinus, volt, ampère, RADIUM'. But the False Artists are the most revealing. Their refrain is *haine à l'art idéal* and their creed is fashion. 'Nous faisons la mode et la suivons. . . . Plus de règles, plus d'études, faisons petit . . . faisons original.' The music is a parody, fairly nondescript, of 'modern' cacophony, but it would not be difficult to understand it—especially in conjunction with 'faisons petit'—as a hit at Ravel. Christopher's first employer is the Queen of Pleasure, and the scenes in her court are a kind of Venusberg orgy, culminating in what is called in the score 'Frénésie de Jouissances', during which couples lie on beds and vocalise 'Ha, ha, ha.' The descriptive symphony in Act II. *La Queste de Dieu*, and the conversion of the Queen into Nicea both suggest Massenet's *Thaïs*; and Camille Erlanger's *Julien l'Hospitalier* (1896) provides obvious parallels with d'Indy's story and some in treatment. The framing of the story in a deliberately archaic way, with a Narrator and a *cappella* chorus, which occasionally comments on the action like the *turba* in the Passion, further complicates the style. In fact *La Légende de Saint Christophe* is an operatic compendium and a key to d'Indy's ideals and pet aversions rather than a unified work of art.

The strength of the *Jour d'été à la Montagne* lay precisely in its spontaneous origin, in d'Indy's strong feeling for 'his own part of the world'. In the case of one of his most attractive pupils, Déodat de Séverac, this regionalist interest was again of the first importance. Séverac, as we have seen, was not whole-hearted in his adherence to the Schola; at least he was not exclusive, but saw the beauties and possibilities of other forms of music. He had gone to the Conservatoire in 1896, at the age of twenty-three, but moved almost immediately to the Schola, where he was a pupil of d'Indy and, for a short time, of Magnard. All his music bears the imprint of the south, his native Languedoc and the half-Spanish Roussillon where he finally settled. Most of what has been preserved (and Séverac either lost or never committed to paper many of his ideas) is in the form of piano suites—*Le Chant de la Terre, En Languedoc* and *Cerdaña* between 1900–10 and *Sous les Lauriers-Roses* just before his death, in 1919. Albéniz, a personal friend, and Chabrier were the strongest influences on Séverac's piano style; but the plainsong melody in *Le Chant de la Terre* and the introduction of the *O Crux ave, spes unica* in what is probably his best single piece (*Les Muletiers devant le Christ de Llivia*, added to *Cerdaña*) show the influence of the Schola. *Par le Mas en fête* and *Le Jour de la foire au mas*, from *En Languedoc*, both have touches of Debussy, but Séverac remains an 'emotive' composer even when he borrows the technique of impressionism. 'Music is useless if it cannot raise us above mere sounds,' he wrote. 'It is merely a game, physical for some and intellectual for others, but a simple game.' Side by side with this fundamentally ethical attitude he had, like Chabrier, something of the sensibility which was to become the fashion in Paris when he was long settled in Roussillon and already a dying man—the feeling for mechanical pianos, wheezing harmoniums, and the whole musical paraphernalia of the cheap provincial café. But whereas Debussy or Satie felt the attraction of a street organ as a kind of rare, supersophisticated sensation, Séverac loved such things for their human associations. In this he resembled Chabrier, and when these two lovers of the things of earth found themselves in accord with the exquisites, one can be sure that their reasons were very different.

Le Cœur du moulin, Séverac's one opera, suffered from a poor libretto in which the mingling of realism and symbolism—in the manner of Bruneau's *Messidor*—was unsuccessful. The folk-songs and dances are admirable but the dramatic element, the building of the story and the characterization, is weak. His only other stage work, *Héliogabale*, was written for the outdoor theatre at Béziers, like Fauré's *Promethée*. He introduced various Catalan instruments into his orchestra on this occasion, apparently with great success, and Fauré himself is said to have been very favourably impressed by a concert performance of the music in Paris.

Séverac's music had always something of the amateur about it. A certain clumsiness, the expression of the naïveté which is one of his charms, gives even his best pieces a personal air which is lacking in some of the more accomplished of d'Indy's pupils. He himself recognized the presence of 'useless dilution' (*un délayage inutile*) in all his music; certainly a fault but not wholly unloveable, rooted as it is in Séverac's meridional volubility. It is the complete antithesis of that professorial quality which distinguishes the music of composers who have spent too much of their time teaching the justly-called 'academic processes' of music. Guy Ropartz, for example, started with very much the same regionalist inspiration as Séverac, only he was a Breton instead of a Provençal. Born in 1864, he studied first with Massenet at the Conservatoire and then with Franck; but at the age of thirty he was appointed director of the Nancy Conservatoire and he has spent the best years of his life there and at the Strasbourg Conservatoire, to which he moved in 1919. Ropartz has cultivated almost every musical genre— chamber and piano music, operas large and small, incidental music for the stage, songs, church works and, with most success, symphonies (four written between 1895–1910). Some of his work is based on Breton folk-song, which he uses effectively in an orchestral genre-picture such as *La Cloche des Morts*. A work such as his fourth symphony is an excellent routine composition by a composer traditional by instinct and training, still inspired by Franck, but developing a distinct and fairly personal dialect of the Franckist idiom away from the rapidly shifting fashions and the new ideas of Paris.

Albéric Magnard was not, strictly speaking, a pupil of the Schola Cantorum, but a private pupil of d'Indy's from 1888–92. He was twenty-one in 1886 when he went to Bayreuth, whence he returned to study music at the Conservatoire. But he found Dubois and Massenet hopelessly out of sympathy with the ruthlessness and idealism which were his form of reaction against the superficiality, the luxury and the atmosphere of facile success in which, as the son of a newspaper magnate, he had been brought up. Magnard spent much of his short life escaping or living down the fact of being his father's son. When he began to compose he was suspicious of the ease with which his works were sometimes accepted for performance, and he was only willing to make use of his position in the cause of other men's music. In 1892 it was he who popularized, by his articles in *Le Figaro*, the early performances of Les Chanteurs de Saint Gervais; but for himself he expected no favoured treatment and the fear of it exaggerated the brusquerie of his manner and his deliberate suggestion of misanthropy.

Magnard was more than a musician. He possessed an all-round

cultivation, he was well-read and had a strong feeling for painting, a veritable passion for light which finds expression in the wide spans, clear vistas and spaced orchestration of his best music. He was a fertile composer, beginning a symphony within a year of going to d'Indy and writing three in the next seven years. It was typical of him to start with a big, serious work; and, apart from the *Promenades* for piano in 1893 and the wind quintet of 1895, he confined himself to orchestral writing and opera (his *Yolande* was given at Brussels in 1893—almost certainly a favour done to his father). The first two symphonies are apprentice's work. Both they, the *Chant funèbre* (1895) and *Hymne à la Justice* (1904) are solid, serious works in the Franck-d'Indy tradition, more severe and less charming than Chausson, clumsier and more halting than d'Indy himself. The wind quintet has more personality and, in spite of thick and awkward passages, the clarinet solo at the beginning of the second movement and the oboe (*nasillard et traînant*) in the third have a colour and character unusual even in Magnard's best music. In the *Promenades*, written in 1893 but not published until 1895, there are interesting foreshadowings of the particular sensibility and even the keyboard technique of the mature Debussy, although the general idiom is nearer that of Chabrier. A suite of piano pieces each based on a different place and all chosen among the favourite objects of Parisian excursions—Versailles, Rambouillet or Villebon—was a novel idea in itself. *Villebon* is based on an ostinato octave figure suggesting bells, and its effects of distance (*dans le lointain*) and contrasting of sonorities make it something like an ancestor of *La cathédrale engloutie*. At the end of *Rambouillet*, which is marked *nuptial* in the Satie manner, Magnard introduces the *sonnerie militaire* which Debussy was to use effectively five years later in *Fêtes*. The *Promenades* stand alone in Magnard's production, a solitary example of the lighter vein and more concrete poetic imagery which he normally eschewed.

He was not concerned with either poetic expression or instrumental colour. Massenet, in the short time that Magnard worked with him, saw that he was a natural contrapuntist. At the height of an era described by Casella as that of 'the harmonic nightmare' Magnard's harmony is comparatively simple and his orchestration deliberately plain and unsubtle. He was a true Franckist in his emotional approach to music but he was original when he wrote that 'art must not be confused with the feelings and thoughts which have given it birth'. Accepting the principle of dramatic content and structure in his symphonies, Magnard nevertheless refused to allow considerations of purely musical structure to be overruled; and this led him into many difficulties which he never wholly solved. He was aware of it and his exasperation found expression in his bitter: 'La musique n'est vraiment belle qu'en nous.' Nevertheless, Magnard came near to finding exterior expression for his *chant intérieur* in a handful of works, in the third and fourth symphonies, a 'cello sonata, and in the opera *Bérénice*.

The third symphony was written in 1895–6 and the fourth between 1911–13. The years between were filled with the composition of another opera, *Guercoeur*, finished in 1900 but lost at the time of the composer's death and only later reconstituted from drafts; with four chamber works—a violin sonata, a string quartet, a trio and a violoncello sonata; and with *Bérénice*, given at the Opéra-Comique in 1911. In 1914 Magnard was killed defending his property at Baron against the invading Germans, a death which earned him more widespread fame than he had ever earned by his music.

Sincerity and concentration are the chief characteristics of both the symphonies. The texture is close, subsidiary incidents are reduced to a minimum and subtle rhythmic effects, which were allowed even by d'Indy and the Schola, are rarely used. When Magnard wishes to break the main six-eight rhythm of the second movement of the third symphony, he does for a short time write in quintuple time; but he writes out his alternate bars of two and three rather than yield an inch to the exotic. The first and third movements of the fourth symphony have themes involving chromatic alteration, but Magnard's harmony is generally sober, conservative even when compared with d'Indy's. His sense of tonality is strong and his contrapuntal gifts appear in the fugues which are scattered throughout his music—in the last movements of the violin sonata, the trio and the fourth symphony, and the first movement of the violoncello sonata. Two of the movements of the third symphony are comparatively light-hearted as their titles, *Danses* and *Pastorales*, suggest; but generally Magnard does not make even so much concession to his listeners. The violin sonata, which was played by Ysaÿe, is a heavy, rhetorical work with much thick writing, such as also mars the piano part of the trio. But the trio has the technical interest of containing variations on a theme which only appears at the end, obviously modelled on d'Indy's *Istar*. Although Magnard sometimes gives the impression of being choked by his own erudition, the weight and power of his music are striking. He may contort his melodies by chromatic alteration and cloud his scores with contrapuntal invention, sometimes introduced for its own sake; but the breadth of design and the sincerity of his music are impressive. There are still traces in the third symphony of d'Indy's transformation of themes, cyclic forms and glowing chorales in the brass, but Magnard was too individual to remain long under the influence of any teacher, even d'Indy.

In *Bérénice* he found a subject after his own heart, classical in its simplicity and theme but intensely emotional and suggesting that discipline of romantic feeling by classical form that was Magnard's ideal. Devising his own libretto, he deliberately confused the Jewish with the Egyptian Berenice, making the mistress of Titus dedicate a lock of her hair to Venus in the last act. In his preface Magnard wrote:

'My score is written in the Wagnerian style. Not having myself the genius necessary in order to create a new lyric form I have chosen among the styles already in existence that which is most in accord with my classical tastes and my wholly traditional culture.'

This conception of Wagner as a classic, and of his music as the culmination of the classical tradition, is in the true spirit of d'Indy and the Schola and has since been acknowledged as the truth, though when first stated it had all the appearance of a brilliant paradox. Magnard's conflation of two classical stories makes a wonderful operatic subject and his actual arrangement of his material is excellent. The drama is largely psychological and, without either action or powerful melodic gift, it could not achieve more than a *succès d'estime* when it was performed in 1911–12. But Magnard's music is often worthy of the grandeur and simplicity of his situations and he made some interesting experiments in the use of abstract musical forms in opera. Thus much of the love music between Titus and Berenice takes the form of a canon at the octave and Titus's bitter meditation in Act II is cast as a fugue; so that *Bérénice* in this respect stands as a kind of middle point between the more vaguely 'symphonic' style of the Wagnerian music-drama and the deliberate use of abstract musical forms in *Wozzeck*. The passion and sincerity of the music are unquestionable; but Magnard found it difficult to discover any middle term between the very full writing, marked by a tortured chromaticism springing ultimately from *Parsifal*, and the deliberately simple, diatonic style, which sounds weak and banal to modern ears.

Four years older than Magnard and very different from him in character, Pierre de Bréville had a greater natural gift for the stage and his *Éros Vainqueur*, produced the year before *Bérénice*, combines the solid workmanship of the Franck tradition with the variety and lyrical grace of the traditional French opera. If the three princesses suggest the imprisoned wives of Dukas's *Ariane et Barbe-Bleue*, the death of Argine in Act III surrounded by the kneeling women is plainly borrowed from *Pelléas*. In a work dedicated to d'Indy it is more surprising to find Eros himself adopting something very like the idiom of Massenet.

Bréville's best and most original work lies in his songs, the earliest of which date from 1883. Here the influence of both Fauré and Massenet is plain (Bréville studied at the Conservatoire before he went to Franck) but his early songs are remarkable for their delicate, precise workmanship and their rhythmic originality. The *Petites Litanies de Jésus* (1896), written for his children, have a simplicity quite unlike Gounod's maudlin piety, and the *Chanson d'Hamsavati* showed that Bréville could use the oriental convention with originality. From 1898–1902 he taught counterpoint at the Schola Cantorum and his easy manipulation of scholastic devices is shown in some of his later songs—the 1912 setting of Henri de Régnier's *Le Secret*, for example (Ex. 45).

Ex. 45

Another song of the same year, van Lerberghe's *Sous les arches des roses* shows how far Bréville could move beyond the normal horizon of the Schola Cantorum (Ex. 46).

Ex. 46

Without possessing a great musical personality he, like Dukas and Schmitt, though on a smaller scale, has made a distinctly individual contribution to French music.

By acknowledging his limitations and working within them, concentrating on fine workmanship, delicate colouring and subtle rhythmic elaboration, Bréville is an example—in many ways a typically French example—to lesser composers, for he has shown himself content to cultivate the garden which is by rights his. His chamber music, without quite the same distinction as his songs, is unfailingly lively and well written; the instruments, the players and the audience are all considered. This is the central artistic tradition of France, from which Berlioz on the one side and Massenet on the other are equally deviations. France has not been a favourable soil for the breeding of earth-shaking master-pieces; Beethoven and Tolstoy, who dwarf the ordinary citizen, are profoundly un-French figures. France has had her giants, but the peculiar glory of French art has been the finding of perfect expression for the ordinary human passions. Chardin's painting, La Fontaine's poetry and Fauré's music all belong to this central, unspectacular, intensely human stream; and so, in its more humble way, does the music of Pierre de Bréville, which has a hundred counterparts in the arts of painting and literature.

A branch of music cultivated strenuously by almost all the composers in any way connected with the Schola Cantorum was the ecclesiastical. In this they were working in the direct Franck tradition, though more in the spirit than in the letter. Franck's own ecclesiastical music was nearer in taste to that of Gounod than to the principles of the *Motu Proprio*, issued in November 1903 by Pope Pius X. This bull, coming just ten years after Charles Bordes's first beginnings with the Chanteurs de Saint Gervais, set the seal of official ecclesiastical approval on the work of the Schola Cantorum in the department of church music. The rediscovery and re-editing of the polyphonic masters was obviously the first step towards that renaissance of liturgical music which was the dream of Pius X; but the bull permitted and even, mildly, encouraged modern composers to turn their attention to liturgical music.

'The Church has always recognized and favoured the progress of art, admitting to a place in its worship all that human genius has discovered of good and beautiful throughout the ages, provided that liturgical laws are observed. Thus more modern music [than that of Palestrina and his contemporaries] is also admitted in the services of the church when it offers a goodness, a seriousness and a gravity which make it not unworthy of the liturgical functions.'

Of the three founders of the Schola Cantorum, Bordes was most concerned, both as creative and executant artist, with liturgical music. D'Indy's output contains a certain proportion of church music, but it occupies a comparatively unimportant place as it does in the output of Fauré and Chausson. The third of the founders, Alexandre Guilmant, was concerned almost exclusively with the organ and may be considered the father of the modern French organ school.

Organists tend to live in a musical world of their own, little affected by the general developments of music in their own age. There are even dynasties of organists, like the Couperins, whose family occupied the organ loft at Saint Gervais from 1655 to 1826. The history of organ music often seems to the outsider too intimately connected with the development of the instrumental mechanism, and to deteriorate in quality as it gains in power and variety of expression. There is no other branch of music, except the liturgical, in which all musicians would admit the inferiority of everything written in the last two hundred years, of organ music written after 1750, to that written before. In fact organ music has, for at least a century, interested nobody but organists. The public may be impressed by the skill and manual (or pedal) dexterity of the modern organist, but the organ, in the words of Saint-Saëns, himself an organist, 'furnishes a harmonious noise rather than precise music'. Nevertheless, within this rather doubtfully musical sphere, the names of Guilmant, Gigout, Widor, Tournemire, Vierne and Dupré have become world-famous, and the distinctive features of the French school—skilled improvisation and great brilliance of effect—are universally recognized even in those circles where they are not valued highly.

Parallel with the activities of the Schola Cantorum, but starting nearly half a century earlier, was the revival of plainchant instituted by the Benedictines of the Abbey of Solesmes. Dom Guéranger (nicknamed Dom Guerroyer by an approving Pope) was the first public figure in this slow and uphill battle, succeeded by Dom Pothier, whose book *Les Mélodies Grégoriennes* was published in 1881. The movement has not been without its own internal dramas and threatened to split into two distinct schools over the question of mensuration. But the work done, first by the Benedictines alone and then by the Schola Cantorum working along the same lines, has borne fruit all over France.

VIII

IN the years immediately preceding the war of 1914–18 there was an unmistakable ferment in the French musical world. The Russian Ballet had given musicians a renewed vision of line, angle and movement, while Picasso, Les Fauves and then the Cubists were revolutionizing the art of painting. The haze of colour and the vague evocative sense of poetry were ceasing to satisfy even those who employed them most skilfully, and Debussy's *Martyre de Saint Sébastien* was followed the next year by a ballet claiming to be a 'plastic apologia of the man of 1913', *Jeux*. In that same year Romain Rolland voiced the feelings of many, particularly the younger musicians, when he wrote that French musical art was 'supreme in the aristocratic qualities but that, with very few exceptions' (and he mentions Florent Schmitt) 'it lacks vigour, red blood'. Even the old Saint-Saëns's attack on the Schola Cantorum (*Les Idées de M. Vincent d'Indy*, 1914) was in a sense a protest of the same kind. Against the emotional criterion of art he championed that of form and claimed that any artist worthy the name should be satisfied by elegant lines, harmonious colours and a fine succession of chords (*une belle série d'accords*). The friendship formed by the leading French composers—Debussy, Ravel and Schmitt— with the young Stravinsky led to an interchange of ideas which was fruitful for both French and Russian music. *Petrushka* in 1911 and *Le Sacre du Printemps* two years later provided object-lessons in an altogether more vigorous and virile conception of music. Stravinsky appeared in fact very much as Gluck had done nearly one hundred and fifty years earlier, the 'peasant from the Danube' startling an over-civilized artistic court with his barbarian violence, directness and power. The barbarian, like Gluck before him, proved a remarkably apt pupil, soon capable of giving his masters a lesson in their own arts of sophistication. Thus it was while working with Stravinsky in Switzerland that Ravel became ac-

quainted with Schönberg's *Pierrot Lunaire* and his settings of
Mallarmé were suggested by Stravinsky's Japanese Lyrics.

In the official world Fauré's acceptance in 1910 of the presi-
dency of a new musical society, the Société Musicale Indépendante,
pointed to a dissatisfaction even among the older generation with
the Société Nationale, founded in 1871 as a genuinely national
body but by now virtually an appanage of the Schola Cantorum.
At the Schola itself there were significant events, too isolated to
form a conscious movement but enough to show that the new
ideals were beginning to penetrate. Albert Roussel, a professor of
counterpoint at the Schola from 1902–14, had come late to music.
He was born at Tourcoing in the north of France in 1869 and became first a professional sailor, interested in music but not whole-
heartedly until 1894, when he was already twenty-five. In 1898
he was introduced to d'Indy and started composition lessons
with him, giving up his naval career. Roussel was in many ways
a typical Northerner. He developed slowly, he had no profusion or facility of ideas, and his early work—especially the orchestral *Resurrection*, inspired by Tolstoy—was coloured by the
heavy, introspective emotion and the self-conscious earnestness of
the Franckist school. *Resurrection* appeared in 1904, but two years
later Roussel wrote a *Divertissement* which was not only remarkable
in itself but also stood out as something alien to the Schola traditions and prophetic of much that was not to become general in
French music for another ten years or more. The instrumental
combination—flute, oboe, clarinet, bassoon, horn and piano—
was itself unusual in 1906. The absence of the 'singing' strings, the
transparent and unpretentious writing, the cocky rhythms and the
pastoral air of the whole short movement owed as little to Debussy
or Ravel as to the gods of the Schola. The oboe theme, with its
direct simplicity, its unequivocal tonality and its predominant intervals of the fourth foreshadowed a type of music whose very
obviousness was a novelty in such an era of sophistication (Ex. 47).

Ex. 47

Two years later the *Poème de la Forêt*, actually written between 1904–6, showed that Roussel was still under the influence of his master d'Indy but also of Debussy. This large orchestral piece may take its place as the third panel in the great nature triptych painted in those years by three different French composers, the other two panels being Debussy's *La Mer* and d'Indy's *Jour d'été à la Montagne*. Roussel's work has neither the technical mastery nor the strongly individual character of the other two but it combines traits of both with a distinctly personal note especially in the second movement, *Renouveau*, which is one of the first of the composer's spring-pieces—green, sour and gay. In his next large-scale work, *Evocations*, Roussel drew largely on the memories and impressions of a journey to India and Cochin China in 1909. Each of the three movements is devoted to a different scene. In the first (*Les Dieux dans l'ombre des cavernes*) the cave-paintings of Ellora inspire a powerful musical frieze. The harps and string arpeggios suggest the weirdness of the scene, a chorale in the brass and woodwind introduces the gods, who then appear—gods of violence, of joy and of sensual pleasure. The chorale appears again to usher them from the listener's imagination and the movement ends, as it began, with the mysterious atmospheric passage for strings and harps. In the second movement (*La Ville Rose-Jaipur*) Roussel depicts the procession of an Indian rajah at a religious festival and makes use of an authentic Indian hymn. This is the most conventional of the three movements but the suggestion of brilliant light, colour and shimmering heat is most effective. The last movement (*Aux Bords du fleuve sacré*) is a dramatic scena with wordless vocalises for chorus and contralto, tenor and baritone solos, the last representing a fakir on the banks of the Ganges at night. The idiom is wholly impressionistic with divided strings, wood-wind triplets and syncopated horn fifths sounding in the distance. Calvocoressi's text is in the pseudo-oriental manner traditional in France and gives a certain old-fashioned air to the movement. On the whole, however, *Evocations*, successfully avoids the pitfalls of mere traveller's music, the superficial impressions and highly coloured souvenirs that too many composers have brought back from the East.

How deeply Roussel was stirred and how fruitfully his imagination was set in motion by his travels is seen not so much in *Evocations* as in his opera *Padmâvatî*, written between 1914–18 though not produced until 1921. In *Padmâvatî* Roussel revived the eighteenth-century French form of the opera-ballet—a series of dances and spectacles linked together by a sung dramatic text, in which the marvellous generally played a substantial part. The Indian setting, the Brahmin, the palace dancing-girls, the temple scenes and the final *Liebestod* of the heroine link the work not so much with Rameau's *Les Indes Galantes* as with the oriental operas of the nineteenth century—*Les Pêcheurs de Perles*, *Le Roi de Lahore*, *Lakmé* or *Thamara*. But Roussel's music for the dances, choruses and pantomimes stands almost alone in Western music for the authenticity of its orientalism. He makes use of Indian scales, or *ragas*, and his melodies are often ornamented with the *melismas* typical of oriental music; but his music never gives the impression of being a pastiche or imitation of the Indian original. Still less does it recall that of the nineteenth-century French operas, where the oriental element is no more integral than the stage sets. Roussel's secret seems to have been that of all those who aim, in Falla's words, at 'authenticity without literalism' in their treatment of traditional music—an ability to use that tradition for their own purposes, to create a parallel, similar effect to that of authentic folk-music.

The loosening and aeration of Roussel's orchestral idiom dates from *Evocations* and the intensification of the composer's visual awareness during his Indian journey, a turning outwards in contrast to the largely introspective habits of the Schola Cantorum. But the most remarkable characteristic of *Padmâvatî*, and one which was to play an increasing part in Roussel's music, is its rhythmic variety and vitality. This is particularly noticeable in the dances and wordless choruses and it is a direct result of the composer's interest in the ballet. The rhythms no longer follow the slow, subtle, sensual patterns typical of Debussy nor the more obvious, four-square gait of d'Indy. Instead, Roussel combines the nervous, muscular, lightweight agility of the eighteenth-century French ballet movements with the exotic oriental rhythms which the Russian Ballet in general, and Stravinsky in particular, had made popular among French musicians. Between *Evocations* and *Padmâvatî* he had written a short ballet for Rouché, the director of the Théâtre des Arts. This was *Le Festin de l'Araignée*, with a scenario not unlike Capek's *Insect Play*. Fabre and Maeterlinck had popularized entomology among writers and Gilbert de Voisins' scenario provided Roussel with opportunities for dramatic as well as decorative music. *Le Festin de l'Araignée* has proved Roussel's most popular work, perhaps because it is in the light, delicate,

pictorial manner, highly articulated and transparently orchestrated, which the average listener has come to expect from a
French composer. Roussel proved in many subsequent works that
he was anything but a La Fontaine by temperament, but the
popularity of the *Festin* has outweighed that of many more typical
works.

Padmâvatî stands out not only by its intrinsic merit but also by
the mere fact of being an opera, the only French opera of lasting
merit written in the decade following Ravel's *L'Heure espagnole* in
1911. In the older composers the new spirit found expression
either in ballet or in a return to chamber music—Debussy's *Jeux*,
Ravel's *Daphnis et Chloé*; ballet versions of *Ma Mère l'Oye* and
Valses nobles et sentimentales; Schmitt's suite for piano duet (later
converted into a ballet) *Une semaine du petit elfe Ferme l'Oeil*; Roussel's own *Festin de l'Araignée*; and Debussy's piano studies and sonatas. After 1910 operas and large orchestral works were out of
fashion, even at the Schola Cantorum, and the cry of the False
Artists in d'Indy's *Légende de Saint Christophe*—'Faisons petit!'—
reflects d'Indy's disgust with a tendency which he deplored but
could not arrest, even among his own flock. Much later, in his
R. Wagner et son influence sur l'art musical français (1930) he spoke of
the thirty years between 1885–1915 as the era of the Wagnerian
ascent (*essor Wagnérien*) and of the period which followed as a 'return
to the depths from which Wagner rescued us', one of the inevitable
valleys in musical history, which he conceived as a noble mountain
chain divided by repellent gulleys.

To a less prejudiced mind than d'Indy's there was plenty in the
gulley, if gulley it was, to charm the ear and engage the intelligence. The three poems by Mallarmé, set by both Ravel and
Debussy in 1913, show the directions in which both composers
were moving. Ravel, inspired by Schönberg's *Pierrot Lunaire*,
wrote for piccolo, flute, clarinet, bass clarinet and string quartet,
and created a subtle and ingenious instrumental web of sound,
against which the voice declaims Mallarmé's cryptic poems, which
themselves aspire to a musical ideal and are for that reason ill-
suited to musical setting. He follows the text with his usual scru-
pulous care, adjusting Schönberg's *Sprechgesang* to the French
language and to the demands of his own personal style. Debussy,
using only the piano, writes a flowing and—at least in the traditional sense—more musical vocal line, moving in the direction of
a greater simplicity just as Ravel aims at the maximum of compli-

cation and sophistication. In 1913 Debussy had only five more years to live and he was already attacked by the cancer which was to cause his death in 1918. In those five years he wrote twelve piano studies and three sonatas for different instrumental combinations, which reveal his ability to renovate his own idiom. The impressionist manner is superseded and in its place a more purely musical, less visually suggestive, style is employed to express either the frustration and melancholy inseparable from a mortal illness or the composer's persistent delight in the simple manipulation of sound-patterns and rhythmic figures. No composer was ever more physically conditioned than Debussy and the sensuous delight in nature, which was the fundamental inspiration of much of his best work after *Pelléas*, here turns not to bitterness but to nostalgia and sardonic humour, the cultivated pagan's natural attitude in the face of pain and approaching death. The violoncello sonata, the first of the three, is predominantly ironical and in the Serenade Debussy assumes the protective masque of Pierrot, a Pierrot 'annoyed with the moon'. This is the ironical Petrushka-Pierrot of Max Jacob's aphorism, the antithesis of the exhibitionist Harlequin whose soul-states are displayed for the public delectation in so much Romantic art. In the sonata for flute, viola and harp, Debussy bade farewell to the hieratic dance, the slow and archaic three-four movement which he had inherited from Satie. The instrumental combination lends itself to exquisite, tenuous and nostalgic effects and the composer himself described the work as 'terribly melancholy—should one laugh or cry? Perhaps both at the same time'.

Ex. 48

Not even in the *Prélude à l'après-midi d'un faune* did Debussy write more beautifully for the flute than in this sonata, especially in the tender, fluttering passages for the lower register, which occur in the opening Pastorale. The last of the three sonatas, for violin and piano, was written between December 1915 and March 1917 under conditions that might have daunted even more detached composers than Debussy—an unsuccessful operation, morphia injections and radium treatment against a background of incessant financial worries and the overwhelming anxiety of the war. Debussy described it as 'the simple play of an idea turning on itself, like a snake biting its own tail', and there is a certain breathlessness, an inability to rise to the old flights as of a mortally wounded bird, which has a beauty and pathos of its own. Léon Vallas has spoken of the music's 'ardent impotence' and this phrase justly describes the pathetic contrast present in the music.

All three sonatas bear the famous signature 'Claude Debussy, *musicien français*', the outward and visible claim to a quality of mind and imagination of which Debussy grew more than ever proud at a time when he saw France and all things French threatened by Germany. Heaven knows, it was not necessary for Debussy to insist on his Frenchness; but this was a gesture, the sort of gesture to please a slowly dying man and make him feel that he was doing something to affirm the national spirit and strike a blow at his country's enemies. It is possible, as Vallas suggests, that the return to the classical form of the sonata—even in Debussy's wholly unclassical spirit—was another gesture of the same kind, a deliberate choosing of the most formal and chastened of patterns in defiance of the sprawling and megalomaniac music of some contemporary German composers.

In the piano studies, dated 1915 and dedicated to the memory of Chopin, Debussy produced his last work for the instrument whose technique he had so thoroughly revolutionized. Many of his orchestral effects are at bottom pianistic, in his songs the piano part is often more important musically than the voice; and in these studies he gives pianists a series of studies in some of the fundamentals of the new technique which he had devised for their instrument. Not all are of equal value, either musically or technically. In Book I *Pour les quartes*, *Pour les octaves* and *Pour les huit doigts* are both more interesting musically and more relevant technically than *Pour les tierces* and *Pour les sixtes*. In Book II *Pour les sonorités opposées* is fundamental to the Debussy technique, while *Pour les notes repétées* and the beautiful *Pour les arpèges composés* are piano pieces in their own right, in which the technical interest is only secondary. The idiom is in some cases that of the Preludes (*Pour les octaves*, for example, is very reminiscent of *Les Collines d'Anacapri*) but the visual, poetic element is either absent or subordinate to the purely musical. This is a weakness in a composer, like Debussy, who drew so much from sense impressions and poetic evocations. Only occasionally, as in *Les Sixtes*, is the influence of Chopin noticeable, and the desolate nostalgic strain, noticeable particularly here and in *Pour les tierces*, is an echo of Debussy's own stricken condition rather than of the romantic melancholy which haunts Chopin's music.

There was a paradox at the very root of Debussy's genius. Pierre de Bréville could write with truth that 'Debussy does not ask of music all that she can give but that which she *alone* can suggest'; and yet this 'purest' of musicians was more dependent than any other on external stimuli. He was a supreme transliterator from one sense to another, the discoverer of exquisite musical counterparts for the impressions of the other senses—sight, touch and smell—the musician who more than any other artist fulfilled Baudelaire's theory of correspondence between the arts. His last works lack this sensual inspiration or have it only in a diluted form, as of impressions remembered but no longer experienced. The memories are coloured with nostalgia, the temperament through which they are filtered has lost tone and resilience and the music correspondingly lacks immediacy because it lacks sensual impetus. The grisaille at which Debussy said that he sometimes aimed in *Pelléas* was then a discipline, a deliberate renunciation of colour; in the last works it has become a sad necessity. It was to this last phase in Debussy's life that J. E. Blanche referred when he said 'c'était une figure ironique et charnelle, mélancolique et voluptueuse'. But the irony is more noticeable than the carnality and the melancholy lay deeper than the voluptuousness.

Voluptuous scene-painting is the chief characteristic of Ravel's *Daphnis et Chloé*. There are those who find in this ballet-music evidence of Ravel's increased stature as a composer and certainly it is planned on a larger scale than any of his other works. But the composer's own statement, that the Greece he envisaged was that imagined by the French painters of the late eighteenth century, shows that he had nothing epic or heroic in mind and that his concern, as always, was with subtlety rather than boldness of design, with charming colours and evocative rhythms rather than with dramatic emotional expression. Like all good ballet music *Daphnis et Chloé* is primarily decorative and sensuous; and it is a mistake to be misled by the greater physical size of the music into thinking that this betokens any change in the composer's musical character. As decorative scene-painting in music *Daphnis et Chloé* is often supremely successful. The orchestra is used with greater power, it is used to explore a wider range of tonal sensations than in any previous work by Ravel; and in this sense *Daphnis et Chloé* does represent an advance, a widening of horizon even though the landscape is the familiar landscape of all Ravel's music. The excitement of the Danse Générale is always a carefully planned excitement, the conception of a brilliant stage manager rather than a spontaneous overflow of energy. This spirit of calculation which marks all Ravel's music diminishes its stature while assuring its effectiveness. In this respect Ravel is the antithesis of Berlioz. His cool head prevents him from ever falling into banalities or committing extravagances, but it also prevents him from soaring any great distance above the ground. His art is compounded of intelligence and fastidious sensuality and within the scope imposed by this personal limitation he is a supreme artist.

In the trio which followed *Daphnis et Chloé* in 1914 he again worked on an unsuspectedly large scale, especially in the last two movements; and *La Valse*, the 'choreographic poem' of 1920, is equally planned for a large stage. Both works are admirable essays in their different genres. The trio combines some extraordinarily conventional features (was it not 'modelled', according to the composer, on a trio by Saint-Saëns?) with an unusual Passacaglia and a delicate Pantoum with a charming mock-sentimental trio. The last movement is an essay in the grand manner—an essay, not the reality of grandeur but a borrowing of the style—so successful that listeners are often persuaded that the grandeur is real and inherent in the music instead of a stylistic experiment. *La Valse*, which was originally to have been an apotheosis of Vienna, finally appeared as a musical impression of a Second Empire ballroom. The valse rhythms and melodic fragments are set in an orchestral background of billowing plush, velvet and lace: the lighting or throwing into relief of the themes has alternately the crude brilliance and flickering uncertainty of a gas chandelier; and the prodigious skill with which the atmosphere is evoked shows Ravel at his most successful as a musical stage-manager.

The suite of piano pieces entitled *Le Tombeau de Couperin*, composed during the war years, is a return to Ravel's small-scale writing. There are six movements: Prelude, Fugue, Toccata and three archaic dances—Forlane, Rigaudon and Menuet. They vary considerably in technical difficulty and harmonic sophistication. The Fugue and the Menuet are simple in both respects and the Menuet harks back to Ravel's early dance-movements and ultimately to Satie. The Prelude and the Rigaudon are written in a style which adapts the technique of the harpsichord to that of the modern virtuoso and in the final Toccata Ravel approaches the style of his own *Scarbo* in several passages. It is interesting to compare *Le Tombeau de Couperin* with Debussy's *Pour le piano* and especially the two Toccatas, superficially similar but fundamentally so different. Ravel's music is wiry and deliberately thin, except in the Lisztian writing at the end; he makes great play with repeated notes and strings of thirds alternating between the two hands, percussive effects suited to the harpsichord. Debussy's Toccata soon dissolves in warm washes of colour, the melody in the upper part of the left hand accompanied with figuration in the right. In the same way Debussy's Toccata moves between wide dramatic extremes while Ravel preserves a more even mood. The quality that Gide missed in the French novel—'the virile *élan* of adventure and exploration, the salty breeze from the sea and the wide horizons and open spaces'—are wanting in *Le Tombeau de Couperin* as in all Ravel's music. But in return there is unfailing charm and skill, aptness of expression and perfect adaptation of means to ends.

The quality for which Gide looked in vain in the French novel was the quality whose absence from French music was deplored by Romain Rolland in the same year, 1913. But Rolland made an exception, Florent Schmitt; and in Psalm 47, the *Tragédie de Salomé* and the quintet there certainly breathed a larger and more vigorous air. But since 1908 Schmitt had written little more than occasional pieces in the smaller forms. *Une Semaine du petit elfe Ferme l'Oeil*, a suite of seven pieces for piano duet, was written in 1912. The primo part, meant for the composer's small son, consists in each piece of a simple five-note sequence and this deliberate restriction of means coupled with the fairy-story atmosphere suggests an obvious affinity with Ravel's *Ma Mère l'Oye*. In fact the last piece of the suite, *Le Parapluie chinois*, is strongly reminiscent of Ravel's *Laideronette*; and though Schmitt has the wit and fineness of technique to carry off successfully what often seems to be an experiment in another composer's manner, it cannot rank among his important or representative works. The orchestral *Rêves* (1913) is far more typical of the composer, disturbed and morbid in atmosphere but subtly and powerfully scored. There was no trace of the newly fashionable aesthetic asceticism, no *dépouillement*, in Schmitt's manner and he remained, as he had always been, a solitary with affinities to all camps and allegiance to none.

A middle-aged composer whose fame began to spread among wider circles in the years before 1914 was Erik Satie. Debussy and Ravel had both been attracted by the aggressive simplicity and paradoxical qualities of his music, the mixture of irony and a certain child-like tenderness in his rare and fantastically-named piano pieces. An eccentric, a wit and a deliberate mystifier is always likely to have a personal following in the comparatively small and closed world in which Parisian artists live. That Satie was opposed to all authority, agin' every form of aesthetic government, was an additional charm in those sophisticated circles where the *esprit frondeur*—the Gallic love of insubordination for its own sake—was well developed. When, at the age of forty, he suddenly announced that he intended to enter his name as a pupil at the Schola Cantorum it was generally regarded as another of Satie's paradoxical gestures. This was in 1905 and three years later Satie had obtained his diploma in counterpoint, signed by d'Indy and Roussel, with a *très bien* appended. In 1911 Ravel and his friends arranged a programme of Satie's music, which included his second Sarabande, the Prelude to *Le Fils des Étoiles* and the third *Gymnopédie*. Satie began to become something of a celebrity and his music, more linear in style after his Schola studies but hardly more solid or intrinsically interesting, was given increasingly extravagant titles. Thus the 1913 pieces were labelled *Descriptions Automatiques*, *Embryons Desséchés*, *Croquis et Agaceries d'un Gros Bonhomme de Bois*, and so on. The running commentary printed above the musical text continued the nonsense tradition, sometimes amusingly but often with an obvious desire to astound, pathetic in a man of Satie's age. To quote a few bars of Chopin's Funeral March and label it as 'a well-known Mazurka by Schubert', as he does in *Embryons Desséchés*, can only be considered amusing by those for whom Satie's wit is an article of faith.

There has been much discussion—as was no doubt intended by the composer—of the exact significance of the titles and commentaries of these piano pieces. Were they a deliberate blind? A parody of the 'exquisite' titles of Debussy's Preludes? From the musical point of view it matters very little. What is the real musical value of these piano pieces? Rollo Myers, in an interesting study of Satie, admits that they are 'of unequal value from a strictly musical point of view and one is conscious at times of a straining after effect and a desire to be facetious at all costs. It is as if Satie, having gained a reputation for buffoonery, was now determined to exploit that vein to the full.' This is a damaging admission when we are asked to believe that absolutely disinterested sincerity was the main quality of Satie's music. Even praise takes on a somewhat negative and equivocal form.

'Each of these pieces [*Heures Séculaires et Instantanées*, 1913], is built on a perfectly clear and well-defined thematic material, of no great musical interest, perhaps, but none the less by no means formless and not nearly so eccentric as the text that accompanies them. In fact, just as in so many surrealist pictures (and also in the writings and paintings of lunatics) however bizarre the subject may be in itself, the treatment is often quite straightforward and uncompromisingly matter-of-fact, so here the music is quite lacking in the hallucinatory quality of the composer's literary inspiration (inspired nonsense) and incapable by itself of suggesting any images whatever.'

Is not this a statement that Satie's material is straightforward and uninteresting, that it has some form but little correspondence with the captions, and that these are comparable with the writings of a lunatic?

It is easy on this side of the Channel to forget the Parisian passion for artistic polemics. Journalists' battles were enjoyed by all Paris in the seventeen-fifties and dignified with the name of the *Guerre des Bouffons*, and the deliberate pitting of Piccinni against Gluck twenty years later was in the same spirit. In the years before 1914 there was a recrudescence of this kind of publicity, with the Italian Futurists' manifesto in 1909 and Guillaume Apollinaire's manifesto and 'Aesthetic Meditations on the Cubist painters' in 1913. Satie was the Guillaume Apollinaire of music, a genuine eccentric, Parisian by adoption but essentially rootless, showman of his own eccentricity and exercising through his bizarre personality a fascination and influence which those who knew him found again in his music. In 1915 Satie met Jean Cocteau, a young man of twenty-four, an ardent admirer of Picasso and wholly in sympathy both with the genuine new aims of painters and also

with the spirit of hoax and publicity with which they were expressed. Like the jugglers and acrobats whom he so much admired
in the music-hall (Satie, too, had written a *Jack in the Box* as far
back as 1900) Cocteau was a virtuoso juggler with words and
ideas. In the Cubists and the Futurists he saw the modern counterparts of the Apollinian and the Dionysian strains which eter-
nally recur in the arts; and in the geometrical, intellectualized
schemes of the Cubists he saw an opportunity for the French
artist to realize his specific mission in the world—to become, as
Gide has put it, the world's drawing-master. In Satie's music
Cocteau found brevity, gaiety, unromantic melancholy and a complete absence of the 'half-lights, muslins, enervating charms and
smells' which he so disliked. If Baudelaire was 'bourgeois' and
Mallarmé's poems could be reduced to 'sept voiles précieux re-
couvrant un objet d'art modern-style', Satie's little piano pieces
were perfectly unmysterious except for the literature attached
to them; and according to Cocteau, 'the spirit of hoax may
quite well be the origin of a discovery'. In any case the idea of
elevating this obscure, middle-aged eccentric, with a handful of
piano pieces and songs to his name, to the position of a *chef d'école*
had precisely that element of hoax and paradox which pleased
Cocteau and was fashionable in Parisian art circles of the day. It
was taken very seriously by those who were not in the secrets of
the aesthetic advance guard but not by Satie himself, willing
though he was to enter into a practical joke which gave his music
publicity and himself a position in the very forefront of the
aesthetic battle. When in 1917 he collaborated with Cocteau and
Picasso in a ballet for Diaghilev this position was assured.

The ballet, *Parade*, was given at the Théâtre du Châtelet on
18 May 1917, and it was during that spring that a handful of
young musicians, dazzled by the twin constellations of Cocteau
and Satie, began to meet at a painter's studio in Montparnasse.
In December of the same year they gave their first public concert.
Satie called them 'les Nouveaux Jeunes'; and it was not until two
years later, in January 1920, that Henri Collet, writing in *Comoedia*,
gave the group—by now considerably enlarged—the name by
which they became famous, *Les Six*. To call them a group is
misleading. They had for a very short time certain general aims
and qualities in common but, like the Russian 'Five' after whom
they were nicknamed, they differed greatly in personal characteristics and they were too typically French in their individual-

ism to remain a coherent body for any length of time. All were under thirty, and this in itself made their subsequent development on very different lines probable. The oldest was Louis Durey, born in 1888. Arthur Honegger, of German-Swiss origin but brought up in France; Germaine Tailleferre, the only woman in the group; and Darius Milhaud, a Provençal Jew, were all born in 1892. Georges Auric and Francis Poulenc, the youngest, were little more than boys in 1917, both born in 1899.

Before examining their music individually it will be as well to say something of their common aims, which were summed up for them in the fashionable manner by Cocteau in his manifesto *Le Coq et l'Harlequin*. Simplicity, terseness and clarity were the qualities at which they aimed in music. Their ideal was consciously masculine (though this cult of masculinity was not wholly unlike that of the Baron de Charlus) and they were opposed to the old-fashioned, decorative paganism of the late nineteenth century. Thus Claudel and Jammes were friends of Milhaud, and Cocteau corresponded with Maritain on the subject of Catholicism. An enthusiasm for negro art, which was already marked amongst the painters, disposed them favourably towards the new American Negro music which was just becoming fashionable in Paris. In 'jazz' they found the stimulation of primitive, masculine energy, in place of enervation, and the *naïveté* and grossness for which their palates craved after too much refinement and sophistication, though this craving was itself merely another refinement of taste. In the music-hall and the circus, already patronized by an earlier generation of painters, they looked, according to Cocteau,

'not for the charm of clowns and negroes but for a lesson in equilibrium. This school, which teaches hard work, strength, the exact use of force (*force discrète*) and a functional elegance (*grâce utile*) is a real *haute école*.'

They even found a counterpart for their aesthetic tastes in a gastronomic preference for under-done meat and extra-dry wines.

On the other hand a more feminine element, seldom absent for long from any French art, could be discerned in a new feeling for prettiness. Pastiche of French eighteenth-century ballet music, with its charming volubility, and the pretty pastel shades of Gounod's early music were cleverly contrasted, or even combined, with negro rhythms and music-hall melodies; and all these varying and disparate elements were employed with that sure sense of

the elegant, the amusing, and the novel which distinguishes the
art of the Parisian dressmaker. In fact the quality shared by all
Les Six was something specifically Parisian rather than French, a
chic which is as foreign to the French provinces as it is to London
or Berlin.

What practical form did these new ideals take? Works were
kept as a general rule small, avoiding at all costs pretentiousness
and anything that could possibly engender boredom. Melodies
were extravagantly simple, imitating or even reproducing the
contours and emotional quality of nursery tunes or music-hall
songs. Rhythms were either correspondingly simple—2/4 or 4/4—
or else very complex, with odd interrupting bars of quintuple or
septuple time. The graceful, flowing 3/8, 9/8 or 12/8 were avoided
and the primitive syncopations of the fashionable 'jazz' were
at first used as occasional decoration rather than part of a
general rhythmic scheme. The continuous dialogue of a musical
movement, shattered by Debussy, was restored in an often aggressive form, the busy chatter of the lesser eighteenth-century composers replacing the sighs, flutters, fragments of distant melody and
dots of harmonic colour. The strings were less used than wood-
wind or the brass and the piano was treated as a percussion instrument. Harmony, like rhythm, was either aggressively simple or
aggressively complex; but always, except in the case of Honegger,
strongly tonal. It was in these two departments, harmony and
rhythm, that the influence of Stravinsky was strongest. The use of
two or more keys simultaneously (bitonality or polytonality)
necessitated the preservation, even the accentuation, of the tonal
sense; and it also implied a linear conception of music, a return to
a primitive form of polyphony. In a sense this proclamation of the
ideals of simplicity, sobriety and linear workmanship was a form
of classicism; certainly it was the end of the 'harmonic nightmare'
and that 'vertical rhetoric' which Casella found to be the dominant
quality of music after 1880, the era of the enigma or puzzle (*la
grande crise française du rébus*, as Cocteau called it). But with the
beauty of simplicity was proclaimed the beauty of banality, of the
commonplace. Thus Cocteau:

'Take a commonplace, clean it, polish it and place it in a light so that
it strikes [the listener or reader] by its youth, by the same freshness and
power that it originally possessed. That is the work of a poet.'

Or Raymond Radiguet, the boy writer who played to Cocteau and his followers rather the same role of fetish or mascot as the boy Maximin to Stefan George and his Munich circle:

'Do your best to be banal. You never find in Ronsard the queerness [*bizarrerie*] which often spoils Rimbaud.'

With such ideas as these it was inevitable that neo-classical pastiche should take the place of what might have been a more serious return to classical ideals and practices. This did not fail to happen, especially in the case of the two composers who were at the heart of the new movement.

Only the youngest members of what was to become the group of Les Six came straight to the world of Cocteau and Satie without any previous affiliations or sympathies. Poulenc and Auric took whole-heartedly to the new aesthetic, in a way that was impossible to those who had already started their musical careers under the twin reign of Debussy and the Schola. Their subsequent careers have shown that much of the aesthetic which came to be regarded as that of Les Six in general belonged naturally and intimately to the younger members alone; and that what was genuine, spontaneous and permanent with them was little more than a passing phase with their companions. To be strictly accurate the historian of music should only speak of Les Six during the year 1920, for it was in the January of that year that Henri Collet invented the nickname and by 1921 one of the members, Louis Durey, had already disassociated himself from the group. However, for convenience the name may well be used to cover loosely the dominant aesthetic of the younger French composers from 1917 to 1927. Durey was twenty-two when he started studying music seriously in 1910 with a professor of the Schola. The war interrupted his work, but he had come under Satie's influence by 1916, when he dedicated to him a *Carillons* for piano duet which is still very much in the manner of Debussy, with a whole-tone ostinato and marked *dans une sonorité voilée de brume*. *Neige* (1918), shows the influence of Ravel, to whom it is dedicated; but the miniature *Inscriptions sur un oranger* of the same year, though they too show traces of Ravel and Satie, have a personal grace and miniature precision which Durey preserved in all his best works. The *Scènes de Cirque* were a tribute to fashion, but the *Images à Crusoé*—a song cycle accompanied by string quartet, flute, clarinet and celesta—have the swaying rhythms and flowing lines of the old style disapproved by Les Six. Durey's writing in his songs (from Guillaume Apollinaire's

Left to right: Germaine Tailleferre, Milhaud, Honegger, Durey,
Marcelle Meyer, Poulenc, Auric, Cocteau

From a painting by Jacques-Emile Blanche

Bestiare, Theocritus and Petronius) is subtle, gentle and at bottom traditional. His first string quartet, dating from 1917, has an extreme bitonal opening, in which tonalities of C and C sharp major occur simultaneously, but his heart does not seem ever to have been wholly with the innovators and all his subsequent music has shown that his natural affinity is rather with the older generation of Debussy and Ravel. His originality and the value of his music lie in his refusal to follow fashion and his ability to use a fundamentally traditional idiom in his own personal way. In this he follows the strongest, and one of the best, of French artistic traditions.

The music of Germaine Tailleferre embodies, as was natural, many of the more feminine characteristics of the new school. Between 1920 and 1924 she produced a *Pastorale* for small orchestra, a string quartet, a violin sonata, a piano concerto and some ballet music, *Jeux de plein air* and *Marchand d'Oiseaux*. Most of her music is based on dance rhythms. Thus the string quartet consists of three short dance movements, pretty though spoiled by rhythmic monotony and a tendency to persistent 2-bar structure inherited from Debussy. The concerto is in the typical bustling manner of the neo-classics, a bright D major—as it might be Scarlatti and Saint-Saëns with a dash of the bitters of Stravinsky. The Ballade for piano and orchestra has a valse in 5-time in the manner of Ravel and its notation shows how easily bi-tonal notation can conceal quite conventional harmony:

Ex. 49

All Tailleferre's music has a fashionable *chic* worn with the pleasant unselfconsciousness of the intelligent Parisienne. She was a talented musician who could probably have composed in any manner which happened to be fashionable; but the vogue for small-scale, short-winded, unpretentious and 'amusing' music was obviously favourable to such a talent. It was indeed a happy time for the little talents, as M. Claude Mauriac says:

'1922! when facility was enthroned and it was only necessary to write in order to have one's talent proclaimed, when anyone printed anything and everyone considered themselves masters if they gave themselves up to their inclinations; when effort was considered superfluous. . . .'

No one would dispute the charm and talent of Tailleferre's music; but who, after all, would dispute the charm and talent of that earlier fashionable lady-composer, Cécile Chaminade?

The most vigorous intelligences made distinctions which may seem casuistical but showed that not all traditional standards were abandoned. Thus Darius Milhaud, writing of Satie's *ballet instantanéiste*, *Relâche* speaks of the

'high degree of authenticity and perfection. . . . No matter what genre he attempted Satie never failed to produce something that fitted that genre completely. There is never any feeling of ambiguity, still less of fake or insincerity, in the whole range of his production . . . and this quality of "authenticity" is something quite different from the actual intrinsic value of the music.'

This, in a thinly disguised form, is a moral judgement; for is authenticity really anything but sincerity? A clever street-urchin scrawls the caricature of his schoolmaster on the classroom wall, impelled by a rage of resentment, and the result may well have a high degree of 'authenticity'. Too much of the music written immediately after 1917 had very little else and its success is a measure of the confusion of values which followed the spiritual upheaval of the war years.

Milhaud himself had many ties with tradition. His fertility was prodigious and he attempted a surprising number of musical genres, both large and small, always with the self-confidence and volubility of the typical Southerner and often with less than the cooler-blooded composer's sense of self-criticism. At the Conservatoire he won prizes for the violin, for fugue and counterpoint and when the war broke out in 1914 he was competing for the Prix de Rome. An early violin sonata (1911) is solid, rich in texture and approached the ideal of the Schola in its solemn chorale themes and general air of high-minded seriousness. His first string quartet, written the following year and dedicated to Cézanne (who had died in 1906), is very different. Here there is a simple diatonic framework, a polyphonic texture, naïve rhythms and a pastoral atmosphere with hardly a suspicion of the sophisticated elements which were soon to enter Milhaud's music. In the piano sonata (1916) appear unambiguously the hall-marks of Milhaud's personal style—successive tenths in the bass, fanfares in the 'wrong' key, jazz 'breaks' and an increasing number of passing bitonalities, though all three movements end diatonically. From 1917–19 Milhaud was at the French Legation in Rio de Janeiro with Paul Claudel, and during those years there appeared two chamber symphonies (*Le Printemps* and *Pastorale*), a second violin sonata dedicated to Gide, a fourth string quartet and a sonata for wind instruments. In 1918 he collaborated with Claudel in a stage work, *L'Homme et son Désir*, in which the theme is obsession and the scene is laid in the tropical forest. Here appear for the first time the large clots or conglomerations of notes, often superimposed thirds and fourths, which became typical of Milhaud's music and of the prodigality or profusion which was becoming increasingly noticeable in it. His style at this time was often paradoxical. Thus the clarinet theme in the last movement of the chamber symphony, *Le Printemps*, is something between a folk-song and a nursery rhyme:

Ex. 50

while the third movement of the fourth quartet is frankly bitonal:

Ex. 51

These chamber symphonies, of which Milhaud eventually wrote
six, are miniatures written for different combinations of instruments, all in three movements, rudimentarily contrapuntal and
increasingly acid harmonically. The third is a Serenade; the fourth
and fifth are for ten instruments, respectively strings and wind
(Stravinsky's Wind Octet was written in 1922, the same year as
Milhaud's fifth symphony): and the sixth is for a quartet of voices,
oboe and violoncello.

The *Machines Agricoles* of 1919 is a setting for flute, clarinet,
bassoon, string quartet and voice of salesman's brochures describing the uses and particular virtues of various agricultural instruments—mowers, seed-drillers, binders and the like. In his memoirs
the composer explains that, 'struck by the beauty of these huge
multi-coloured iron insects, modern brothers of the plough and
the sickle', he wished to celebrate them in the same spirit as that
of the Georgics. There had always been a strong pastoral vein in
Milhaud's music and in these pieces he combined this with the
objective, impersonal style of the shop catalogue, which it was
fashionable to exalt at the expense of the hermetic poetry of the
Symbolists. The Seedsman's Catalogue (*Catalogue des Fleurs*) was
another essay of the same kind, a set of primitive inventions in
two or three parts. The Begonia is a typical example:

Ex. 52

In his other songs of this period—*Soirées de Petrograd* and *Chansons bas de S. Mallarmé*—Milhaud attempted successfully the thumbnail sketch in a manner derived from Chabrier's songs and Ravel's *Histoires Naturelles*. The fifth string quartet, dedicated to Schönberg, and Five Studies for piano and orchestra appeared in 1920. In the fourth quartet (1918) Milhaud had written polytonal passages in a block style (Example 51). Now he aimed at genuine polyphonic polytonality, four real melodies developing in four different but occasionally converging keys. Although the whole first movement of the fifth quartet is to be played cantabile and with great expressiveness, at one point the violins play in A and C sharp major respectively, the viola in C natural and the violoncello in F. This, for what it is worth, is real polytonality, as opposed to the passing polytonal combinations used by Stravinsky; but it is significant that, inasmuch as polytonality has survived to our day, it is in the form favoured by Stravinsky rather than in this strict and logical style. Milhaud's extraordinary fertility found expressions in many other directions, including the stage. *Le Boeuf sur le Toit* (1920) he called a cinema-symphony; it is a sophisticated cabaret entertainment based on South American airs and the tango and rumba rhythms. *La Création du Monde* (1923) was a negro ballet, written after Milhaud's discovery of Harlem on an American visit in 1922 and his exploration of the music that accompanied Parisian night-life in the Rue de Lappe or the Boulevard Barbès. 'My orchestra was modelled on those of Harlem', he writes in his memoirs, 'and consisted of seventeen soloists. I used the jazz style without reserve, mingling with it a classical sentiment.' The 'nigger Bach' that resulted from this mésalliance still possess a nostalgic beauty, romantic in character rather than classical.

The search for the exotic linked with the Romantics all this post-war reaction against Romanticism. The desire to escape from his own era, by a flight into space or time, is one of the distinguishing marks of the Romantic; and the primitive negro world played much the same part in the imaginations of artists between 1905 and 1925 as the Middle Ages had played a hundred years earlier. Even the deliberate embracing of the symbols of modern life— as in Milhaud's Agricultural Machines or Honegger's Pacific No. 231—had a defiant and aggressive quality and a self-consciousness which quite remove any of the results from the domain of the classical. Milhaud himself was basically an expressionist, concerned 'not to render the visible but to render visible' the human being mysteriously hidden in his emotions. Boris de Schloezer finds Milhaud's music 'saturated with psychology' and he compares his subjective, violently lyrical and theatrically declamatory style with those of other Jewish composers, Bloch and Schönberg. Certainly many of Milhaud's affinities were with the German and Central European expressionists rather than with the more formal and intellectual ideals of the Latin artists. He himself considers that the basic element of his music is a 'Mediterranean lyricism'; but it is difficult to account on this hypothesis for many of his works and for traits in almost everything that he has composed. Many of the stage-works, in particular—*L'Homme et son Désir*, *La Création du Monde* and the later *Maximilien* and *Christophe Colomb*—are anything but Mediterranean.

Milhaud shared these un-French affiliations with Arthur Honegger, who studied with Widor and d'Indy and refused formally to regard Cocteau's *Le Coq et l'Arlequin* as a gospel, preferring to take what suited him and leave the rest. He never had a great interest in the art of the fair or the music-hall, but pursued from the beginning the architectural forms of chamber music and the symphony. Although born and brought up in France, he retained in his spiritual make-up, and expressed in his music, the solid Germanic culture of Zürich, the home of his family to which he often returned. His spiritual descent from Beethoven and Wagner is clearly to be seen in his early chamber music—a string quartet and a violin sonata written in 1917–18. Honegger marks the first movement of the quartet 'violent and tormented', and he uses a rich contrapuntal texture and tense, crossing rhythms to achieve a vigorous and strongly emotional expressiveness. Both in the quartet and the violin sonata the use of canonic imitation and a sophisticated but still recognizable chorale reveal the pupil of d'Indy. The second movement of the sonata is a Presto in 2/4 time with strongly *martellato* rhythms and diatonic scale passages in contrary motion which suggest a cross between Bartok and a Beethoven Bagatelle. The second violin sonata (1919) is largely homophonic and an unexpected fugato in the first movement is the only contrapuntal incident, while a viola sonata belonging to the following year has an almost atonal first movement followed by two largely diatonic movements (Ex. 53 opposite).

In fact, Honegger had not yet found himself and, with plenty to say, was still casting about for his own individual way of saying

it. His friendship with the *nouveaux jeunes* helped him to clear his
mind and thin out his vocabulary. The *Pastorale d'été* (1920) is a
simple construction based on two main ideas, lyrical and rustic,
entrusted to the horn and the bassoon respectively. The orchestration is clear and uncomplicated and the ostinato rhythms give the
whole piece an air of rural tranquility. Obvious tribute to the
advertised ideals of the Six was paid by Honegger in the clarinet
sonatina of 1922 and the piano concertino of 1924, but far more
interesting and individual were the two orchestral works of 1921.
Le Roi David was originally conceived as incidental music for a
play by René Morax, though its great success led the composer
to make a concert version which is virtually an oratorio. The

Ex. 53

original orchestration was for wood-wind, brass, double bass,
piano and harmonium and the effect aimed at by the composer
is alternately one of lyrical simplicity and harsh, primitive grandeur. The first is represented chiefly by the various psalms,
some of which are sung to a diatonic, folk-like melody with
more complicated chromatic harmonies in the instrumental accompaniment. The Lament of Gilboa is the only movement in
which Honegger approaches the oriental style, with elaborate
antiphonal *melismas* for the voices. Occasionally the style is
marred by a too obvious and literal pastiche of a Bach cantata, as
in *Loué soit le Seigneur,* and the final movement contains a chorale
tune which confirms Honegger's indebtedness to Bach. The whole
work, which has movements of great beauty and real grandeur,
stands half-way between Florent Schmitt's *Psalm 47* and Walton's

Belshazzar's Feast. The Dance before the Ark has the cumulative, orgiastic character of a primitive festivity and achieves an impression of exultant vitality equal to that achieved, with far larger resources, by Schmitt and Walton. The lyrical passages are deeply felt and their simplicity is not an affectation. But how far Honegger still remained from having really found a finally personal style can be seen from the inclusion of Bach pastiche in *Le Roi David*, and from the *Horace Victorieux* which was his other main work of 1921. This is 'mimed symphony', powerful and concentrated in manner, in the direct line of Honegger's earlier chamber music and quite untouched, apparently, by the anti-emotional bias of the Six. *Pacific 231* (1924) revealed still another side of Honegger's character and, although he has disclaimed any interest in the actual imitation of the noises emitted by an engine of the Canadian Pacific Railway, his ingenious imitation of them and his masterly method of handling a large orchestra cannot fail to suggest a similarity to Richard Strauss. Honegger aimed, in his own words, at

'. . . the translation into sound of a visual impression and a state of physical enjoyment. . . . Starting from objective contemplation . . . the speed increases steadily and reaches lyrical ecstasy at 75 miles an hour, with 300 tons hurtling down the track.'

This intoxication with speed and mechanical beauty had, of course, been preached by Marinetti and the Italian Futurists ten years earlier; but it is surprising to find it allied with a deep interest in the traditional musical forms and textures. Perhaps this breadth of sympathy, which has been a danger to Honegger, is also one of his chief virtues; and it certainly set him apart from composers like Auric or Poulenc, whose ideals he appreciated but never whole-heartedly shared.

Francis Poulenc's musical personality has no precedent in musical history; and that his personality predominated in the music usually attributed to Les Six generally is shown by the fact that he alone has continued to write in a style that has no doubt developed greater solidity, but is still recognizably the same as that which shocked or amused Paris—and very soon all Europe and America—in the years following the first war. He is a musical clown of the first order, a brilliant musical mimic and an adroit craftsman, who pieces together the most heterogeneous collection of musical styles to form an unmistakably personal style of his own. Unlike other French composers—with the exception of Chabrier—he has humour rather than wit and, like every clown, his tongue is never so firmly in his cheek as in his moments of pathos. He carries Satie's *blague* a step further and reveals his personality in the ingenious and individual arrangement of his works, which often resemble the nests of a musical jackdaw. An admirer has imagined Poulenc at work and murmuring to himself:

'Ici je ferai du Ravel, là du Chabrier; à ce moment j'imaginerai un Debussy première manière . . . ailleurs je recommencerai mes Poèmes de Ronsard ou je penserai au style avec lequel Mme. X entre dans un salon, ou bien je composerai un Le Nain. Ceci débutera comme *Mavra*: cela fera très Marie-Laure.'

And yet the result has an unmistakably personal character. Poulenc was largely self-taught as a composer, though his piano lessons with Ricardo Viñes contributed to the forming of his taste and the development of his acute sense of style. He was only eighteen when his *Rapsodie Nègre* was performed in 1917. This was followed the next year by *Mouvements Perpetuels* for piano and a sonata for two clarinets, and in 1919 by settings from Guillaume Apollinaire's *Bestiaire* and Cocteau's *Cocardes*. In these pieces the melody is simple, the harmony generally diatonic, and dissonance is used as a form of accentuation or a seasoning. The sonata was followed by one for clarinet and bassoon and another for horn, trumpet and trombone, both in 1922: they are treated as two- or three-part inventions and as experiments in timbre. Appollinaire's animal poems are the nearest French equivalent to Edward Lear's nonsense rhymes and Poulenc's music matches their humour and neat, unpretentious form very well. Cocteau's guying of Mallarmé suited Poulenc even better, revealing the close connection between clinical and poetic methods of free association and the near relationship of both to nonsense. The first of the *Cocardes*, which are scored for viola, cornet, trombone, bass drum and triangle, is called *Miel de Narbonne* and runs as in Ex. 54 (on next page).

In the *Mouvements Perpetuels* and again in his ballet *Les Biches* (1923) Poulenc showed a different side of his musical character, a frank and often charming exploitation of the 'pretty' and a deliberate return to the facile and surface emotions which we call sentimental. The pleasant chatter of the minor eighteenth-century composers and the pretty elegance of Gounod's early music are

combined in Poulenc's individual manner to form works whose
appeal and quality are comparable with the pictures of Marie
Laurencin or, in an earlier day, Boucher. Like Boucher, Poulenc
in these early works was wholly in sympathy with the public for
which he worked, the smart Parisian society which had taken to
its heart Diaghilev and his Russian ballets and wanted before all

Ex. 54

else to be amused. It must have been a relief to the unmusical
to have no longer to sit through *The Ring*, but, instead, to be
confronted with little chamber works, lasting hardly as many
minutes as *The Ring* lasts hours; and to be told that these pleasing
and witty creations are the last word in aesthetic modernity.
Seriousness, which was in fashion in the days of the Wagnerian
ascendancy and only took a slightly different colouring during

the era of *Pelléas*, was now replaced by a frankly hedonistic approach and the journalistic champions of the new mode wrote charmingly of 'the aesthetics of pleasure' and 'the rights of prettiness'.

These same journalists soon coupled with the name of Poulenc that of Georges Auric and as soon dubbed the two of them, in the traditional journalistic manner, *les sportifs de la musique*. Certainly there is an atmosphere of physical bustle, a display of muscularity and an absence of all fine sentiments in much of their music, which often seems to be envisaged more as a game than as an emotional communication. But it is a game in the sense that the French speak of a *jeu d'esprit* or a *jeu de mots* rather than in any Anglo-Saxon sense. Auric studied both at the Conservatoire and with d'Indy and was early prolific, composing according to one account more than three hundred songs and piano pieces between the ages of twelve and sixteen. In 1917 he came under Satie's influence, but it was only in the songs published in 1920 that his personality became distinct. Both *Alphabet* and *Les Joues en Feu* are settings of poems by Raymond Radiguet. *Alphabet* is a thumbnail collection strongly influenced by Satie, but less perverse and more straightforwardly witty. (Thus in *Le Papillon* Auric parodies the obvious Grieg instead of some wholly irrelevant composer). *Les Joues en Feu* are more solid matter. In general the voice part is simple and diatonic while the accompaniment is violently discordant. Thus in No. 1 the voice does no more than modulate from the tonic to the sub-dominant and back. In No. 3 the keys of B major and E flat major are first contrasted and then combined. The good and bad points of bitonal writing can be seen very clearly by contrasting two passages from different works by Auric. The first comes from one of the *Quatre Poèmes by* Georges Gabory (Ex. 55 on next page).

Here the voice and the right-hand of the piano part are in B major while the accompaniment figure in the left hand is in B flat major. The voice has the simplest diatonic melody, which fits conventionally with the right-hand part of the piano, no more than a series of conventional broken chords. The left hand is in the most distantly related key and is nothing more than another accompanying figure. Instead of having two or three lines of real melodic interest there is only one melodic line with an accompaniment half right and half 'wrong'. Contrast this with a passage from Auric's ballet *Les Fâcheux* (1923) (Ex. 56 on next page).

Here there are two lines of real melody, one in B major and the other in A flat major, and the keys are related, though the relationship implies bi-modality rather than bi-tonality. (The relative minor of B major, G sharp minor, is enharmonically identical with A flat minor). The lesson of this comparison is that any music which employs two or more different modes or tonalities simultaneously must be genuinely polyphonic. In his two most successful ballets, *Les Fâcheux* and *Les Matelots* (1925), Auric wrote strongly

Ex. 55

rhythmic music with great verve and motor energy. He avoids any length, either of phrase or development, and in his keys and time-signatures generally prefers the simplicities of the old *comédie-ballet* or the early *opéra-comique*. He included Messager among his models and with Poulenc he created something like a new comic style. Like Poulenc he makes great play with unexpected elements, often effectively introduced by way of contrast. Thus in

Les Fâcheux Orphise's dance in D flat major, highly ornamented and marked 'very slow and expressive', stands out in strong relief against the quick staccato movements which make up most of the ballet.

In the formation of the musical character and the technical development of Les Six it is almost impossible to exaggerate the influence of Stravinsky. He and Satie, both interpreted by Cocteau, provided the new aesthetic. A list of the instrumental combinations and the subjects chosen by Stravinsky for his works from 1913 to 1917 is like an advance list of the French works composed between 1917 and 1921. There are the children's pieces, simple and sophisticated; the animal studies; the flirtation with jazz. The combinations—contralto and three clarinets, or voice, flute, oboe, clarinet, bassoon, violin, viola, violoncello and bass—have the same freakish chamber music quality, which was probably suggested in turn to Stravinsky by *Pierrot Lunaire*. The influence of Satie has already been discussed. Stravinsky certainly underwent it and it was partly a dose of Satie's violently purging ideas that led to the sudden abandonment of the richness and complications of *Le Sacre* in favour of the little dehydrated masterpieces that followed. The war favoured drastic changes. There was neither the money nor the public for large, expensive ballets and operas. Making a virtue of necessity, Stravinsky created a new taste, while Satie found his pseudo-ascetic ideas justified by circumstance. Of the works produced by him in these last years before his death in 1924, *Socrate* is certainly the most interesting. In the ballets *Parade*, *Mercure* and *Relâche*, Satie's music is only a subordinate part of spectacles in which the spirit of aesthetic nihilism (in the form of Dada) or hoax joins with a peculiarly Parisian form of humour and the holiday moods and fantasies of Picasso. It is very difficult to attribut any real meaning to some of the eulogies of these pieces. Thus Cocteau writes, of the themes of three dances from *Parade*, that 'a metronomical unity governs each of these enumerations, which are superimposed upon the simple outlines of each character and upon the imaginative ideas evoked by them'. Surely no German Doctor of Music and Philosophy ever wrote more high-sounding nonsense about music. But in *Socrate* Satie's mainly negative qualities—'no humbug, no repetition, no furtive caresses, no feverishness or miasma', in Cocteau's words—are combined with a genuine, if tenuously expressed, feeling. The text is taken from Victor Cousin's translation of passages from the Platonic dialogues and is divided into three parts—Portrait of Socrates, By the banks of the Ilyssus and Death of Socrates. The music is written for cor anglais, horn, trumpet, harp, tympani and strings, and requires four women's voices. It takes the form of continuous chanting, melodic psalmody rather than recitative, and the extreme monotony of this was plainly deliberate. In Rollo Myers's words, 'the instrumental accompaniment seems strangely independent of what is being sung and consists mainly of recurring patterns based on bare harmonies in which sevenths, fourths and fifths are predominant'. There are moments, as when Socrates drinks the hemlock, where the philosopher seems to be joining hands over the centuries with Debussy's *Damoiselle Élue* and these are the most effective in the work; though effect, in that sense, was not Satie's aim. As we have seen, his admirers claim for this, as for all his music, a high degree of 'authenticity' and with this moral rather than artistic praise and a bouquet of well-deserved negatives we may take leave of this composer.

IX

'The average Frenchman is born an anarchist, slowly evolves into a socialist, then into a bourgeois of the Left, and so passes gradually across the Centre to become a man of the Right. He begins as a sceptic, professes atheism in the wildness of his youth, conforms as he approaches maturity and dies in the faith of his ancestors.'

IN 1921 Saint-Saëns died, full of years and malice but incorrigibly skilful and fertile almost to the end. He was followed three years later by Fauré and in 1925 by a third *chef d'école*, Satie. Les Six were beginning to go their own individual ways (they had never really done anything else) and Stravinsky had moved from Switzerland and set up his headquarters in Paris.

Three great figures of the pre-war musical world were still active in composition, Ravel and d'Indy for another decade and Florent Schmitt up to the present day; but in each case their finest and most characteristic period was well behind them and they no longer set the pace or the tone of French musical development. Roussel, on the other hand, emerged quietly and late in his life as an unmistakable master of a tough, but delicate style, terse and impersonal, the most important French composer between the two German wars. But his roots were deep in the past and neither the character of his music nor his personal temperament was such as forms a new school. This role, as so often in the history of French music, was reserved for a foreigner, the man of multiple (and therefore weak) nationality, Stravinsky. Two fundamental characteristics of Stravinsky made a strong appeal to young French composers: his intellectuality and a sense of style rendered all the more intriguing by being displayed in an unpredictable succession of widely differing manners. The final evaluation of Stravinsky does not belong to this study, neither does that of the music written by French composers under his overwhelming influence. A generation must elapse before it is possible to see any work of art in a true historical perspective, for it is as true in the aesthetic as in the spiritual hierarchy that many that were last shall be first and many that were first shall be last—and perhaps nowhere more true than in France, where Parisian fashion can do much to make or unmake a reputation.

Before saying something of the later works of those leading composers whose early careers have already been sketched, some idea
must be given of the wealth and variety of lesser composers, in
whom French music has continued to be particularly rich. Few of
them have made any name outside their own country, except
among professional musicians or among amateurs of French
music. They are of many different ages and temperaments and
owe allegiance to widely divergent schools or to no school at all;
but all have in common certain characteristics which we recognize as French—precise and finished workmanship, a nice adjust-
ment of means to ends, an elegant and generally discreet sense
of orchestral colour and a preference for clear and thin texture.
Of the older generation, pupils of Massenet, Reynaldo Hahn is
the most distinguished. His operettas and *opéras comiques* were
variously successful, but *Ciboulette* (1923) and *Mozart* (1925) are
classics of their kinds and combine an elegant musicianship with
a pretty wit and a gift for charmingly nostalgic melody. Hahn
is chiefly remembered for his songs, and his settings of Verlaine
written in 1891-2, when he was a boy of hardly eighteen, are
comparable with those of Fauré and Debussy, not always for their
purely musical qualities, but for the fidelity and sureness with
which they treat the text and evoke the particular atmosphere of
Verlaine's poetry with the minimum of musical apparatus. These
Chansons Grises were followed by ten settings of Leconte de Lisle,
Études Latines, almost equally successful but inferior inasmuch as
Leconte de Lisle is a less musical poet than Verlaine. Hahn, a
Venezuelan Jew by birth, was a friend of Marcel Proust for whose
early *Les Plaisirs et Jours* (1896) he wrote four piano pieces. He also
shared Proust's admiration for Ruskin and wrote an ode on his
death in 1900, for female voices and harps. Some of his incidental
theatre music is in the best French tradition of this difficult, if
subsidiary, art, and his piano concerto has much of the unpretentious melodic charm and the drawing-room elegance of his master
Massenet. An equivalent figure in English music might be Roger
Quilter and a comparison of the two would reveal many of the
similarities and the differences between French and English musical taste. Hahn was born in 1874 and died in 1947.

Conductors and professors of music have often proved more
successful composers in France than in other countries. It is only
necessary to compare the names of Pierné, Rabaud, Emmanuel,
Grovlez, Roger-Ducasse and Caplet with a representative list of

contemporary conductors and professors in England or Germany to see the difference; for the compositions of Sir Hamilton Harty and Sir Donald Tovey, Salomon Jadassohn and Felix Weingartner are rarely played in their own countries, never abroad. Even the fact that composers of the eminence of Fauré and d'Indy held official positions as heads of the two most important musical educational establishments argues a difference between musical life in France and in other countries. In no other country is tradition so strong and in no other country have apparent revolutionaries so soon proved to be traditionalists at heart. The innovations of individual composers are often adopted and assimilated into the traditional, and traditionally expanding, idiom in less than a generation; and the conventional antithesis between academic forms and vital creation is nowhere more meaningless than in France. Thus Ravel long before his death suffered from being regarded as an academic composer, not because his original contributions to music were forgotten or despised but because they had already been assimilated into the classical idiom and vocabulary of the French composer. The pupils of Fauré and d'Indy and the composers who, without being pupils, were closely connected with Debussy or Ravel, themselves taught, wrote, played or conducted, and contributed to popularize by precept and example the musical idiom and vocabulary which had for a short time been the private property of their masters. None of this could happen in a country where musical tradition is weak, as in England, or rigid, as in Germany.

Of the same generation as Reynaldo Hahn, Gabriel Pierné and Henri Rabaud were, respectively, conductor and professor before they were composers. Pierné, who won the Prix de Rome in 1882, was a fecund composer in all departments of music until his death in 1937 at the age of seventy-four. He had worked with Franck as well as at the Conservatoire, but his music is at its best when it is least pretentious and takes the form of incidental stage or ballet music rather than the big classical forms. Rabaud, a pupil of Massenet and Prix de Rome scholar in 1894, made his name by a single work, the opera *Mârouf* (1914). This is an engaging work, old-fashioned in conception and form and in direct descent from the orientalism of Bizet's *Djamileh*, but brilliantly orchestrated and enlivened with well-judged dissonances, which gave an impression of 'modernity' without altering the traditional harmonic basis of Rabaud's idiom. A *Procession Nocturne* (1899), based on

Lenau's *Faust*, already showed a remarkable orchestral sense and an ease in manipulating the current idiom of the time, and was temperately praised by Paul Dukas. A fantasy on Russian themes reveals the same skill and the composer's instinctive following of musical fashion. Rabaud was successively professor of harmony at the Conservatoire, conductor of the Opera and finally, in 1920, followed Fauré as Director of the Conservatoire. It is in the light of these high official posts that his music must be judged. If it is academic by French standards, the composer of *Mârouf* would hardly be considered academic in any other country.

The chair of History of Music at the Paris Conservatoire, held until 1909 by Bourgault-Ducoudray (see pp. 34 and 87) was taken over in that year by another scholar-composer, Maurice Emmanuel, who combined a deep scholarship in ancient Greek, Gregorian and folk-music with an original and voluble creative gift which he exercised in many different forms of composition. A *Sonate Bourguignonne* written in 1893, when he was over thirty, is chiefly inspired by folk-music; but his piano sonatinas, written during the nineteen-twenties, combine an original instrumental style with a charming yet forceful musical idiom, based on scholarship but more lively and personal than that of most scholars. After the 1914–18 war Emmanuel wrote in the larger forms and published two symphonies (1919 and 1931) and in 1929 an opera, *Salamine*, based on Aeschylus. By many he will probably be best remembered for an excellent little book on Debussy's *Pelléas et Mélisande*, which contains interesting reminiscences of his youthful days at the Conservatoire with Debussy.

A conductor who was also a pianist and taught the piano for ten years at the Schola Cantorum is Gabriel Grovlez, the author of pleasant and ingenious miniatures for the piano. Grovlez, Louis Aubert and Roger-Ducasse were among the most gifted of Fauré's pupils at the Conservatoire and though all of them belong to the generation born in the late eighteen-seventies and were therefore inevitably influenced by Debussy, all three have preserved an individual character in their music. Aubert has written some effective songs (*Crépuscules d'Automne*) and orchestral music (*Habañera*, 1916) and was the first pianist to play Ravel's *Valses nobles et sentimentales*. Roger-Ducasse is the most distinguished of these lesser composers of the older generation, who have combined a traditional attitude to the fundamental problems of tonality and form with a free use of modern condiments, colouristic and harmonic. After some early chamber works he has written a considerable number of orchestral pieces. A *Suite Française* (1907) is pleasantly written and well or-chestrated, with a hint of Chabrier in the Bourrée and an effective use of the oboe d'amore in the Recitativo. *Le Joli Jeu du Furet*, an orchestral adaptation of a choral piece, is a vigorous and witty scherzo, in the same line as Dukas's *Apprenti Sorcier*; and in *Nocturne de Printemps* Roger-Ducasse pays a graceful and imaginative tribute to impressionism. His *Orphée*, an ambitious combination of music, choreography and pantomime, is generally known only in orchestral fragments, which show unfailing skill and distinction in the handling of ideas insufficiently characterized to stand alone in the concert hall. An *Epithalame*, written in 1923 for the marriage of Margaret Damrosch, makes use of the fashionable dance-rhythms, including a fox-trot and a tango, which are later com-bined in an impressionistic picture of the modern ballroom, possibly suggested by Ravel's *La Valse*. Roger-Ducasse's more scholastic side has found expression in the contrapuntal style of some of his piano works. In his early *Jardin de Marguerite* (1905) he followed the fashion, set by Massenet, of writing a sequel or epi-logue to a famous story. Massenet had contented himself with imaginary portraits of Des Grieux and Cherubino in later life; but Roger-Ducasse, more ambitious, imagines Faust in his old age returning to the garden where he had known and loved Marguerite. It is the same garden as Zola's Paradou in *La Faute de l'Abbé Mouret* and the voices of the good and evil flowers, of the evening and of the two idealized lovers are woven into a big choral work with orchestral preludes and interludes. The vocal writing is often beautiful and effective, the idiom owing much to both Fauré and Debussy; but the text and the general conception of the work are unmistakably in the nineteenth-century operatic tradition.

André Caplet, winner of the Prix de Rome in 1901 at twenty-three, was a friend and champion of Debussy, and his music is generally that of a gifted and sensitive disciple. He was chosen to conduct the first performance of *Le Martyre de Saint Sébastien*, and much of his subsequent music derives its character and inspiration from this hieratic manner of Debussy's. His early songs had shown a more traditional, though real and individual, poetic sense; but his last works, especially the Mass for three voices *a cappella* and *Le Miroir de Jésus* for string quartet, harp and three voices have the tenuous, archaic beauty and the deliberate hieratic (rather than properly religious) quality which we associate with Debussy's later manner. Caplet died suddenly in 1925 at the age of forty-seven, as a result of wounds and gas-poisoning in the war of 1914–18.

Two independent figures, Charles Koechlin and Georges Migot, are interesting for the profoundly traditional character of their most original works. Koechlin, a pupil of Massenet and Fauré, has published comparatively little. His sonatinas and other piano pieces combine a child-like simplicity of manner—an affinity with nursery rhyme, folk-song and the naïve melodies of medieval secular music—with free rhythm and passages of experimental harmony and modality. His chamber music, including three string quartets and a sonata for two flutes, is polyphonic and more original than it at first appears; but Koechlin never insists, never raises his voice and by this quietistic attitude, reflected in the fact that the greater part of his work remains unpublished, he has forfeited the interest of all but a few connoisseurs. Large orchestral works, *Les Heures Persanes* and *L'Abbaye*, are highly praised by those who have heard them, but are not published. It seems probable that Koechlin, who is also a writer on musical subjects and a theorist, resembles Satie in being more important as the embodiment of an ideal than for the actual quality of his music. The purity and child-like innocent charm of his smaller works reflect a rare disinterestedness and a musicianship to which years of practice have given all the appearance of being second nature. As with Satie, so with Koechlin the distinctive quality of his music springs from a moral attribute of the composer's character.

Migot, who was born in 1891, is almost twenty-five years younger than Koechlin, but he too has formed his idiom from unusual sources, chiefly medieval and oriental as the titles of many of his works suggest (*Le Livre des Danceries*, *Le Tombeau de Du Fault*, *Hagoromo*, *Le Paravent de laque aux cinq images*.) His multiple interests and enthusiasms, musical and otherwise, are reflected in his music which is diffuse and lacks strong personality.

The medieval, or at least the archaic, element was strong in the last works of d'Indy and Saint-Saëns and has been constant in the later works of Florent Schmitt. None of these older and already highly respected composers was quite untouched by the new musical fashions of the nineteen-twenties, though they all favoured the same single aspect of what was a complex and multiform movement. It was not to be expected that they should start to write in the manner of Satie or that they should renounce the solidly constructed technique and the distinguished manner of a lifetime in favour of studio jokes or smart, drawing-room *gamineries*. But the element of classical or medieval pastiche appealed to the scholar in d'Indy and in Saint-Saëns, who could claim familiarity with the idea and even experience of putting it into practice a full quarter of a century before it was made fashionable by Stravinsky and Les Six. Saint-Saëns paid his tribute in the three sonatas—for oboe, clarinet and bassoon respectively—which close the long list of his works. D'Indy had still something to say in his own familiar manner before he turned to neo-classicism, and in the *Symphonia Brevis de Bello Gallico* (1919), the *Poème des Rivages* (1922) and the quintet (1924) he distilled the last drops of that honey which he had gathered so assiduously in the garden of Franck. The *Diptyque Méditerranéen* (1926) is, on the composer's own showing, an essay in impressionism. 'This work', he wrote in the score, 'has no other purpose than that of noting in music two impressions of light.' The two movements, entitled Morning Sun and Evening Sun, recall the first and last movements of the *Jour d'été à la Montagne*, but the manner is closer to that of Debussy, and the whole work, by its deliberately and exclusively sensuous character, lacks the very quality which is d'Indy's strength and his most personal contribution. In 1927, when he was nearer eighty than seventy, this enemy of artistic frivolity and personification of austere idealism wrote a small comic opera, *Le Rêve de Cinyras*, in which memories of old-fashioned gaieties are to be found in comic juxtaposition to the composer's more weighty manner—by no means a great work, but a charming and belated substitute for that crop of musical wild oats that d'Indy never sowed in his youth. After this improbable excursion d'Indy seemed to accept his age and for the last five years of his life, until his death in 1932, he cultivated serenely that corner of the traditional musical field which lay closest to the fashionable highway. The *Suite en parties*, the concerto for flute, piano and strings, and the *Trio en forme de suite* reveal even by their titles their neo-classical affinities. The concerto is the most personal, neat and serene, as befits the old age of a great teacher who had spent the whole of his life in the service and practice of music.

Florent Schmitt, like d'Indy, had still in 1918 a wholly unfashionable attitude to music, which was not to be seriously modified until he had expressed to the full his personal thoughts and feelings and was content to allow old age its due, to write for

the sake of amusement or because composition was one of the
habits of a lifetime to which age put no natural stop. The oriental
vein of *Psalm 47*, the *Tragédie de Salomé* and the *Danse des Dévadasis*
was continued in the *Légende* for violin and orchestra (1918), the
suites arranged from the incidental music written for Gide's translation of *Antony and Cleopatra* (1920) and the film *Salammbô* (1925),
and the orchestral *Danse d'Abisag* of the same year. The harsh,
brooding atmosphere of these works and their strong pictorial and
literary characteristics continued that fusion of the romantic and
the impressionist traditions which had marked Schmitt as a solitary before and further emphasized his solitariness in the post-
war world. But Schmitt himself was not lacking in sympathy
with the younger generation. A vein of humour and fantasy, already visible in the *Semaine du petit elfe Ferme l'Oeil*, found new
expression in works whose titles (perhaps more often than their
content) show the composer's awareness of changed fashions. The
violin sonata of 1918 (*Sonate libre en deux parties enchaînées, ad modum
clementis aquae*), *Fonctionnaire M.C.M.xii* and the suites '*sans esprit de
suite*' and '*en rocaille*' (1933 and 1935), the small chamber works
often written for freakish combinations (quartets for saxophones,
for flutes, and for trombones and tuba) all reveal a considerable
concession to the mode of the day. They are unfailingly well-
written, pleasant and generally apt; but they lack not only the
characteristic profuseness and violence of the works of Schmitt's
youth and maturity, but any strongly personal flavour. Like the
ageing Strauss, and for the same reason, Schmitt possesses so
effortlessly the technique of composition that he can please or
amuse himself and his listener in almost any genre long after the
need to compose—the need, that is to say, for self-expression—has
ceased to exist. In this sense the neo-classical and the deliberately
frivolous, the typical aesthetic fashions of the years between 1920
and 1940, revealed themselves as marks of failing vitality, not remarkable in the older composers who were content to give to the
amusements of their old age a fashionable colour. But they were
serious in younger men, many of whose mature works had no
greater life or urgency than these elderly triflings of a generation
who, in their day, had proved their worth in far more formidable
fields. The great athlete may well take to croquet in his old age;
but what can be said of an age whose champions in their prime are
content to pit their strength and skill against nothing more formidable than croquet-hoops? And this has been true of too large a

proportion of French composers in the years between the two wars.

Ravel's best work was already done by 1920. During the next fourteen years, until he was finally incapacitated in 1932 by a tragic illness, he continued to write, always with skill and his own very personal form of taste. He even achieved universal celebrity, bordering on notoriety, with a *tour de force*, *Bolero*, in 1928; but after *La Valse* it is only occasionally that his musical ideas are worthy of their presentation or that his works excite more than professional admiration and the astonishment of a public greedy for what were in their day novel effects. The sonatas, for violin and violoncello and for violin and piano, and the G major concerto are clever trivialities in which Ravel paid a pathetic tribute to the fashions of the nineteen-twenties. His vanity, which found expression in his dandy's sense of dress, was piqued when he found himself no longer among the leaders of musical fashion and, having no longer a strong personal impulse behind his music, he was content to experiment in the latest fashions. In *L'Enfant et les Sortilèges*, however, he followed his own bent and gave free rein to his taste for the exquisite and the fantastic. The clocks and mechanical toys of *L'Heure Espagnole* found worthy and charming descendants in the toys, the furniture and the animals of Colette's fantasy. Here, too, in the music of the Princess, there appears almost for the last time that vein of shy but sophisticated emotion which lies so close to sentimentality, the coquetry of a heart perhaps too tender with an artistic sense whose fastidiousness was offended by any natural expression of feeling. In the concerto for the left hand Ravel's flagging inspiration was once again stimulated by a technical problem and, in spite of the weakness of the scherzo section, the work as a whole has a sonorous splendour and moments of strength which recall the trio of eighteen years before. If Ravel had died in the same year as Debussy, if the trio and the *Tombeau de Couperin* had been his last works, would his reputation be different from what it is to-day? Hardly; and both he and his friends and admirers would have been spared the painful spectacle of a consummate artist sinking, first below the level of his own best works and then into the five years of silence which preceded his death in 1937.

The neo-classicism of Stravinsky, from which Ravel had borrowed in his chamber music, has been a large component part in much of the output of the three composers of the original Six who have continued active since 1920. Activity has, indeed, been perhaps the most notable feature of Milhaud, Poulenc and Honegger, whose production has been as regular and profuse (and often, severe critics might add, as perfunctory) as that of any minor composers of the eighteenth century. Concertinos, quartets, sonatas and sonatinas; operas and operettas of all dimensions; cantatas, oratorios and masses; the cinema and the radio, *a cappella* and *Ondes Martenot*—the profusion has been bewildering, an apparent cornucopia. But this horn of plenty proves on closer examination to be mainly filled with imitation fruit, with plastic pomegranates and pears of papier mâché. Some of these are amusing drawing-room ornaments, some have been useful though ephemeral properties in the studios and theatres, where a quick wit, a sense of 'good theatre' and of the 'contemporary' have been more in demand than the fruits of contemplation or a sense of poetry and eternal values. The ease and speed with which Milhaud, at nearly sixty, has already produced a body of music comparable in size with that of Saint-Saëns at eighty-four, invite comparisons of diligence, certainly, but also of quality. All this music, despite personal characteristics of Milhaud, Poulenc and Honegger, has one fundamental quality in common: that it seems planned—in haste, one would say—with only the most superficial consideration for the quality of the material or the nature of the musical genre attempted. In a piece of chamber music by Poulenc, an oratorio by Honegger or a concerto by Milhaud the most heterogeneous elements are combined, the most difficult problems solved (or shelved) by means of a technical dexterity and a self-confident fluency which is, in the last resort, sheer bluff. This bluff has no doubt an artistic quality (did not Cocteau proclaim the possibilities of hoax?) but more than bluff is needed to treat of Antigone and Joan of Arc, to write a mass or a string quartet comparable in musical quality with the great masses and quartets of the past. The cinema, the radio and the ballet have created a large demand for heteronomous music; music for use, in which the quality of the composer's material is less important than his technical assurance. The evil of this attitude has spread widely; but its origin lies not in the cinema, the radio or the ballet but in the original conceptions of *musique d'ameublement* and *Gebrauchsmusik*. The standard demanded of music designed to be listened to only incidentally (or not at all) has spread rapidly, and reaction against the self-conscious solemnity and quasi-pontifical pretensions of many nineteenth-century artists has resulted in an attitude of casual, easy-going intimacy with the Muse, who has her own way of avenging herself on disrespectful composers. A renaissance of light music is wholly admirable in itself, nowhere more so than in France; but it should not be synonymous with a lowering of artistic standards nor should such music, light in weight rather than in heart, find its way into every corner of the musical field. A mass or a string quartet may well be light-hearted—*hilarem datorem diligit Dominus* —but too many of these composers' works are light-minded. There are, of course, exceptions and Honegger's Symphony for Strings and Poulenc's *Tel jour, tel nuit* are examples of music composed under an emotional pressure and with a sense of responsibility unusual in either composer, even when engaged on subjects and texts of the utmost solemnity. But not even half a dozen swallows make a summer and music in France between the German wars experienced as hard and lean a winter as in the rest of Europe.

This winter followed in France a singularly long and beautiful autumn, glorious for the mists of Debussy and the mellow fruitfulness of Fauré's old age, and it was cheered by the gleam of Roussel's sun. A winter sun, Roussel's music gives more light than heat, revealing the nakedness of the surrounding country without immediately increasing its fertility. But any attempt to chronicle the great period of French music between the death of Berlioz and the death of Fauré must end with Fauré's autumn sunsets and the hope implicit in Roussel's wintry radiance. Between 1918 and his death in 1924—that is to say, between the ages of seventy-three and seventy-nine—Fauré wrote six chamber works, three sets of songs, his last Barcarolle and Nocturne, the *Fantaisie* for piano and orchestra and the suite *Masques et Bergamasques*. The chamber music includes a second violin sonata, two violoncello sonatas, a trio, a quintet and a string quartet; and the songs are contained in *Le Jardin Clos*, *Mirages* and *L'Horizon Chimérique*. Fauré was by now deaf and the extreme refinement of expression, the often elliptical utterance of a man who was writing primarily for himself and had lost interest in surface charm, have led to these works being compared with the last quartets of Beethoven. The comparison disregards the great difference in the two composers' ages as well as the personal and racial differences which make them antipodal examples of the Germanic and the Latin genius; but it is true that these last works had in each case a quality different from anything

else written by either composer, and contained ideas to which
succeeding generations of composers may turn and turn again
without exhausting their significance. Norman Suckling has written of these last chamber works by Fauré that

'their opening movements are vigorous without protestation, their
finales without effervescence; and the intervening andantes distil an
atmosphere of peaceful intensity where every vibration is significant
without being insistent.'

Technically they are marked by a great sobriety. The material
is compressed, the expression concentrated; and only the attentive
listener will unfailingly distinguish between the power of tranquil
thought, which is the true character of the music, and the distinguished monotony that is the superficial listener's main impression. Harmonically Fauré returned to a new simplicity; there is
hardly a trace of his old ingenious chromaticism or of the shot-silk
effects of surface. In this, and in his preference for small melodic
cells rather than long melodic lines, Norman Suckling discovers
a possible parentage of Stravinsky's 'neo-diatonic' and 'neo-classical' styles and he quotes as an example the following passage from
the string quartet:

Ex. 57

There are exceptions to this extreme compression, moments when
Fauré's old eloquence returns to him, as in the Andante of the
second violoncello sonata and the middle of the thirteenth
nocturne. His writing for the piano retained many of its original
characteristics, especially his favourite use of the broken chord and
the enclosing of the melodic line in scale passages passing from one
hand to the other and often extended over a wide range. The
occasional harmonic crabbedness, already noticed in the ninth

Nocturne, is to be found again in the eleventh Barcarolle and in the *Fantaisie*, whose most extraordinary feature is its rhythmic angularity and variety.

In his last songs Fauré sometimes returns to types which he had created many years earlier and a comparison between his earlier and his later usage is instructive. Thus the opening of *Exaucement*, first song in *Le Jardin Clos*, recalls very closely the *Soir* of nearly twenty years earlier, but in an ascetic version. Instead of the warm, rich D flat major broken chords in semi-quavers there are open quaver figures in a simple C major and the voice part is correspondingly less laden. The *Lydia* of fifty years ago lives again in the *Diane, Seléné* of *L'Horizon Chimérique* and in the first song of *Mirages*; and the ingenious student of Fauré's style will find other examples to add to these. *Le Jardin Clos*, like the earlier *Chanson d'Eve*, was composed of poems by Charles van Lerberghe, *Mirages* of four poems by the Baronne de Brimont and *L'Horizon Chimérique* of four poems by Jean de la Ville de Mirmont, a young man killed in the war of 1914–18. All the poems set by Fauré after *La Chanson d'Eve* are poems of the interior life, religious in a pantheistic sense, or verbal patterns inspired by the esoteric modes of feeling introduced by the Symbolists. Love poems are rare and, when they occur, ethereal. References to the visual world—roses, dawn, dusk, swans and water—generally suggest a symbolical interpretation. Both ardour and nostalgia are outgrown and in some of the best of these songs—*O Mort, poussière d'étoiles, Inscription sur le sable* and all *L'Horizon Chimérique*—Fauré was facing the only future event on which any man of his age can count with certainty. The prospect of death filled him with as little perturbation now as in 1888, when he wrote the *Requiem*, but neither does he make any pretence of stoicism. The note of anguish that sounded in the *Libera me* is echoed in *L'Horizon Chimérique*, where the embarking on a sea voyage is an unmistakable allegory, rendered doubly moving by the mating of the words of an 'early dead' poet with the music of an old man on the point of making the same journey.

> Hors du port qui n'est plus qu'une image effacée,
> Les larmes du départ ne brûlent plus mes yeux.
> Je ne me souviens pas des mes derniers adieux,
> O ma peine, ma peine, où vous ai-je laissée?

To give in words anything approaching the quality and flavour of this music written by Fauré in his old age is impossible. It is far easier to suggest by description, analysis and analogy the character of Debussy's or Ravel's music, where the personal manner is even more noticeable than the general sense of style. Fauré grew less communicative in his music as he grew older. His music becomes increasingly less of a personal effusion as it takes on more and more the character of the landscape to which he retired— 'those Provençal-Savoyard surroundings which', in Norman Suckling's words, 'accentuated the identity of the French Spirit with that of civilized humanity'. Civilization is no longer a word with wholly happy associations; but Fauré's music has the qualities of the finest, latest flowering of a genuine civilization. They are the qualities of a period which, in literature, would be called 'silver' or Alexandrine; he is an Ausonius rather than a Virgil, a Callimachus or a Theocritus rather than a Pindar. He was the last great traditionalist in French music, more human and fruitful than Ravel, more sane though less original than Debussy and more wholly, unequivocally French than either—a central figure while the centre of the path of artistic tradition was not yet reserved for the timid and the impotent.

If Fauré embodied all the finest qualities of a great silver age of Latin civilization, Roussel had the more difficult task of coming to terms with the barbarian invaders of music. By age and formation he, too, belonged to the silver age, whose high standard of craftsmanship and refined palate he never lost; but all his best and most personal work was done in the Dark Ages after 1918, whose chaos and welter he dominated by sheer force of natural musical breeding. All his mature work has the quality of distinction which is so noticeably absent from that of the younger composers newly arrived upon the scene, in France as elsewhere. This distinction was largely the fruit of discipline. Roussel, passing through the hands of d'Indy and teaching for years at the Schola Cantorum, could reflect as Renan reflected on his years at Tréguier and Saint-Nicolas du Chardonnet. He could even (though there is no vestige of evidence that he did) adopt the same slightly sardonic attitude towards the younger generation of composers as Renan adopted towards those whose rejection of the old discipline he felt to be altogether too facile.

'The fact that a Parisian street-urchin dismisses with a joke the beliefs from which Pascal's reason never succeeded in detaching him should not be taken to imply that Gavroche is the superior of Pascal. I confess that I sometimes feel humiliated by the thought that I needed five or six years of passionate study, a knowledge of Hebrew and the Semitic languages, Gesenius and Ewald to reach precisely the same result as this little creature achieves from the outset. . . . But Father Hardouin used to say that he had not risen at four o'clock every morning for forty years in order to share the opinions of the rest of the world.'

The solidity of Roussel's technique and his ability first to envisage and then to achieve precisely the effect that he desired are the fruit of the old disciplines; only his sensibility became increasingly attuned to that of the younger composers and of the post-war world generally. The *Divertissement* of 1906 proved prophetic, both in its general temper and in its dimensions, for much of Roussel's most characteristic work was to be in chamber music or in small orchestral forms. But it was with the orchestral *Pour une Fête de Printemps* in 1921 that Roussel took his stand unequivocally with the younger composers. The opening chord, a simultaneous statement of the tonalities of A natural and E flat major, could be paralleled in the music of Strauss, but its uncompromising appearance at the very beginning of a work not otherwise notably revolutionary showed the direction in which Roussel's idiom was developing. He himself was quite conscious of his change of front. Of his second symphony which appeared in 1922, he wrote:

'Impressionism had exercised its charm upon me. My music was perhaps too attached to exterior factors and picturesque processes which, as I have come to think, robbed it of part of its own specific veracity. I resolved (during the years between 1914–18) to broaden the harmonic sense of my writing and tried to move towards a conception of music as willed and realized for its own sake. My Symphony in B flat (No. 2) was, I willingly admit, a rather hermetic work. . . .'

The *Suite in F* (1927) and the *Petite Suite* (1929) were further stages on Roussel's path towards a completely successful realization of himself in the two big orchestral works of 1930 and 1935, the third and fourth symphonies, to which should be added the intensely personal Sinfonietta for string orchestra of 1934. In his symphonies Roussel was bold enough to set his main emotional climaxes in the slow movement, an unusual sign of confidence and indeed of strength. The rude vitality of the opening movements gives little hint of the contained emotional force of these slow movements, as expressed in the fugue of the third symphony and the big crescendo of the fourth. Roussel's harmonic idiom is astringent and gives the impression of a ruthlessness which is often the result of his

contrapuntal habits of thought rather than of any harmonic
theory. His dance movements, as in the *Petite Suite* or the Scherzo
of the third symphony, are light-hearted without frivolity, comparable in robust vigour with the scherzos of Beethoven and
Bruckner, in whom the peasant origins of the dance were still
strong. The last movements stand half-way between the efferves-
cent, gay finales of Haydn and Mozart and the powerful affirmations of Beethoven and the nineteenth-century symphonists, for
whom the end must at all costs crown the work and reassert its
predominant character. Roussel, in fact, could claim in these
works to be capturing a large measure of the classical spirit without
the attachment of any 'neo-classical' label.

He was never at his best in writing for the piano, and the concerto of 1928 is an ungrateful work in which the solo instrument
is treated largely percussively. The best of his chamber music
written after 1918 is in the *Serenade* (1925), the second trio (1929)
and the string quartet (1932), works in which the composer's
elegant and fastidious side found perfect expression and close
musical thinking is matched with great refinement of sensibility.
His ballet music for *Bacchus et Ariane* (1930) and *Aeneas* (1935)
combines the spare lines and chaste melodic contours suggested by
the classical subjects with beautiful instrumentation in which
some of the glories of the old impressionist orchestra are revived.
Another classical subject inspired *La Naissance de la Lyre*, a dramatic cantata which stands half-way between Roussel's two works for
the stage, *Padmâvatî* and the comic opera *Le Testament de la Tante
Caroline*.

Roussel's best work falls outside the strict scope of this study,
but there is an irresistible poetic appeal and a dramatic rightness
in ending with a composer in whose music the two streams which
had flowed strongly in France since the eighteen-nineties—the
impressionist and that of the Schola Cantorum—combined to
force their way powerfully along the new and unfamiliar channels
of the years between the two German wars. 'Innovation within
the traditional framework', the formula suggested by André
Coeuroy to sum up the achievement of Fauré, is in a slightly different sense applicable to Roussel also. And if it is legitimate to
describe this, as Coeuroy goes on to do, as a 'typically French
proceeding', then it is in the music of Roussel that the sanest and
most deep-rooted traditions of French art are to be found in these
latter years.

BIBLIOGRAPHY

BELLAIGUE, C. *Gounod*. Paris, 1910.

BIRON, FERNAND. *Le chant grégorien dans l'enseignement et les œuvres musicales de V. d'Indy*. Ottawa, 1941.

BONNEROT, J. *Saint-Saëns, sa vie et son œuvre*. Paris, 1914.

BORGEX, L. *Vincent d'Indy; sa vie et son œuvre*. Paris, 1912.

BOSCHOT, A. *La vie et les œuvres de Alfred Bruneau*. Paris, 1937.

BRUNEAU, A. *Massenet*. Paris, 1935.

Musiques d'hier et de demain. Paris, 1900.

CAILLARD, C. F. *et* DE BERYS. *Le Cas Debussy*. Paris, 1909.

CALVOCORESSI, M. D. *Musicians' Gallery*, London, 1933.

CARRAUD, G. *La vie, l'œuvre et la mort d'Albéric Magnard*. Paris, 1921.

CEILLIER, L. *Roger-Ducasse, le musicien—l'œuvre*. Paris, 1930.

COCTEAU, J.[1] *Le Coq et l'Harlequin*. Paris, 1926.

Portraits-Souvenir. Paris, 1935.

Rappel à l'Ordre. Paris, 1926.

COEUROY, A. *La musique française moderne*. Paris, 1922.

CORTOT, A. *La Musique française de piano*, 2 vols. Paris, 1930–2.

DEAN, WINTON. *Bizet*. London, 1948.

DEMUTH, N. *Albert Roussel*. London, 1947.

DESAYMARD, J. *Un artiste auvergnat, Emmanuel Chabrier et son œuvre*. Clermont Ferrand, 1908.

DUKAS, PAUL. *Écrits sur la Musique*. Paris: 1948

DUMESNIL, R. *La musique contemporaine en France*, 2 vols. Paris, 1930 .

FAURÉ-FREMIET, P. *Gabriel Fauré*. Paris, 1929.

FERROUD, P. O. *Autour de Florent Schmitt*. Paris, 1927.

GEORGE, A. *Arthur Honegger*. Paris, 1926.

GOSS, M. *Bolero*. New York. 1940.

GOURMONT, R. DE. *Promenades Littéraires*. Paris, 1904.

HAHN, R. *Notes: Journal d'un Musicien*. Paris, 1933.

HERVEY, A. *Alfred Bruneau*. London, 1907.

HOÉRÉE, A. *Albert Roussel*. Paris, 1938.

INDY, V. D'. *César Franck*. Paris, 1906.

R. Wagner et son influence sur l'art musical français. Paris, 1930.

INDY, V. D' and others. *La Schola Cantorum, son histoire depuis sa fondation jusqu'en 1925*. Paris, 1927.

Cours de composition musicale.

JACOB, MAX. *Art Poétique*. Paris, 1922.

JANKÉLÉVITCH, V. G. *Fauré et ses mélodies*. Paris, 1938.

Maurice Ravel. Paris, 1939.

---

[1] *A Call to Order*. Essays written between 1918 and 1926 and including 'The Cock and Harlequin,' etc. Translated by Rollo Myers, London, 1926.

JULLIEN, A. *Musiciens d'aujourd'hui*. Paris, 1892.

KOECHLIN, C. *Gabriel Fauré*. Paris, 1927.

LALOY, L. *Claude Debussy*, Paris, 1909.
 La musique retrouvée, 1902–27. Paris, 1928.

LORRAIN, M. G. *Lekeu, sa correspondance, sa vie et son œuvre*. Liége, 1923.

MARLIAVE, J. DE. *Etudes Musicales*. Paris, 1917.

MASSENET, J. *Mes Souvenirs*. Paris, 1912.

MAUCLAIR, C. *La religion de la musique*. Paris, 1909 and 1919.

MAURIAC, C. J. *Cocteau—ou la Vérité du Mensonge*. Paris, 1945.

MELLERS, W. *Studies in Contemporary Music* (Fauré, Koechlin, Satie). London, 1948.

MILHAUD, D. *Notes sans musique*. Paris, 1949.

MYERS, R. *Erik Satie*. London, 1948.

OULMONT, C. *Musique de l'Amour*, 2 vols. Paris, 1935.

PROD'HOMME, J. G. *et* DANDELOT, A. *Gounod, sa vie et ses œuvres*. Paris, 1911.

REYER, E. *Quarante ans de musique*. Paris, 1909.

ROHOZINSKI, L. (ed.). *50 ans de musique française, de* 1874 1925, 2 vols. Paris, 1925.

ROLAND-MANUEL. *Ravel*. Paris, 1948.

ROLLAND, R. *Musiciens d'aujourd'hui*. Paris, 1908.
 La Foire sur la Place (*Jean Christophe V*.).

SAINT-SAËNS, C. *Portraits et Souvenirs*. Paris, 1900.
 Les idées de M. Vincent d'Indy. Paris, 1914.

SAMAZEUILH, G. *Paul Dukas*. Paris, 1913.

SCHNEIDER, L. *Maîtres de l'opérette: Hervé et Lecocq*. Paris, 1923.

SELVA, B. *Déodat de Séverac*. Paris, 1930.

SÉRÉ, O. *Musiciens français*. Paris, 1921.

SERVIÈRES, G. *Edouard Lalo*. Paris, 1925.
 La musique française moderne. Paris, 1897.

SUCKLING, N. *Fauré*. London, 1946.

TIERSOT, J. *Un demi siècle de musique française. Entre les deux guerres,* 1870–1917. Paris, 1918.

VALLAS, L. *Claude Debussy et son temps*. Paris, 1932.
 Vincent d'Indy. Paris, 1946.

WYZÉWA, I. DE. *La Revue Wagnérienne*. Paris, 1934.

PERIODICALS

Revue Musicale. The following numbers are particularly valuable as they are either wholly or largely dedicated to the study of one composer.

December 1920 and May 1926. Debussy.

October 1922. Fauré.

April 1923. Milhaud's essay on polytonality.
December 1923. Chausson.
March 1924. Satie.
March 1925. Milhaud.
April 1925. Ravel.
April-May 1929. Roussel.

TABLE OF EVENTS 1870–1925

The date assigned to each work is, where possible, the date of performance or publication.

	BORN	DIED	MUSIC	OTHER ARTS
1870	Guillaume Lekeu Florent Schmitt		Delibes: *Coppélia* Castillon: *Pianoforte Quintet*	Verlaine: *La Bonne Chanson*
1871	(Marcel Proust)	Daniel Auber	Foundation of Société Nationale de Musique Gounod: *Gallia* Saint-Saëns: *Le Rouet d'Omphale* Castillon: *String Quartet* *Pianoforte Trio*	Zola: *La Fortune des Rougon* (Les Rougon Macquart, 1871–93) Rimbaud: *Bateau ivre* Renan: *La Réforme intellectuelle et morale*
1872		(Théophile Gautier)	Bizet: *Djamileh, L'Arlésienne* Massenet: *Don César de Bazan* Saint-Saëns: *La Princesse Jaune* *1st Violoncello Sonata* Castillon: *Pianoforte Concerto* *Pianoforte Quartet* *Pianoforte Trio* *Violin Sonata* Franck appointed professor of organ at Conservatoire Lecocq: *La Fille de Mme Angot*	
1873	Déodat de Séverac Roger-Ducasse	Alexis de Castillon	Delibes: *Le Roi l'a dit* Bizet: *Jeux d'Enfants* Franck: *Rédemption* Massenet: *Les Erinnyes* *Marie Magdeleine* Saint-Saëns: *Phaëton* *Violoncello Concerto* *1st Violin Concerto* Lalo: *Fiesque*	Rimbaud: *Une Saison en enfer*

	BORN	DIED	MUSIC	OTHER ARTS
1874	Reynaldo Hahn	(Jules Michelet)	Saint-Saëns: La Danse Macabre Bourgault-Ducoudray: Fantaisie D'Indy: Piccolomini	Foundation of the Société Anonyme des artistes, peintres, sculpteurs et graveurs (Boudin, Pissarro, Monet, Sisley, Morisot, Renoir, Degas, Cézanne) First Impressionist Exhibition Flaubert: La Tentation de Saint Antoine Zola: La Curée, La Ventre de Paris Verlaine: Romances sans paroles Barbey d'Aurevilly: Les Diaboliques Lautréamont (Isidore Ducasse): Les Chants de Maldoror
1875	Maurice Ravel	Georges Bizet	Bizet: Carmen Massenet: Ève Lalo: Symphonie espagnole Duparc: Lénore Saint-Saëns: Pianoforte Quartet Fourth Pianoforte Concerto d'Indy: Jean Hunyade	Taine: Origines de la France contemporaine Zola: La Conquête de Plassans, La Faute de l'Abbé Mouret
1876		Félicien David	Delibes: Sylvia Franck: Les Éolides	Second Impressionist Exhibition Mallarmé: Prélude à l'après-midi d'un faune Huysmans: Marthe

	BORN	DIED	MUSIC	OTHER ARTS
1877			Gounod: *Cinq Mars* Massenet: *Le Roi de Lahore* Chabrier: *L'Étoile* Saint-Saëns: *La Jeunesse d'Hercule* *Le Timbre d'Argent* *Samson et Dalila* (Weimar)	Third Impressionist Exhibition: use of the term 'peintres impressionnistes' Flaubert: *Trois Contes* Zola: *L'Assommoir*
1878	André Caplet		Gounod: *Polyeucte* Saint-Saëns: *Etienne Marcel* Fauré: *1st Violin Sonata* d'Indy: *La Forêt Enchantée* *Pianoforte Quartet* Franck: *Three Pieces* Bourgault-Ducoudray appointed professor of musical history, Massenet professor of composition at Conservatoire	Universal Exhibition Sully Prudhomme: *Justice*
1879			Franck: *Béatitudes* (in private) Chabrier: *Une Education manquée*	Fourth Impressionist Exhibition Huysmans: *Les Soeurs Vatard*
1880		Jacques Offenbach (Gustave Flaubert)	Franck: *Pianoforte Quintet* Lalo: *Trio in A minor* Delibes: *Jean de Nivelle* Saint-Saëns: *Septet* *Suite Algérienne* *Violin Concerto in B minor*	Fifth Impressionist Exhibition Translation of Tolstoy: *War and Peace* Zola: *Nana*

BORN	DIED	MUSIC	OTHER ARTS
1881		Gounod: *Le Tribut de Zamora* Massenet: *Hérodiade* Chabrier: *Dix Pièces pittoresques* Offenbach: *Contes d'Hoffmann* Fauré: *Ballade* Dom Pothier: *Les Mélodies grégoriennes*	Sixth Impressionist Exhibition Flaubert: *Bouvard et Pécuchet* Verlaine: *Sagesse* Maupassant: *La Maison Tellier* Huysmans: *En Ménage*
1882		Gounod: *Redemption* Fauré: *1st Pianoforte Quartet* Chausson: *Trio* Lalo: *Namouna*	Seventh Impressionist Exhibition Huysmans: *A vau-l'eau*
1883	(Edouard Manet)	Franck: *Le Chasseur Maudit* Chabrier: *España, Trois Valses Romantiques* Delibes: *Lakmé* Saint-Saëns: *Henry VIII*	Japanese Exhibition Renan: *Souvenirs d'enfance et de jeunesse* Villiers de l'Isle Adam: *Contes Cruels*
1884		Gounod: *Mors et Vita* Massenet: *Manon* Reyer: *Sigurd* (Brussels) Debussy: *L'Enfant Prodigue*	Foundation of the Salon des Indépendants Leconte de Lisle: *Poèmes tragiques* Verlaine: *Jadis et naguère* Maupassant: *Au soleil* Translation of Dostoevsky's *Crime and Punishment* Huysmans: *A Rebours*

BORN	DIED	MUSIC	OTHER ARTS
1885	(Victor Hugo)	Franck: *Les Djinns* *Prélude, chorale et fugue* Saint-Saëns: *1st Violin Sonata* Massenet: *Le Cid* Chabrier: *La Sulamite*	Laforgue: *Les Complaintes* Maupassant: *Contes et nouvelles, M. Parent, Contes du jour et de la nuit, Bel Ami* Translation of Tolstoy's *Anna Karenina* Zola: *Germinal* Régnier: *Lendemains*
1886		Saint-Saëns: *Third Symphony* *Carnaval des Animaux* d'Indy: *Chant de la Cloche* *Trumpet Septet* Franck: *Violin Sonata* Fauré: *2nd Pianoforte Quartet* Chabrier: *Gwendoline* (Brussels)	Eighth (and last) Impressionist Exhibition Translation of Dostoevsky's *Possessed* Mendès: *Richard Wagner* Bloy: *Le Désespéré*
1887	Jules Pasdeloup (Jules Laforgue)	Saint-Saëns: *Proserpine* Lalo: *Symphony in G minor* Fauré: *Requiem* *2nd Pianoforte Quartet* Satie: *Sarabandes* Chabrier: *Le Roi malgré lui* d'Indy: *Symphonie cévenole* First performance in Paris of *Lohengrin*	Mallarmé: *Poésies complètes* Translation of Dostoevsky's *Idiot* Huysmans: *En Route* Laforgue: *Moralités Légendaires* First volume of the Goncourt Journal published Dujardin: *Les Lauriers sont coupés*

BORN	DIED	MUSIC	OTHER ARTS
1888 Louis Durey	Alkan	Lalo: *Le roi d'Ys* Bordes: *Trio basque* Franck: *Psyche* *Prélude, aria et finale* Satie: *Gymnopédies*	Verlaine: *Amour* Renan: *Drames philosophiques* Maupassant: *Le rosier de Mme. Husson* Translations of: Poe, Dostoevsky (*Brothers Karamazov*), and Schopenhauer Zola: *La Terre*
1889	(Villiers de l'Isle Adam) (Barbey d'Aurevilly)	Franck: *Symphony* Chabrier: *Gwendoline* (Karlsruhe) Massenet: *Esclarmonde* Debussy: *Petite Suite*	Universal Exhibition Verlaine: *Parallèlement* Moréas: *Premières Armes de symbolisme* First translations of Ibsen appear Villiers de l'Isle Adam: *Nouveaux Contes cruels*
1890	César Franck (Vincent Van Gogh)	Franck: *String Quartet* *Three Chorales* Reyer: *Salammbô* Saint-Saëns: *Ascanio* Bourgault-Ducoudray: *Rhapsodie cambodgienne* Debussy: *Petite Suite* Satie: *Gnossiennes* Chausson: *Symphony* *Pianoforte Concerto* d'Indy: *1st String Quartet*	Maupassant: *Inutile beauté, Notre coeur,* *La vie errante* Régnier: *Les Jeux rustiques et divins* France: *Thaïs* Villiers de l'Isle Adam: *Axel*

	BORN	DIED	MUSIC	OTHER ARTS
1891	Georges Migot	Léo Delibes (Theodore de Banville) (Arthur Rimbaud) (Georges Seurat)	Saint-Saëns: *Africa* *1st Quartet* *2nd Trio* Bruneau: *Le Rêve* Bourgault-Ducoudray: *Thamara* Chabrier: *Bourrée fantasque*	Mallarmé: *Pages* Verlaine: *Bonheur* Huysmans: *Là-Bas* E. de Goncourt: *L'Art Japonais au xviiie siècle*
1892	Darius Milhaud Arthur Honegger Germaine Tailleferre	Edouard Lalo Ernest Guiraud (Ernest Renan)	Massenet: *Werther* Lekeu: *Fantaisie sur deux airs angerins* *Violin Sonata* Dukas: *Polyeucte* Magnard: *Suite dans le style ancien* Foundation of the *Chanteurs de Saint Gervais* Debussy: *Fêtes galantes* (1) Fauré: *La Bonne Chanson*	Claudel: First published poems (*Larmes sur la joue vieille*)
1893		Charles Gounod (Hippolyte Taine) (Guy de Maupassant)	Saint-Saëns: *Phryné* Bruneau: *L'Attaque du moulin* Debussy: *Damoiselle élue* *String Quartet* First performance of *Walküre* in Paris	Hérédia: *Les Trophées* Mallarmé: *Vers et prose* *A travers l'oeuvre de Nietzsche* (extracts) published France: *La Rôtisserie de la Reine Pedauque* Samain: *Au Jardin de l'Infante*

BORN	DIED	MUSIC	OTHER ARTS
1894	(Leconte de Lisle) Guillaume Lekeu Emmanuel Chabrier	Massenet: *Thaïs; La Navarraise* *Le Portrait de Manon* Debussy: *Prélude à l'après-midi d'un faune* *String Quartet* Magnard: *First Symphony* *Yolande* *Wind Quintet* Franck: *Hulda* Foundation of the Schola Cantorum by Bordes, Guilmant and d'Indy, 6 October	Louÿs: *Chansons de Bilitis* France: *Le Jardin d'Épicure*
1895	Benjamin Godard	Magnard: *Promenades* (1893) Revival of *Tannhäuser* (after 1861 fiasco)	Leconte de Lisle: *Derniers Poèmes* Laforgue: *Poésies Complètes* Translation of d'Annunzio's *Il Piacere* Huysmans: *En Route*
1896	Ambroise Thomas (Paul Verlaine)	Saint-Saëns: *5th Pianoforte Concerto* *2nd Violin Sonata* Dukas: *Symphony* Chausson: *Poème* Franck: *Ghisèle* Erlanger: *Julien L'Hospitalier*	Translation of d'Annunzio's *Il Trionfo della Morte* Louÿs: *Aphrodite* Jarry: *Ubu Roi*

BORN	DIED	MUSIC	OTHER ARTS
1897		Massenet: *Sapho* Bruneau: *Messidor* d'Indy: *Fervaal-Istar:* 2nd String Quartet Chausson: *String Quartet* Satie: *Pièces Froides* Dukas: *L'Apprenti Sorcier* First performance of *Fliegende* *Holländer* and *Meistersinger* in Paris	Mallarmé: *Divagations* Bloy: *La Femme Pauvre* Gide: *Les Nourritures Terrestres*
1898	(Stéphane Mallarmé)	Saint-Saëns: *Déjanire* Fauré: *Pelléas et Mélisande* Ravel: *Sites auriculaires* d'Indy: *Chansons et Danses*	Huysmans: *La Cathédrale* Louÿs: *La Femme et le pantin*
1899	Ernest Chausson	Massenet: *Cendrillon* Magnard: *Second Symphony* Chabrier: *Briséis* Debussy: *Chansons de Bilitis*	Mallarmé: *Poésies*
1900	Francis Poulenc Georges Auric (Albert Samain)	Debussy: *Nocturnes* Fauré: *Prométhée* Séverac: *Le Chant de la Terre* Charpentier: *Louise* Caplet: *Suite persane* First full performance of *Tristan* in Paris (first act in concert form, 1884)	Universal Exhibition Louÿs: *Les Aventures du roi Pausole*

	BORN	DIED	MUSIC	OTHER ARTS
1901		(Henri Toulouse-Lautrec)	Saint-Saëns: *Les Barbares* Massenet: *Grislidis* Dukas: *Pianoforte Sonata* Bruneau: *L'Ouragan* Debussy: *Pour le Piano*	Huysmans: *Sainte Lydwine de Schiedam*
1902		(Emile Zola)	Saint-Saëns: *Parysatis* Massenet: *Le Jongleur de Notre Dame* Debussy: *Pelléas et Mélisande* Roussel: *Trio*. First peformance of *Siegfried* and *Götterdämmerung* in Paris	
1903		(Paul Gauguin)	Debussy: *Estampes* (1) *Ariettes oubliées* Ravel: *String quartet* Dukas: *Variations on a theme of Rameau* Roussel: *Resurrection* d'Indy: *L'Etranger*	Huysmans: *L'Oblat* Picasso's 'Blue' period Exhibition of Oriental Arts
1904			Debussy: *Fêtes galantes* (2) Saint-Saëns: *Hélène* *2nd Violoncello Sonata* Schmitt: *Psalm 47* *Le Palais hanté* d'Indy: *Violin Sonata, Second Symphony* Séverac: *En Languedoc* Magnard: *Quintet* *String Quartet* *Overture* *Chant funèbre*	Exhibition of French Primitives

	BORN	DIED	MUSIC	OTHER ARTS
1905			Debussy: *La Mer* / *Images* (1) / Ravel: *Sonatine* / *Miroirs* / d'Indy: *Jour d'été à la Montagne* / Massenet: *Chérubin*	'Les Fauves.' Apollinaire meets Picasso and Max Jacob
1906		(Paul Cézanne) (José Maria de Hérédia)	Ravel: *Introduction et Allegro* / *Histoires naturelles* / Roussel: *Divertissement* / Saint-Saëns: *L'Ancêtre* / Massenet: *Ariane* / Magnard: *Pianoforte Trio* / *Hymne à Vénus*	Loüys: *Archipel*
1907			Debussy: *Images* (2) / Massenet: *Thérèse* / Dukas: *Ariane et Barbe-bleue* / Schmitt: *La Tragédie de Salomé*	
1908		(Sully Prudhomme)	Debussy: *Children's Corner* / Ravel: *Gaspard de la Nuit* / *Rapsodie espagnole* / *Ma Mère l'Oye* / Schmitt: *Pianoforte Quintet* / Roussel: *Poème de la forêt* / *Violin Sonata*	France: *Ile des Pingouins* / Braque's 'Cubist' pictures shown

BORN	DIED	MUSIC	OTHER ARTS

1909	Ernest Reyer
	Charles Bordes
		Saint-Saëns: *La Foi*
		Massenet: *Bacchus*
		Séverac: *Le Cœur du moulin*
		Roger-Ducasse: *String Quartet*
		   Suite française
		   Variations plaisantes
		Caplet: *La Masque de la mort rouge*
		Debussy: *Rondes de Printemps*
		First complete performance of
		   Rheingold in Paris (fragments,
		   1893; concert version, 1901)
			Diaghilev's *Ballet russe* in Paris
			First Futurist Manifesto

1910	Louis Bourgault- Ducoudray	Debussy: *Préludes* (1) Massenet: *Don Quichotte* Schmitt: *Lied et Scherzo* Séverac: *Cerdaña* *En Vacances* Bréville: *Eros vainqueur* Roger-Ducasse: *Prélude d'un ballet* Hahn: *La Fête chez Thérèse*	Claudel: *Cinq Grandes Odes*

1911		Debussy: *Le Martyre de St. Sebastien*
		Ravel: *L'Heure Espagnole*
		   Valses nobles et sentimentales
		Magnard: *Violoncello Sonata*
		   Bérénice
		First complete performance of
		   the *Ring* in Paris	

	BORN	DIED	MUSIC	OTHER ARTS
1912		Jules Massenet	Ravel: *Daphnis et Chloé* Roger-Ducasse: *Pianoforte Quartet* Dukas: *Le Péri* Roussel: *Evocations* Milhaud: *1st String Quartet*	Claudel: *L'Annonce faite à Marie*
1913			Debussy: *Préludes* (2) *Jeux* *Three Songs* (Mallarmé) Ravel: *Three Songs* (Mallarmé) Roussel: *Festin de l'Araignée* Fauré: *Pénélope* Magnard: *Fourth Symphony* Roger-Ducasse: *Au Jardin de Marguérite*	Apollinaire: *Alcools* *Les Peintres cubistes* Proust: *Du Côté de Chez Swann*
1914		Albéric Magnard	Rabaud: *Mârouf* Caplet: *Les Inscriptions Champêtres* First performance of *Parsifal* in Paris	Gide: *Les Caves du Vatican*
1915			Debussy: *En blanc et noir* *12 Etudes* Ravel: *Pianoforte Trio*	
1916			Debussy: *Violoncello Sonata* *Sonata for flute, viola and harp* Honegger: *Violin Sonata*	

BORN	DIED	MUSIC	OTHER ARTS

1917	(Edgar Degas)
	(Léon Bloy)
		Debussy: *Violin Sonata*
		Fauré: *2nd Violin Sonata*
		Ravel: *Le Tombeau de Couperin*
		Honegger: *String Quartet*
		    Le Chant de Nigamon
		    Prelude to Aglavaine et Sélysette
		Satie: *Parade*
		Poulenc: *Rhapsodie nègre*
		Durey: *Scènes de Cirque*
			Apollinaire: *Calligrammes*
			Valéry: *La Jeune Parque*

1918	Claude Debussy
	(Guillaume Apol-
	linaire)
		Fauré: *1st Violoncello Sonata*
		Schmitt: *Rêves*
		    Légende
		Poulenc: *Mouvements perpetuels*
		    Sonata for Pianoforte Duet
		    Sonata for Two Clarinets
		Honegger: *Le Dit des jeux du monde*
		Durey: *String Quartet*
		    Images à Crusoë
		Migot: *Trio*	

1919		Satie: *Socrate*
		Poulenc: *Le Bestiaire*
		    Cocardes
		Honegger: *1st Violin Sonata*
		Saint-Saëns: *2nd String Quartet*
		Migot: *Les Agrestides*
		Milhaud: *Le boeuf sur le toit*
		    Machines agricoles	

BORN	DIED	MUSIC	OTHER ARTS
1920		Ravel: *La Valse* Poulenc: *Pianoforte Suite* Schmitt: *Antoine et Cleopâtre* Tailleferre: *Pastorale* Honegger: *Pastorale d'été* 2nd Violin Sonata Sonata for Violin and Violoncello d'Indy: *La Légende de Saint Christophe* Migot: *Cinq Mouvements d'eau*	Colette: *Chéri* Cocteau: *Le Coq et L'Harlequin*
1921	Camille Saint-Saëns	Fauré: *Piano Quintet No. 2* Roussel: *Pour une Fête de printemps* Honegger: *Horace Victorieux* *Le Roi David*	Giraudoux: *Suzanne et le Pacifique* Valéry: *La Soirée avec M. Teste* *Charmes*
1922	(Marcel Proust)	Fauré: *L'Horizon Chimérique* 2nd Violoncello Sonata Roussel: *Symphony No. 2*	Le Corbusier: *Vers une Architecture* Romains: *Les Copains*
1923		Auric: *Les Fâcheux* Fauré: *Trio* Roussel: *Padmâvatî* Milhaud: *La Création du Monde* Poulenc: *Les Biches*	
1924	Gabriel Fauré	Satie: *Relâche* Fauré: *String Quartet* Poulenc: *Les Biches* Honegger: *Pacific 231*	First Surrealist manifesto
1925	Erik Satie	Ravel: *L'Enfant et les Sortilèges*	Duhamel: *Confession de Minuit*

INDEX

(Page numbers in heavy type indicate the more important references. Music examples are separately indexed at the end.)

INDEX TO MUSIC EXAMPLES

Oxford Paperbacks